Understanding industria

This book provides a critical review of the perspectives which have most influenced our understanding of industrial organisations in the period since 1945. Four main approaches are identified: *systems thinking* considers organisations as systems of inter-related parts; *contingency theory* emphasises the influence of an organisation's context or environment on its structure and functioning; *action approaches* analyse organisations in terms of the orientations and actions of organisational members; *labour process theories* focus on the means whereby labour is controlled. Combining exegesis and critique, in each case a detailed account is given of the arguments and main contributors to the approach, and an extensive critical literature is used to identify the main strengths and weaknesses.

These debates are placed in their appropriate institutional, intellectual and socioeconomic contexts, thereby also providing an overview of the development of industrial sociology in the post-war years. The author concludes his review of these contributions to industrial sociology by arguing that 'organisation' is best seen as created and sustained by the ongoing negotiation of the terms of the employment relationship, though within certain limits and constraints.

This well-documented discussion of the leading theoretical perspectives in the field offers the reader a masterly guide to the sociology of organisations. It will be of interest to students of industrial sociology, organisational behaviour, industrial relations, and business and management, and to teachers and researchers in these areas. Richard Brown has been teaching and undertaking research in industrial sociology for more than thirty years and has published extensively on these topics.

Richard Brown is Professor of Sociology, University of Durham.

Understanding industrial organisations

Theoretical perspectives in industrial sociology

Richard K. Brown

London and New York

First published in 1992
by Routledge
11 New Fetter Lane, London EC4P 4EE

Simultaneously published in the USA and Canada
by Routledge
a division of Routledge, Chapman and Hall Inc.
29 West 35th Street, New York, NY 10001

Typeset in Baskerville by LaserScript, Mitcham, Surrey
Printed in Great Britain by
Biddles Ltd, Guildford and King's Lynn

British Library Cataloguing in Publication Data
A catalogue record for this book is available from the British Library.

Library of Congress Cataloging in Publication Data
Brown, Richard K., 1933–
    Understanding industrial organisations: theoretical perspectives
    in industrial sociology/Richard K. Brown.
    p. cm.
    Includes bibliographical references and indexes.
    1. Industrial sociology. 2. Industrial organisation. I. Title.
    HD6955.B74   1992
    302.3′5 dc20   91-42664
                                                                  CIP

ISBN 0–415–01781–5
      0–415–01782–3 (pbk)

Contents

To Jane

Acknowledgements

The Economic and Social Research Council awarded me a personal research grant (F00242002) for the academic year 1983–4 which enabled me to undertake reading and research for this book and to write the initial drafts of several chapters. I am grateful to them for making possible a period of sustained work on one project, something which cannot easily be managed otherwise. The book was completed during two terms of research leave in the autumn of 1988 and the spring of 1991; I am grateful to the University of Durham for granting this leave and to my colleagues in the Department of Sociology and Social Policy for supporting my applications and covering for my absences.

During the long period of preparing this book I have received much encouragement and support from a succession of editors at Tavistock Publications and, since 1988, at Routledge. I am grateful in particular to Andrew Franklin, who first expressed interest in the project; to Gill Davies, who continued to believe over a long period that I would eventually produce a complete text when all the evidence appeared to suggest otherwise; to Rosemary Nixon and to Talia Rodgers; and most recently to Chris Rojek, who has provided much appreciated encouragement for what he could have been forgiven for thinking a lost cause.

Over the past twenty-five or more years I have discussed much of the material to be found in this book with undergraduate and, especially, postgraduate students. It is impossible to mention them all by name, but I am grateful for their interest and the part they have played in forcing me to try to clarify my ideas. They have contributed to my education as I hope I may have contributed to theirs. I am also very grateful to all those colleagues and friends with whom I have discussed these issues, and to those on whose work I have drawn in writing the book. I apologise if I have in any way misrepresented their ideas or overlooked some of their contributions to these debates. I would like to acknowledge, too, the thoughtful and helpful comments made at different stages during the book's development by two (anonymous) readers; I regret that I have not been able to respond to all their suggestions as fully as I would have liked.

I greatly appreciate the help I have received from Ann Scott, Lynda Nurse and Donna Harris, each of whom has produced excellently typed drafts of one or more chapters at different stages during the book's preparation.

Jane Brown read the whole text in draft and it has benefited greatly from her comments. Any errors of commission or omission are of course entirely my responsibility. My family have had to live with this (incomplete) book for far too long. I am very grateful for their forbearance and their encouragement. Jane has contributed more to the completion of this project than she will ever acknowledge, or than I could have hoped for. My greatest thanks, as always, are to her.

Richard Brown
Durham
August 1991

Introduction – sociologists and industry

ICL forced out of Europe
Over 3,000 jobs at risk as Lewis's puts up shutters
Ford chief fears big drop in car sales
Murdoch set to seal deal
W.H. Smith puts squeeze on pay-outs as profits fall
Rolls Royce to shed 1,500 jobs
Virgin plan to appeal to Europe over BA tactics
TWA in plea to quit London

Industrial organisations dominate industrial societies. They are, indeed, one of the most distinctive features of such societies. Though large-scale industrial organisations did not figure to any great extent in the earliest stages of industrialisation in Europe and the United States of America, their importance was apparent well before the end of the nineteenth century; and during the present century their influence has become increasingly pervasive. Many small enterprises still exist, of course, but for most people in societies like our own paid work means employment as one of hundreds or thousands of others in a large industrial corporation, or – for a considerable minority – in an equally large or larger public sector organisation. For industrialisation and the urbanisation which accompanied it have seen not only the domination of the economy by large industrial and commercial organisations, but also the parallel growth of central and local government, and the development of organisations to provide mass education, mass communications, mass leisure and mass representation, all employing large numbers of people.

It should be no surprise then that the examination of a few issues of national newspapers at the end of January 1991 can produce a selection of headlines like those at the start of this chapter. The activities of industrial organisations are, rightly, seen as something in which readers will be interested and about which they should be informed. Whilst only a small minority may be directly affected by competition between airlines for shares of the transatlantic market, or by W.H. Smith's freeze on dividend payments, and even fewer directly affected by threatened redundancies at Lewis's or Rolls-Royce, the actions, and success or failure, of these and other enterprises will have consequences for the lives of many more people in Britain and abroad.

It is significant that the writers of such headlines could safely assume considerable familiarity with industry among their readership: readers could be expected to know that BA was British Airways and that ICL manufactured computers; that Virgin and TWA were also airlines (among other things in the case of Virgin), and that Rupert Murdoch was head of the transnational media group News International and engaged in refinancing the company's borrowings. Much of this familiarity is deliberately fostered, of course, by the organisations themselves through advertising and public relations activities with such success that the identities of many large corporations, even those which do not sell direct to the public as (say) Ford do, are truly 'household names'. It is significant too that the headlines record events with international ramifications such as the exclusion of ICL from a European advisory group of leading computer firms because of its takeover in 1989 by the Japanese Fujitsu group.

It should be no surprise, either, that sociologists have been concerned to investigate these developments. In this as in other areas of sociology the aim has been to go behind the headlines and common-sense understandings to identify underlying trends and patterns of cause and effect, both intended and unintended. An interest in industrialisation, and in the evolving patterns of work and employment in industrial enterprises, can be traced back to the first emergence of sociology as a distinct discipline, an emergence which represented a response to the industrial, and democratic, 'revolutions' in Europe. In the works of the 'founding fathers' of the subject there are insights and theoretical formulations which have continued to influence research to the present day: Marx's analysis of wage labour, Durkheim's discussion of the division of labour, and Weber's ideal type of bureaucracy are the most obvious examples. However, as we shall see, it is very much more recently that such an interest in industry and industrial organisations in general has come to be complemented by detailed research in particular industrial enterprises and the development of concepts and theoretical approaches which provide a more nearly adequate basis for understanding the variety of patterns of social relations and social processes within them.

The focus of this book is on these attempts to understand and account for the social characteristics of industrial organisations, the social relations and interaction within such organisations, and their interconnections with the wider society. It is therefore concerned with a central area within industrial sociology. In undertaking a critical review of sociological research and writing on industrial organisations, however, I have necessarily set certain limits to the materials I wish to consider. I am concerned primarily with research and writing in Britain in the period since the Second World War; and I have organised my discussion around certain influential theoretical perspectives concerned with understanding industrial organisations rather than attempting to review all the substantive topics on which industrial sociologists have had something to say. Let me discuss these limits in a bit more detail.

Industrial sociology in Britain scarcely existed as such before the Second World War. There was, however, a significant tradition of research on psychological and social problems in industry (Seear 1962). I have made no attempt to assess these bodies of work or their legacy (see Rose 1988, esp. Pt 2, for such an assessment). My attention is concentrated on the period after 1945 when explicitly sociological research on industrial organisations was being undertaken for the first time. The focus is deliberately, but not exclusively, on British research and writing. Partly this represents a pragmatic decision to limit the field to be covered. More importantly, however, it reflects the fact that the main debates to be reviewed have either been relatively self-contained within British sociology or had British protagonists for each of their main positions. Of course, there is no intention of ignoring the important influences on industrial sociology in Britain which have originated elsewhere, especially in the USA, and such work will be discussed as appropriate.

The focus is upon the attempts by industrial sociologists to provide conceptual frameworks with which to investigate, analyse and explain the structure of and processes within industrial organisations. This book is not intended to be a comprehensive text book on industrial sociology. In contrast to the situation even fifteen years ago there is now a good choice of such books, together with complementary volumes of readings. This book is more narrowly focused than a text book. There is no attempt to cover the whole heterogeneous range of empirical questions and materials which commonly feature in books and courses on industrial sociology. My focus, the study of industrial organisations, has always been a central concern of industrial sociology, but it does not comprise the whole of the subject as conventionally understood. We shall give relatively little attention to work on industrial conflict, for example, which has been the other major focus for theoretical developments in industrial sociology, though such issues will not be neglected altogether.

In this chapter I shall outline the ways in which industrial sociology has developed in Britain since 1945, referring both to the institutional setting and social and economic context within which research was conducted and to the intellectual background against which it grew. There were, of course, major changes in all these areas during the forty-five year period under review, and this provides an important context for the material discussed in the rest of the book. I shall indicate the major substantive concerns of industrial sociology, as embodied in text books and reviews of the field. During the whole of the period, but more especially since the 1960s, the question of the scope of a sociology of industry has been contentious and there have been at least latent boundary problems with other branches of the social sciences or other sub-disciplines within sociology. The final section of the chapter will identify and outline briefly the theoretical perspectives and debates to be considered in the body of the book.

In undertaking this brief review I have defined 'industrial sociology' in much the same way as have most of its practitioners: that is pragmatically as a somewhat disparate and unintegrated collection of topics and questions centred on social relations in work organisations (and in practice often limited to male employment in large-scale organisations in mining and manufacturing). Such a focus can include topics which go well beyond the individual industrial enterprise (for example, trade union organisation, industrial relations, and the ownership and control of industry). It has at times extended to a more general consideration of the nature of industrialism and industrial society, and – in addition to this tendency to merge with a sociology of industrial societies – there have been questions of overlap with other 'sub-disciplines'.

Such a pragmatic definition is not particularly desirable or defensible. Indeed I shall argue both that greater coherence can be found for the study of many of the questions traditionally included in industrial sociology by taking the employment relationship as the analytical starting point; and that such a study ought in any case to be located within the wider framework of a sociology of work. For present purposes, however, it is sufficient to take the conventional view of the scope of industrial sociology as the starting point for the discussion.

THE GROWTH AND DEVELOPMENT OF INDUSTRIAL SOCIOLOGY IN BRITAIN SINCE 1945

The institutional context

Industrial sociology as such did not exist in Britain before the end of the Second World War. Indeed, with the exception of a very thin, though often distinguished, succession of scholars, sociology itself hardly existed as a distinct and recognised area of study and, with the possible exception of the London School of Economics, it had no secure institutional base in British universities. Seear has noted, in her review of social research in industry, that in the interwar period 'sociology, as understood today, was not studied at all in the majority of British universities' (1962, 171; see also Garrett 1987). Only thirty-three students graduated in 1938–9 in Britain in the group of social science subjects including sociology, social administration and anthropology (Heyworth Committee 1965, 9). The situation with regard to social research in general was perhaps slightly better; for example, there was the fifty-year-old tradition of studies of poverty and town life, and the work of bodies like Mass Observation in the late 1930s and the war years (see Kent 1981). Research in industry, however, was hampered not only by the weak position of the 'human sciences' in British academic life but also by the strongly practical orientations of most managers and industrialists, and the barriers of social class and intellectual training between them and the academic world (Seear 1962).

Psychological research in industry was established earlier. The first major impetus to research on behavioural problems in industry was provided by the First World War. The need for an increased output of munitions led to the setting up of the Health of Munitions Workers Committee in 1915 and the initiation of a series of psychological studies of working conditions, and of problems such as fatigue and monotony, which continued until the late 1940s. The Health of Munitions Workers Committee was succeeded by the Industrial Fatigue Research Board in 1917 (from 1921 financed through the Medical Research Council) and this became the Industrial Health Research Board in 1929. The parallel development of the National Institute of Industrial Psychology (NIIP) from 1921 further strengthened this stream of applied psychological research in industry, though the NIIP's reliance on consultancy work for funds led to an emphasis on employers' problems such as selection and on individual services such as vocational guidance. As Rose has shown in his lively account of 'human factor industrial psychology', the investigators of questions about individual behaviour were more than once led to the consideration of social factors and, in a broad sense, of sociological explanations (Rose 1988, Pt 2; also 1975, Pt 2).

The Second World War stimulated renewed interest in the contribution psychological research could make to war production and indeed this included repetition of investigations of the relationship between hours of work and output which had been carried out in the First World War (Rose 1988, 80). Though there was scarcely any research in industry which could be labelled 'sociological' (for a possible exception in the armed forces see Paterson 1955) there were two innovations which had an important influence on later developments. Psychiatrists and psychologists played an important role in dealing with psychological problems among service personnel and in developing methods of officer selection; some of them went on to undertake social research in industry, notably as members of the Tavistock Institute of Human Relations. Secondly, operational research in the RAF and elsewhere during the war demonstrated the value of systematic analysis of problems based on first-hand observation; some of those involved in or aware of this work went on to secure and administer government support for social research on industrial problems in the post-war period (see Stansfield 1981).

It was such government funding which was of vital importance in the subsequent establishment of *social* research in industry in Britain on at least a semi-secure footing. The post-war concern with the low levels of productivity in British industry, especially in comparison with the USA, led to the setting up of a Committee on Industrial Productivity in 1947; recognition that industry's problems were social as well as technical meant that one of the Committee's four panels was concerned with 'human factors'. This panel made grants for research on the foreman (NIIP 1951), on joint consultation (NIIP 1952; Scott 1952; Jaques 1951), and for the support of research in mining and on the problems of the older worker, among other issues (see Seear 1962; Stansfield 1981).

The Human Factors Panel was disbanded in 1951, but succeeded two years later, so far as research funding was concerned, by two tri-partite (management, trade unions, universities) joint committees of the Medical Research Council (MRC) and the Department of Scientific and Industrial Research (DSIR) – 'Human Relations in Industry' and 'Individual Efficiency in Industry' respectively. A major part of their funds was provided from American Conditional Aid money, which came with the proviso that the research supported had 'to be related directly to increasing productivity and industrial efficiency . . . and to show promise of producing applicable results in three years'. The Human Relations Committee concentrated its funding on projects on 'management organisation, technical change, incentives, training and promotion, and the problems of special groups in industry' (Seear 1962, 178; Stansfield 1981). Among those whose early work was supported by this Committee, and its successor from 1957, the DSIR Human Sciences Committee, were Scott and his colleagues in Liverpool, Woodward, Burns, Lupton, Cunnison and Klein. This array of names demonstrates the importance of the Committee's contribution to establishing research in industrial sociology in Britain (DSIR/MRC 1958, 3).

Thus opportunities and support for university based social research in industry were very limited until the expansion of higher education in the 1960s. The Clapham Committee in 1946 had recommended increased support for social sciences and earmarked grants were provided between 1947 and 1952. As the Heyworth Committee discovered nearly two decades later the major part of this additional money had been used to establish additional teaching posts, and many of them were in economics (Heyworth Committee 1965, 5–8, 80–5). The University of Liverpool appears to have been an exception in channelling most of the money into research posts and this must have contributed to the successful establishment of an industrial sociology research group there.

The early 1960s marked a distinct watershed in the development of sociology and sociological research in Britain, and this change can be attributed to two main factors: the expansion of higher education in the wake of the Robbins Report (1963) and the establishment of the Social Science Research Council (SSRC) following the recommendations of the Heyworth Committee (1965). The findings of the Heyworth Committee provide a useful summary of the situation for the 'Sociology Group' of subjects, which included social anthropology and social administration, at a time when the expansion of higher education, and of sociology, was just beginning. The Report records that in 1962–3 there were 259 teaching and 67 research staff in this Group, receiving a total of £300,000 in external research funds. In the same year 341 students graduated with first degrees (ten times as many as in 1938–9); 156 students were pursuing higher degrees by research and a further 88 by advanced courses.

It is not possible to apportion research staffing and expenditure between industrial and other areas of sociology, and some research in industrial sociology will have been carried out in other departments, for example of management, business studies or industrial relations. Some indication of the scale of sociological research on industry and work-related problems at the time can be gained from a survey of professional sociologists carried out in 1966–7. This showed that in each of the three periods considered – 1945–60, 1961–6 and 1966 – more than a fifth of all research 'projects' were in 'industrial sociology and the sociology of work' (Carter 1968, 18).

There has, unfortunately, been no comparable survey of professional sociologists since Carter's. Some indication of the continuing high level of interest in work, industry and employment can, however, be gained from an analysis of information in the periodic registers of members of the British Sociological Association (BSA). This shows that during the considerable expansion of teaching and research in sociology during the past three decades the proportion of sociologists with involvement in research in the sociology of work and industry has remained relatively high (10 per cent on the most cautious estimate). The absolute amount of resources – personnel and financial – devoted to industrial sociological research must have grown considerably.

Nevertheless it has never been easy to find resources for research in industrial sociology in Britain. There have always been pressures to focus research on applied problems where there is likely to be some perceived benefit for practitioners, or for society at large. However, it is probably true to say that finance as such has not been the most intractable problem. In the earlier part of the post-war period there was a shortage of trained and experienced researchers, and with very few exceptions the absence of an even moderately secure institutional base. Even since the expansion of higher education in the 1960s there have been problems for those engaged in full-time research arising from insecurity of employment and the lack of a recognised career structure. The establishment by the SSRC (now the ESRC – Economic and Social Research Council) of the Industrial Relations Research Unit at the University of Warwick in 1970, with a rolling five-year programme, and of the Work Organisation Research Centre at the University of Aston in 1982 for five years, represented recognition of and attempts to meet these problems. The expansion of business schools and management education in practice provided some additional relatively secure and well-financed 'homes' for research in industrial sociology. None of these developments can be regarded as solving the problems.

At all times those wishing to investigate social relations in present-day industry have faced the additional problems of securing access to the sites where they wished to carry out field-work and collect data. Securing access has typically meant not only obtaining management's permission to interview, to consult records, to undertake observations, or whatever, but also securing the approval and cooperation of trade union representatives. It would be difficult if not impossible to establish how often research facilities have been refused (but see C. Brown *et al.* 1976), but the need to secure access is likely to change research intentions in two ways: it may be a further reason for emphasising the practical contributions research can make, and it may lead to the avoidance of topics and issues which are controversial and divisive. Not all research in industrial sociology requires access to organisations; for example, some research on labour markets can be carried out using home based interviews; but without the cooperation of managements and trade unions research would be greatly restricted.

The intellectual context

Even a brief and incomplete account of the institutional context for social research in industry in Britain demonstrates how much the situation has changed during the past forty years. The changes in the intellectual context for industrial sociology during the same period were if anything even more marked. The starting point of any attempt to chart these changes must be the 'Human Relations Movement', though this tradition of research and theorising about social relations in industry was not altogether clear-cut in content and message (see Landsberger 1958; Rose 1988). A number of strands can be distinguished. The principal report of the research at the Hawthorne plant in Chicago of the Western Electric Company, *Management and the Worker* (Roethlisberger and Dickson 1939), had been published just before the Second World War. Its findings, or a version of them, had already been popularised, together with supportive material from his own work, by Elton Mayo (1933). Mayo's writings, especially his further volume, *The Social Problems of an Industrial Civilization* (Mayo 1949), and works which drew on them such as J.A.C. Brown's *The Social Psychology of Industry* (1954), continued to be more widely read and quoted than the longer detailed account. Mayo was alarmed by the social disorganisation and conflict which he saw as deriving from the breakdown of the 'established' society of the pre-industrial period; he saw the solution to these problems of 'anomie' lying in the development of social skills and in providing at the workplace the possibilities of belonging to cohesive small groups, with a common purpose, which did not exist in the outside world.

This vision was not necessarily or completely shared by those responsible for the research which followed the Hawthorne Experiments, though their varied investigations could be and were seen as within the Human Relations tradition (see Rose 1988, 103–182; Parker *et al.* 1981, 85–91; and Chapter 4). Indeed the most clearly sociological work within the tradition was a study of change and conflict in the New England shoe industry produced as part of a major community study of 'Yankee City', which did show awareness of the influence of wider economic and social factors, though their importance was not altogether satisfactorily acknowledged (Warner and Low 1947).

Certain assumptions, common to all or most strands in the Human Relations tradition, influenced the content and form of early sociological research in industry in Britain. Workers were to be seen as more than narrowly 'economic men': they had social as well as economic needs and their behaviour was affected at least as much by social factors. In particular the small groups to which they belonged and with which they identified were important sources of influence, as were those in positions of authority – supervisors and immediate managers. It was necessary to have knowledge and understanding of the 'informal' organisation to understand what actually happened in industry – sometimes almost to the exclusion of consideration of the 'formal' organisation altogether. Thus Human Relations research tended to be focused on the exploration of face-to-face small group relations and dynamics, on supervisory 'leadership' and on the opportunities for direct personal participation in group activities. It neglected the wider economic and institutional context within which such social relations existed and the technological, market and other conditions and constraints within which managers, supervisors and others had to act. This neglect made it easier to assume that there were no inherent conflicts of interest within the enterprise and to attribute those conflicts which did occur to faulty communications, poor leadership, or personal inadequacies or failings among members of the organisation.

The Human Relations approach in studies of industry and work was clearly compatible with the dominant emphasis on functionalist analysis which characterised sociology in general in the 1940s and 1950s. Indeed among the rather sparse references to other social theorists in the work of Mayo and Roethlisberger and Dickson it is noticeable that Durkheim, Pareto and the social anthropologists Malinowski and Radcliffe-Brown are cited, all of them customarily regarded as important contributors to 'functionalism' in sociology. Whereas familiarity with American industrial sociology, largely reflecting the Human Relations approach, may have been fairly widespread, it is doubtful how much the more general theoretical discussions in sociology influenced British sociological research in industry in the first decade or more after the War. References to the work of Parsons, for example, can be found (e.g. Jaques 1951, 335), but most early research was descriptive and, at most, only implicitly drawing on or contributing to any body of more general assumptions or propositions.

From its beginnings the Human Relations approach, and the normative functionalism which it implied, did not go unchallenged either in Britain or in the USA (see Landsberger 1958, esp. 28–47). It was more difficult in Britain than in the USA to regard industrial conflict as inevitably pathological and trade unions as misguided; Britain had different political traditions and trade unions were more securely established within the system of industrial relations. Though interpretations of the sources and nature of the conflicting interests of employers and employees continued to differ, the legitimacy of both sets of interests was fairly widely recognised. Nor was the Human Relations movement the only source of underlying assumptions and more general ideas in industrial sociology. To give only two important examples: Marx's arguments about class and class consciousness were clearly of relevance to the industrial situation and had limited and partial acceptance; some of Weber's writings were available in English and his formulations, perhaps especially the discussion of bureaucracy, were drawn on selectively.

Three books published in the 1950s can be used to illustrate the ways in which ideas from these various sources were combined. Scott and his colleagues in Liverpool probably showed the greatest influence of Human Relations ideas in their attempt to elaborate a view of the industrial enterprise as a social system. In their study of a steel plant, *Technical Change and Industrial Relations*, and elsewhere, however, they explicitly rejected the view that social relations in industrial enterprises can or should be characterised by 'harmony' (Scott *et al.* 1956, esp. 263–81; also Scott *et al.* 1963, 10; and see Chapter 2 below). *Coal is our Life* is a study of work, leisure and the family in a mining community in West Yorkshire using the fieldwork methods of social anthropology but showing a clear awareness of Marxist ideas about class, class conflict and class consciousness (Dennis *et al.* 1956). Most explicitly of all Lockwood's *The Blackcoated Worker* used a conceptual framework derived from Weber's discussion of class and status to discuss a question – the class consciousness of clerical workers and the patterns of their trade union membership – which originated in Marxist debates; and this study showed no obvious influences from Human Relations approaches or functionalist sociology (Lockwood 1958).

From the late 1950s sociology changed rapidly in ways which had a direct effect on the content and conduct of research in industrial sociology. A number of writers, notably Dahrendorf (1958) and Rex (1961), made influential critiques of normative functionalism and the consensual model of society to which it could lead: approaches later labelled 'conflict theory'. Dahrendorf's fuller elaboration of his ideas in *Class and Class Conflict in an Industrial Society* (1959) was presented as a revision and updating of Marx's analysis of capitalist society, but it can be seen as more nearly Weberian than Marxian in inspiration. Such a judgement could also be made about Rex's book. Work such as theirs reflected and reinforced interest in the development within sociology, including industrial sociology, of the analytical perspectives which could be derived from Marx's and Weber's work.

This developing theoretical pluralism in sociology fairly rapidly solidified as three 'perspectives' – functionalism, conflict theory, and the social action approach or 'interactionism' – and, in many ways unfortunately, such a categorisation has subsequently been enshrined in influential text book introductions to the subject (e.g. Haralambos 1980; see also Watson 1980 and 1987). The extent of the differences, or even incompatibility, between these 'perspectives' was sometimes exaggerated and often left unclear (but see the valuable discussion in Cohen 1968, esp. 236–9). Despite such ambiguities, however, a number of important debates in industrial sociology in the 1960s and 1970s came to be organised around the problems raised by these three approaches and their supposed incompatible interpretations of society. For example, the social action approach advocated by Goldthorpe and his colleagues was explicitly contrasted with the assumptions of neo-Human Relations and the implicit functionalism of the 'technological implications' approach (Goldthorpe *et al.* 1968, 178–86, and see Chapter 4). In the analysis of industrial conflict both a pluralist approach derived from or at least compatible with the social action perspective and a more 'radical' perspective drawing on Marxian analysis of class conflict were counterposed to the consensus assumptions of Human Relations (Fox 1973; Hyman 1975).

Very rapidly, however, the ground shifted to produce an even more variegated picture. Theorists developed ideas derived from continental philosophy and other sources, and explored the implications of the theoretical positions taken by Marx, Weber, Durkheim and other early social theorists. The relatively limited prescriptions of the social action approach as advocated by Goldthorpe and others, for example, which could be seen as derived primarily from Weber's work, were developed with reference to the writings of

Schutz and others to produce a variety of phenomenological perspectives in sociology which demanded a radically different
approach to sociological research (see Lassman 1974). Similarly
the traditional account of Marx's analysis of capitalist society,
which had been based on a rather limited reading of his extensive
writings, was largely superseded by a variety of Marxisms –
structuralist, humanist, and so on – and by developments such as
'critical theory' (see the accounts in Bottomore 1979; and Craib
1984).

A great deal of this work was theoretical or conceptual and it
cannot be said that it had an obvious immediate impact on the
research carried out by most industrial sociologists or on the ways
in which they analysed their findings. A few studies did use a
thorough-going phenomenological approach in research on
organisations (see Chapter 4), but more common was the attempt
to incorporate a recognition of the potential importance of the
actor's 'definition of the situation' within studies which otherwise
had a more conventional theoretical framework. Similarly, whilst
there was research on the sociology of work which utilised structuralist Marxist ideas (e.g. Willis 1977), the majority of industrial
sociologists sympathetic to Marxian approaches were more conventional in their use of them (e.g. Beynon 1973; Nichols and
Beynon 1977).

The publication of Braverman's *Labor and Monopoly Capital* in
1974, however, did eventually lead to a major shift in the theoretical framework adopted by many industrial sociologists in
Britain, and the analysis it advocated came to influence the work
even of those who were unsympathetic to this basic approach.
Debates about the analysis of the capitalist labour process replaced
discussions of the adequacy and limitations of the social action
approach as the central, though by no means the only, controversy
within this area of sociology. As we shall see in more detail in
Chapter 5, what Braverman offered was an approach drawing on
aspects of Marx's analysis of capitalism which had largely been
neglected in sociology up to that time; and he was able to show that
Marx's work provided the basis for an illuminating, though by no
means uncontentious, interpretation of contemporary industrial
organisations.

Although much of the work which has been produced in the
wake of Braverman's book has been critical of his arguments,
sometimes in quite major ways, during the 1980s the 'labour

process' debate was probably the most popular theoretical point of reference for British industrial sociologists. Much of the literature published in the past decade has been focused on one or other of the issues raised by Braverman's work. However, the dominance of the issues and approaches identified by Braverman, though considerable, must not be overstated nor expected to continue indefinitely. In his review of the 'sociology of economic life' in *Recent British Sociology* (1980, 53–108) Eldridge, for example, made no reference to Braverman's arguments, and he has stated elsewhere that he regards the prominence given to Braverman as unjustified (Eldridge 1983). Similarly, when considering 'directions for the future' for research on the sociology of economic life Gallie acknowledged these debates as only one strand among many others and saw no need to advocate further research specifically within this framework (Gallie 1985, 512–13).

The 1990s will probably be dominated by new debates. The various changes in the organisation and management of work and of workers, which have given rise to terms like 'flexible specialisation' and 'the flexible firm', represent a clear challenge to some of Braverman's central contentions and have already stimulated a range of theoretical responses. Debates around the controversial notion of 'post-modernism', and the influence of the writings of social theorists such as Foucault, have provided further challenges to established ways of understanding industrial organisations and could provide the bases for new perspectives. No attempt will be made here to describe and discuss these developments (for one such discussion in the context of the study of organisations see Clegg 1990); as yet there are no bodies of research and writing on organisations from within these new perspectives to compare with those which are the subject of this book; and it is too soon to evaluate the contributions which such research and writing might make. We can be certain, however, that the sociological analysis of industrial organisations will continue to develop; and many will welcome the ways in which such changes may lead to a renewed appreciation of earlier research and writing, some of which has been neglected during more recent debates.

The economic and social context

The relationship between the approaches and content of research in industrial sociology since 1945 and the social and economic conditions in the society in which this research was being carried out is complex; a full exploration of this question would require much more detailed treatment than can be provided here. However, suggestions can be made as to the links which do exist (see also Brown 1984). Certainly, among those who have worked in the area for some time there is a growing awareness of how the unarticulated assumptions behind much earlier research in industrial sociology, including their own, have been called into question in the changed Britain of the past decade or so.

Distinguishing historical periods is always perilous, but it can be suggested that the post-war industrial history of Britain divides into three overlapping episodes. Initially there was a period of austerity, lasting from 1945 until the mid-1950s (rationing finally ended in 1954), characterised by material shortages and only slowly growing standards of living; by major economic and social changes such as nationalisation of key industries and the establishment of the 'welfare state'; and by a time of relative advantage for many British industries as compared with overseas competitors who had still not recovered from wartime devastation, and in some cases defeat. Secondly, there was something approaching two decades of 'affluence', the 'long boom', the period of 'you've never had it so good' and the 'white heat of technological revolution', with economic growth, full or near-full employment, and rising standards of living. Finally came the period from the mid-1970s when economic growth and full employment could clearly no longer be taken for granted and Britain's declining economic position relative to most other industrial societies became increasingly apparent. Of course, each of these periods overlaps with its neighbours; the affluent 1960s was also the decade in which poverty was 'rediscovered' and the incidence of strikes increased; the decline in employment in manufacturing industry in Britain and the increase in unemployment both started in the 1960s and pre-date the first oil price rise of 1973 which, with its disruptive effects on the whole world economy, is probably the most obvious date for the start of the present period.

Not surprisingly it can be argued that, perhaps after a slight time lag, each of these periods roughly coincided with distinct episodes in the development of higher education and support for social research. Thus, the university system expanded slowly until the end of the 1950s, and research funding was sparse; the 1960s brought the rapid expansion of higher education in universities, polytechnics and other colleges, and the establishment of the SSRC; conversely since the mid-1970s 'rationalisation' has replaced expansion in higher education, and universities, polytechnics and the research councils have been faced with cuts and uncertainties in funding which have had clear adverse consequences for research activity, as well as so much else.

Some of the links between economic and social conditions and industrial sociological research are equally direct, perhaps especially where there is a clear public interest in research in certain areas. The immediate post-war period saw the demand for research which would improve the productivity of British industry and, for example, projects were supported on the resistance to and acceptance of technical changes and innovations, and the effectiveness of financial incentives. There was also interest in research on the newly nationalised industries (Acton Society Trust 1951, Clegg 1950). In the largely fully employed economy of the 1960s and early 1970s, when there was also a 'resurgence' of strikes in Britain and Western Europe, sociological research was expected to explain the causes of industrial conflict. Research was also directed to questions of industrial democracy and new forms of work organisation, which were seen as potential means to improve worker commitment and management–worker relations.

In the most recent period, since the mid-1970s, the changes in the world of work have perhaps been even more far-reaching and extensive than in the decades following the Second World War, and in Britain their extent and nature have been significantly affected by the actions and inactions of the Thatcher Governments of the 1980s. It is only possible to list some of the more important developments: the continuing high levels of unemployment; the catastrophic decline in manufacturing industry; the advocacy of and support for 'enterprise', self-employment and small business, which have helped bring about a major reversal in the previous long term trend for self-employment to decline relatively and absolutely; legislative changes in industrial relations and the responses of trade unions to them and to the loss of members due to unemployment and industrial restructuring; changes in the organisation and management of work designed to increase flexibility, and to encourage employee involvement and commitment, though on management's terms; and changes in the composition of the labour force brought about by early retirements, high levels of youth unemployment, and the increasing numbers of women in employment, especially in part-time jobs.

Some of the responses of sociologists and other social scientists to these changes have been immediate and direct, for example increasing interest in and research on the labour market, and on redundancy and unemployment. Of probably greater long term importance, however, has been the widespread acceptance, in response to changes such as the increases in men's unemployment and in women's employment, of the importance of studying all forms of work and not just employment. This has provided a more satisfactory basis for defining a field of study; it also makes it more likely that those studying industrial organisations, only one albeit an important context for work, will acknowledge the significance of the interrelations between employment and work in all sorts of other settings.

Not all research activity has reflected these changes in industry and employment nor been directed towards publicly identified problems, even though the chances of gaining research funding are generally greater for research focused in such a way. As we shall see the questions which have attracted the interest and attention of industrial sociologists have to some extent arisen from developments within the subject itself; as one theoretical perspective appears to become exhausted, or as the assumptions based on a current theoretical framework are called into question by the findings of empirical research, new perspectives are explored. Occasionally the publication of a particular book or article has proved especially influential. More general social movements have also had their effects.

All these influences can be seen at work in the quantitative growth and qualitative development of research on women's work during the past two decades (for recent reviews see Beechey 1986, 1987; also Brown 1976). Changes in the occupational and industrial structure have been important. Women have become much more prominent in the labour force, in absolute terms and even more so relatively, since the 1960s. Equal pay and equal opportunities have been the subject of legislation and remain issues of public debate. Within sociology the question of gender, about which 'malestream' sociology was seriously deficient, has acquired increasing importance. Empirical findings in such areas as the labour market and the recruitment and control of a labour force have demanded that gender differences be fully considered, whilst the essential contribution made by women's (unpaid) work to the production and reproduction of all labour forces has slowly been recognised. Feminism and the women's movement have changed the intellectual climate in general and explicitly advocated research which takes gender seriously.

Thus the identification and selection of research problems, and of the conceptual frameworks within which they are to be formulated and investigated, must always be seen as *in part* conditioned by the context within which those processes occur. Equally it is important to be aware of the things which are taken for granted and the questions which are not asked. In the 1960s, for example, researchers tended to take full employment and relative economic prosperity for granted – and they were not alone in that! It is now possible to see that the situation then was in some ways atypical and had occurred due to the coincidence of a specific set of historical conditions. Recognition that this was the case should ensure that current research avoids a similar mistake. Even for the study of a particular workplace, the changing international division of labour, the policies of transnational corporations, the state of the world economy, and the actions and inactions of the state may all be relevant to a full and adequate account of what appears to be a specific local situation. The criticism that industrial sociologists allowed their enquiries to stop at the plant gate is a long-standing, and too often justified, one; it has been given greater force by the economic and social changes of the last two decades.

THE SCOPE OF INDUSTRIAL SOCIOLOGY

At the start of the 1960s three surveys were published of the condition of industrial sociology at that time. Two of them (Tréanton and Reynaud 1964; Smith 1961) were explicitly international in coverage, and the third (Burns 1962) ranged almost as widely. From them one can gain a clear idea of the substantive concerns of industrial sociologists up to that time and of the ways in which they defined their field of study. Although there seemed to be considerable agreement as to what industrial sociology was 'about', and this definition has not changed greatly since then, neither these early nor later surveys and summaries have given the subject real overall coherence or demarcated it clearly from other academic specialisms. Whether or not this is seen as a 'problem' (other than for writers of text books and designers of syllabuses) it is clear that industrial sociology has faced the perennial question of defining its boundary with other areas within sociology and its distinctiveness in relation to other subjects within the social sciences.

Both Smith and Tréanton and Reynaud began their reviews with reference to *Management and the Worker* and the Human Relations tradition, and both emphasised how much the subject had developed since that starting point (see also Smith 1959). In their report on the literature of the subject published between 1951 and 1962 Tréanton and Reynaud, for example, referred to studies of formal organisations and bureaucracy; professionalisation; trade unions, industrial relations and strikes; workers' participation and its political implications and connections; and the relations between the labour movement and economic development. Their bibliography was organised into an even more extensive list of sub-headings.

Smith was primarily concerned with the organisation and content of teaching, and of text books, rather than research, and despite the considerable diversity of definitions of the subject and of syllabuses he unearthed, he was able to suggest two broad headings under which teaching could be developed: 'the social structure of large-scale industry' and the 'mutual relations between industrial and social institutions'. Under the first were to be included 'work units' (the influence of technology; management structures; social relations among workers; the factory as a social system); the enterprise, trade unions and industrial relations; and work cultures and socialisation. The second considered a number of ways in which industry and industrialisation related to other aspects of the social structure of society, thereby merging 'into that part of general sociology which is concerned with the structure of industrial societies' (Smith 1961, 71–2). Thus the apparent concomitant of the very necessary development of industrial sociology away from a narrow preoccupation with the face-to-face social relations in the workplace, isolated from the wider organisational, economic and social context, was the abandonment of any clear boundary between the sociology of industry and the sociology of industrial society. Yet there was no obvious focus around which industrial sociology could be organised either, except possibly the factory/workplace as a social system, and that raised other problems.

In his introduction to Smith's book Reynaud took up the same themes and suggested that industrial sociology is perhaps not only the application of a hierarchy of analytical methods to a more or less clearly defined field, but also the discovery of certain phenomena which are the driving force of industrial society, and the affirmation that this society, as an industrial one, has its own particular dynamic.

(Smith 1961, 19)

He went on to develop the ambitious notion that industrial sociology might be 'striving . . . to give a strict sense to the concept of industrial society'.

Its subject is not the enterprise, the trade union or the industry; it will have to examine the industrial nature of our societies, the structures related to that nature and the sequence of their transformations, and, in short, to put together a structural and historical model which will account for them.

(Smith 1961, 21)

In what is still an outstanding brief discussion of the problems and methods of industrial sociology Burns made the same distinction between two areas: on the one hand 'the *external* references of the industrial system' and a 'concern with industrialism as the characteristic institution of modern advanced societies and as the prime mover of social change in them'; and on the other 'the *internal* order of industry and the situation arising within it', 'the internal structure of industrial concerns and the roles and situations prevailing in industrial milieux' (Burns 1962, 185). His account makes fewer claims than Reynaud's as to the centrality of industrial sociology for sociology in general, but does suggest that research on the internal relationships of industry may be an essential component in understanding the nature of industrialism:

there is a growing connexion . . . between studies of the internal structure and institutions of industrial undertakings, those of the way in which the industrial system is evolving, and those, again, of the way in which industrialism processes society and its members. There is, in fact, an explicit seeking after a synthetic view of the institutional patterns in modern society which derive from and contribute to its essentially industrial character.

(Burns 1962, 208)

By the 1960s, therefore, the sociological study of industry had developed to a state where there were a number of key unresolved questions about its scope and boundaries. If, as the enthusiasts asserted, it provided a key to understanding the peculiar nature and dynamics of industrial societies, could it remain distinct from a (general) sociology of industrial societies? If a more limited view were to be taken, that it should be concerned with the internal relations of (especially large-scale) industrial organisations, surely the lesson of research had been that these could not and should not be studied in isolation from the wider institutional context? Was it satisfactory, in any case, to take a common-sense understanding of 'industry' as a basis for a field of study? What about other contexts in which people were employed and/or in which work was carried out – government, hospitals, agriculture, voluntary organisations? Was what happened in (mostly large-scale manufacturing) industry really so distinctive?

In the text books on the subject which appeared over the next twenty years the authors had in practice to confront these questions, by virtue of what they included in or excluded from their coverage of the field, even if they did not do so explicitly. Approaches varied considerably and it cannot be claimed that a consensus has emerged, though some interesting clues as to the possible bases for one can be discerned. No one has taken up the challenge suggested by Reynaud, but most authors have seen the subject as involving a good deal more than the study of industrial organisations more or less in isolation.

Perhaps the widest coverage was offered by the earliest British text book (Parker *et al.* 1967, 1981) which discussed, briefly and on the whole descriptively, 'Industry and . . . ' education, the family, social stratification, the community and the polity, as well as industrial organisations and roles, and aspects of occupations; but such coverage was at the expense of any overarching framework. Eldridge (1971) adopted a quite different approach, though in its own way also eclectic: he traced the ways in which some of the central problems raised in the work of the great nineteenth and early twentieth century social theorists, especially the issues of anomie and alienation, had been taken up within industrial sociology and continued to underlie current preoccupations. The most theoretically single-minded, but also limited, approach to the study of industrial sociology was Fox's carefully titled *A Sociology of Work in Industry* (1971) where a social action perspective was used to build both an account of the organising of work and a discussion of industrial conflict and its regulation.

In more recently published texts the substantive coverage has widened again, for example to include sociological studies of occupations (Watson 1980), social stratification and class consciousness (Hill 1981) and images of the working class (Hirszowicz 1981). All three of these authors located their discussions of social relations in industry within accounts, though brief ones, of salient characteristics of 'industrial' or 'capitalist' society. In other respects, however, for example the amount of attention given to trade unionism, industrial conflict and industrial relations, there are considerable differences in treatment. Both Watson and Hill, however, focused on the social relations of employment as a key point in their analysis – 'the implicit contract between employer and employee' (Watson 1980, 67; 1987, 100–1), and 'employment and the social relations involved in production' (Hill 1981, 257). Their subsequent arguments differ considerably, but I shall argue in Chapter 6 that such an analytical point of reference can provide industrial sociology with a coherence that most approaches to it in the past have lacked. Such a starting point has the potential advantage, which Watson comes closer to realising than Hill, of directing attention to forms of employment other than the conventional ones which have been the most frequent subjects of research; it directs attention to the service sector as well as manufacturing, part-time employment as well as full-time, women's employment as well as men's, small and marginal enterprises as well as large, established corporations, and so on.

The fissiparous and eclectic tendencies of industrial sociology have been increased by the fact that a number of important and interesting specialist debates have developed concerning topics within the fields it normally covers. Some of these debates have taken on a life of their own and given rise to very considerable bodies of literature, so that they can only with difficulty be treated as an integral part of the industrial sociology. For example, the question of the ownership and control of industrial enterprises has understandably attracted the attention of industrial sociologists interested in the social relations and distribution of power within large-scale public and private corporations. It has also, however, been of interest to social scientists – economists, political scientists and others – whose prime concern may be to understand the consequences of differences in the pattern of ownership and control for economic decisions by organisations or their relations with government. Ever since Berle and Means (1932) first argued that the large joint stock company would in important ways be different from the ideal typical capitalist enterprise because it was not for the most part owned by the executives who effectively controlled it, a debate has raged as to the extent of the separation of ownership and control, and as to its likely or actual consequences (see Scott 1979, 1985). This debate has not been very well integrated with other topics in industrial sociology. Other examples of such specialised areas of research are the question of industrial democracy and worker participation (see the reviews by Ramsay 1982 and Brannen 1983), and a number of the issues relating to trade union membership and government (discussed by Banks 1974; Undy *et al.* 1981).

Industrial sociology derives its identity and any coherence it can claim from its place within the discipline of sociology. It uses sociological concepts and analysis to explore and try to explain action and interaction within one area of social life. As we have seen there can be problems as to how that area can best be defined and delimited, but in whatever way that is done no sociologist should want to deny other social scientists the right to investigate the same subject matter using their own disciplinary concepts and techniques.

The development of such specialised areas of study as those described above may have tended to fragment industrial sociology but it did not challenge the viability of the subject itself. In the cases of 'industrial relations' and what can most conveniently be labelled 'organisational behaviour' the situation was rather different. Both of these areas of study are defined primarily in terms of the substantive problems to be investigated, which therefore permits a variety of disciplinary approaches to that subject matter. The subject matter of industrial relations – management–worker relations, collective bargaining, trade unions – is of interest to historians, psychologists, economists, political scientists, lawyers and others, as well as to sociologists; and this is also the case for 'organisational behaviour' – the ways in which organisations are structured, and the social processes which occur within them. In each of these subjects there developed both a substantial corpus of research and writing and an institutional presence in university and polytechnic departments and specialised research units. If the development of industrial relations and organisational behaviour as subjects of study meant no more than that researchers from a variety of disciplinary backgrounds were focusing their attentions on the same subject matter as sociologists there would be no particular challenge to industrial sociology; indeed the stimulation to be derived from such multi-disciplinary endeavour should be welcomed. In each case, however, some scholars have claimed more than that.

Industrial relations

Industrial relations has been the longer and more securely established of these two areas of research and teaching. University chairs in the subject were established in the inter-war period, and since 1945 the study of industrial relations has developed considerably. Though first degrees in the subject are still relatively rare – courses as part of other undergraduate degrees are much more common – there are a number of taught graduate courses, and industrial relations features in the syllabus of management studies, in extra-mural teaching, and elsewhere. Most of those involved in the academic study of industrial relations have come to it from other disciplines, including sociology, and in many cases their academic identity has remained with the original subject. Industrial relations provides them primarily with a substantive area for research on problems of interest to their original discipline and amenable to its analytical techniques. For some, however, industrial relations has been the prime focus of academic identity and it is the attempt to establish industrial relations as 'an intellectual discipline in its own right' rather than 'a field of study to be cultivated with the well-tried methods of other disciplines' (Flanders 1970, 85) which has given rise to the issue of the relationship between industrial sociology and industrial relations in its most acute form.

During the first two decades after the Second World War research in industrial relations was almost uniformly descriptive and often strongly historical; the major exception was probably the research on industrial relations issues, such as wage determination, by economists. The complexity of the institutions and procedures of industrial relations in Britain and elsewhere, such as trade union organisation and collective bargaining arrangements, was such that it was a major task to provide a full, and properly scholarly, account of them. In this context the activities of sociologists could be subjected to rather hostile criticism and regarded as at best premature and more probably as having little to offer to the study of 'the system of industrial relations in Great Britain, its history, law and institutions'. The editors of a book with that title, which for many years provided the most authoritative account of industrial relations in Britain, commented on the work of sociologists as follows:

> We are aware that our concentration on the formal institutions of industrial relations may arouse criticism from those who have been affected by the teachings of the new school of 'human relations in industry'. This school applies the techniques of sociology and social psychology direct to 'situations' which it discovers in factories and other places of work. There is no *a priori* reason why this method should not be preferred to ours. The school is, however, in an early stage of development, and has still to provide material which could be used for teaching. Moreover, much of its published work shows a deplorable lack of historical understanding and, sometimes, a failure to appreciate the nature of the 'situation' studied due to ignorance of the formal institutions which surround it. Accordingly the study of the institutions seems to us a proper preliminary to the use of these more adventurous methods.
>
> (Flanders and Clegg 1954, v–vi)

Important changes in the relationship between the subjects of industrial relations and industrial sociology took place during the 1960s. It is probable that the rapid expansion of sociological teaching and research, and of the social sciences more generally, would have brought this about, but the process was undoubtedly hastened and publicised by the work of the Royal Commission on Trade Unions and Employers' Associations (the Donovan Commission) which sat from 1965 to 1968. As one of a number of *Research Papers* the Commission asked Alan Fox, lecturer in industrial sociology in the University of Oxford, to write 'an assessment of the contribution which industrial sociology can make towards understanding and resolving some of the problems now being considered by the Royal Commission' (Fox 1966, i). Fox's arguments were widely noted and well received. His assessment – not surprisingly perhaps – was a very positive one. He emphasised the importance of knowledge of 'the particular pattern of social organisation that has evolved in the situation concerned' for an understanding of industrial relations behaviour and argued that the

'structural determinants' of behaviour, which he saw as the particular concern of sociology, must be identified and changed if
desired changes in industrial relations practice were to be successfully achieved (Fox 1966, 33).

Even more influential was the analysis embodied in the *Report* of
the Commission itself (Royal Commission 1968). The Commission
drew a basic distinction between the 'formal' system of industry-
wide collective bargaining embodied in official institutions and
the 'informal system' of bargaining over piecework, additions to
basic wage rates, and overtime earnings at the factory level, which
was seen as largely out of the control of employers and their
associations and of unions. The development of this 'informal
system' in conditions of full employment had led to increasing
numbers of unofficial and unconstitutional strikes. The Commission saw the solution to these problems of disorderly industrial
relations as lying in voluntary action by the parties themselves,
management and unions, with state assistance but without
coercion, to secure the necessary institutional reforms and to
establish orderly and effective collective bargaining procedures,
and agreed bilateral control over levels of pay and working
practices.

In the light of such an analysis it would have been difficult to
continue to argue that sociological investigations of industrial
'situations' had little or nothing to offer to the study of industrial
relations. Instead influential voices amongst students of industrial
relations argued that the subject should develop its own theoretical framework and direct research to actual patterns of
behaviour as well as the more 'formal' institutional framework
within which they occurred. The Commission's views had been
strongly influenced by the writings of Allan Flanders (who had
been jointly responsible for the previously quoted negative judgement on sociology). In 1965 Flanders had published a pamphlet
Industrial Relations: what is wrong with the system? (1970, 83–128)
which not only dealt with the then current problems of British
industrial relations practice but also made a powerful case for
regarding industrial relations as a subject which has its own distinctive body of theory.

Although Flanders sidestepped the question of making a 'case
for treating industrial relations as an intellectual discipline in its
own right', he went on to argue:

Even if the subject is regarded as no more than a field of study
to be cultivated with the well-tried methods of other disciplines,
its development must depend on the mutual support of theory
and research. At its simplest, theory is needed to pose the right
questions and research to provide the right answers, granted
that a constant interplay has to take place between the two. . . .
The drawback of relying on the theory of any one of the several
disciplines that have impinged on industrial relations is that it
was never intended to offer an integrated view of the whole
complex of institutions in this field. Theoretically speaking,
these disciplines tear the subject apart by concentrating attention on some of its aspects to the exclusion or comparative
neglect of others. And a partial view of anything, accurate as it
may be within its limits, must of necessity be a distorted one.
Hence the significance of the notion of a system of industrial
relations which expresses the subject's inherent unity.

(Flanders 1970, 85)

The next question was 'system of what?'. To answer this Flanders
referred to Dunlop's *Industrial Relations Systems* (1958), a book
which drew explicitly on the ideas about social systems developed
by the influential American social theorist, Talcott Parsons.

'Not until recently has it been explicitly stated that a system of
industrial relations is a system of rules' (Dunlop 1958, 13–16).
These rules appear in different guises: in legislation and statu-
tory orders; in trade union regulations; in collective agreements
and arbitration awards; in social conventions; in managerial
decisions; and in accepted 'custom and practice' . . . . In other
words, the subject deals with certain regulated or institutionalised relationships within industry. Personal, or in the language
of sociology 'unstructured', relationships have their importance
for management and workers, but they lie outside the scope of
a system of industrial relations.

(Flanders 1970, 86)

However, not all rules and relationships in industry are part of this
'system of industrial relations', but only those relationships which
are 'either expressed in or arise out of contracts of employment
(or service), which represent, in common speech, jobs. The study
of industrial relations may therefore be described as a study of the
institutions of job regulation' (Flanders 1970, 86).

This is not the place to provide an extended critique of Flanders's arguments, nor of the 'Oxford School' of industrial relations to which he made such a key contribution (for critical comment see, among others, Fox 1973; Hyman and Brough 1975; Goldthorpe 1977; Gabriel 1978). Perhaps the most important point of criticism has been Flanders's neglect of power as a factor in the relations between employers and employees, a neglect which allows him to attribute to the outcomes of collective bargaining a legitimacy, acceptability and 'fairness' which they did not possess. Although he accepts that there are inherent conflicts of interest in the relations of employers and employees – and in this respect clearly differs from Human Relations thinking – Flanders's ideas seem to have a strong affinity with a pluralist normative functionalism. It is assumed that such conflicts can be regulated and contained within a normatively approved institutional framework; there is no sense of irreconcilable conflicts, of contradiction, nor of inequalities of power which enable one party to impose solutions on others.

Despite disclaimers, and despite the use of terms and concepts which seem to be predominantly 'sociological', Flanders did appear to be attempting to establish the subject of industrial relations as a discipline which was distinct from those disciplines, including sociology, which had previously 'cultivated' this field. By implication industrial relations would now supplant those disciplines in the study of this area of social life. Although management–worker relations, industrial conflict, and so on do not constitute the whole of the subject matter of industrial sociology, they do make up a substantial part of it. An industrial relations 'discipline' which was in effect very sociological in outlook would clearly overlap if not compete with the work of industrial sociologists. Indeed, in subsequent years the outcome of research in industrial relations was to lead researchers to give increasing attention to questions of management organisation and strategy (see, for example, Thurley and Wood 1983) and thus further increase the area of overlap – or competition.

Organisational behaviour

An interest in the 'theory' of organisations can be traced back to the earliest years of this century, if not much earlier. At that time the emergence of large-scale organisations in industry, government and elsewhere stimulated attempts to identify the common characteristics of such forms of social life. Weber's ideal type 'bureaucracy' dates from this period; the rather different 'theories' of Weber's contemporaries had a strong normative element and attempted to provide guidance to businessmen, politicians, and others as to how such enterprises should be structured and regulated (see Pugh *et al.* 1964; Albrow 1970; Pugh 1971). Weber's writings on bureaucracy are probably the most important point of reference for the development within sociology of a concern with the sociology of organisations. This overlapped with industrial sociology in so far as it was concerned with industrial and commercial enterprises, but differed from it in pursuing comparative studies of organisations of all sorts – industrial, religious, educational, governmental, charitable, or whatever – in order to develop generalisations applicable across the whole range of organisational forms (see, for example, Etzioni 1961; Blau and Scott 1963).

The establishment of 'organisational behaviour' as a distinct subject with an institutional base in universities, polytechnics, business schools and research institutes in Britain is more recent, dating from the 1960s, but it drew heavily on this sociological tradition as well as on other social science disciplines. Leading advocates have described it in the following terms:

> Organizational behaviour is the study of the structure and functioning of organizations and the behaviour of groups and individuals within them. It is an emerging inter-disciplinary quasi-independent science, drawing primarily on the disciplines of sociology and psychology, but also on economics, political science, social anthropology, and production engineering.
>
> (Pugh *et al.* 1975, 1)

Pugh and his colleagues went on to argue that it was necessary to integrate the three levels of organisational analysis (organisational, group and individual) which had previously been dealt with separately by sociologists, social psychologists and psychologists respectively. Only in this way could a number of problems be adequately tackled. For example:

> One of the most common views held by practising managers is that the structure of an organization is a reflection of the personality of its chief executive. We know of no evidence

bearing on this hypothesis because it cannot be tackled in terms of the separate disciplines of psychology and sociology. The sociologist, with his conceptual limitation against accepting that an individual can more than marginally affect an organization, tends to regard the hypothesis as naive; while the psychologist's conceptual limitations make him regard the notion of organization structure with suspicion, as being unreal, since it cannot be reduced to behaviour. But to anyone who has not had the benefit of a specifically sociological or specifically psychological training, it seems an eminently reasonable hypothesis and well worth further study. But this can only be done by people who are equally at home in the structural and individual traditions and who are, therefore, prepared to develop a balanced model of the relationship between the two.

(Pugh *et al.* 1975, 25)

A number of comments can be made about this position. It is doubtful whether most sociologists or psychologists are as blinkered as these authors suggest. The literature of industrial sociology contains a number of illuminating studies of the importance of the role and behaviour of the chief executive for social relations and social processes within organisations (e.g. Gouldner 1955; Guest 1962), and a classic *sociological* analysis of precisely this question of the influence on an organisation's structure and performance of 'the character of the head of the concern' (Burns and Stalker 1961, 210 *et seq.*). More generally, Abrams (1982, Ch.9) has argued persuasively that it is possible to account 'sociologically for the individual in particular' if the problem is treated historically, and has demonstrated how this is done by reference to revolutionaries such as Victor Serge, Lenin and Rosa Luxemburg.

It must be doubted whether it is helpful to regard the study of organisational behaviour as a discipline or sub-discipline, capable of developing its own concepts and analytical frameworks, rather than as a field of study to which scholars from different disciplinary backgrounds can helpfully contribute. It is not self-evident that the answer to the problems identified by Pugh and his colleagues lies in creating a new 'discipline' rather than in inter-disciplinary work and/or the development within disciplines of approaches to problems previously regarded as outside their remit – as Abrams has done for 'the historical sociology of individuals'. Further, some aspects of the ways in which 'organisational behaviour' has developed are open to criticism. For example, it has tended to imply an overdetermined and reified view of the organisation (significantly the reference is to 'behaviour' rather than 'action'); the sources and nature of conflict within organisations have been inadequately conceptualised; and, although this is not always nor necessarily the case, some of the crucial distinguishing characteristics of different types of organisations can be overlooked in the quest for generalisations applicable to organisations in general (see Silverman 1968, 1970; Albrow 1968; Chapters 2 and 3 below; but see also Donaldson 1985, 1988; Hinings 1988).

Nevertheless, whatever the validity of these criticisms, 'organisational behaviour' is by now well established and in contention as the academic specialism within which studies of industrial organisations should be carried out. It is in evidence particularly in business schools and management centres. There must be suspicion that this is because it is, or appears to be, less critical of management in particular, and society as it is presently constituted in general, than sociologists deservedly or not have gained the reputation for being. (It should be said that Pugh and his colleagues explicitly reject the view that 'organisational behaviour' is or should be primarily concerned with management's problems (1975, 16).) Whatever the reason, there is here a considerable overlap with, if not a challenge to, a central area of interest within industrial sociology.

In exploring the scope of industrial sociology we have identified a number of areas of difficulty. There is no clear boundary between the study of 'industry' and the study of 'industrial society'. A number of topics conventionally within the scope of industrial sociology have developed a 'life of their own' and acquired a large specialist literature at least some of which is not sociological in orientation. In two areas, both of which are central to industrial sociology as conventionally understood and practised, rival '(sub-) disciplines' have developed concerned respectively with the study of industrial relations and the study of organisational behaviour.

As has already been suggested, this may be no cause for alarm. The social world does not come neatly packaged with disciplinary labels attached, but has to be constituted as a subject for study. There will always be boundary problems, and the need to reconsider and possibly change the limits to one's area of enquiry. Whereas it might be convenient for teachers and students to have a clear analytical point of reference and a clearly delimited field of study, some of the most fruitful work in science, social and natural, has typically been done on problems on the margins of two or more disciplines.

Indeed, what might be thought a more serious ground for concern is that the work of industrial sociologists has been restricted in ways which have little or no theoretical justification. Industrial sociological research for the most part has been concerned with large-scale enterprises rather than small, with manufacturing industry rather than the service sector, manual work rather than non-manual, men's work rather than women's. In each respect there are important exceptions, and there have been changes for the better in all these respects in recent years. Nevertheless the exceptions and changes are not yet numerous and substantial enough to defuse altogether the criticism that there have been and remain some serious distortions and lacunae in the ways in which industrial sociologists have in practice pursued their interests.

No subject develops in an entirely neat and systematic way; among other things, personal interests (intellectual and material), external influences, and chance see to that. The rather *ad hoc* development of industrial sociology, however, reflects – to put it no more strongly – the absence of any clear analytical point of reference and the lack of an agreed definition of what it is about. The term 'industry' itself is unhelpful; it suggests manufacturing, and on the whole manufacturing of a traditional 'smokestack' sort, whereas the problems with which sociology deals in this context – questions of the way work is organised and controlled, the nature of employer–employee relations, and so on – are problems to be found in all contexts in which people are employed. For this reason, among others, I shall argue in the conclusions to this book that a focus on the employment relationship and on organisations, of all sorts, within which people are employed, would provide a much more coherent and theoretically defensible definition of this field of study within sociology. This would be even more the case if sociological analysis of the social relations and social organisation of employment were to be undertaken in the context of a more general sociology of work. This would allow explicit recognition to be given to the fact that the employment relationship is only one, though in our sort of society the most important, context within which work is carried out; and would enable illuminating comparisons to be made, and important interconnections to be explored, between work as an employee and work in other settings, domestic, charitable, and so on.

FOUR THEMES

We began the discussion in this chapter by considering those, mostly large and powerful, industrial organisations which 'get their names in the paper'. The study of industrial organisations of all sorts has been of long standing interest to sociologists and has been a central, perhaps the central concern within that part of the subject conventionally known as the sociology of industry. It is with the attempts by industrial sociologists to develop a satisfactory theoretical framework or perspective within which to analyse industrial organisations that the remainder of this book is largely concerned. This means that some of the other concerns of industrial sociologists, particularly the analysis of industrial conflict and the institutions of industrial relations, will only be considered in so far as they impinge on, and in the context of, these attempts to 'understand' industrial organisations.

The discussion is structured around four themes or approaches, each of which contains an important organising idea or concept which has been used in empirical work and theoretical discussions to provide accounts of why organisations are as they are and why social relations and social processes within them occur as they do. These four perspectives do not exhaust all the possible ways in which industrial organisations have been conceptualised but they include and allow discussion of the most important bodies of work contributing to a sociology of industrial organisations. They also allow us to consider most of the key theoretical and methodological issues which have been at the centre of debates about organisations. Perhaps the most important such issue has been the competing claims of theories emphasising the structural and constraining nature of organisations as compared with those which emphasise that organisations are socially constructed and sustained by the actions of relatively autonomous human agents. It will be helpful to keep in mind this basic difference in approach during the discussion of the four perspectives, and we shall return to it in the final chapter.

The materials to be considered in relation to each of these approaches are quite diverse and it is important to be aware of the differences of view within each perspective and of the ways in which they have been developed and changed over time. There is, however, sufficient coherence and common ground in each case for the discussion to be arranged in this way.

In Chapter 2 we look at attempts to understand industrial organisations as 'systems'. The idea that the factory could be conceptualised as a 'social system' has a long history. The focus of the concluding chapters of *Management and the Worker* (Roethlisberger and Dickson 1939), it was taken up and developed in some of the earliest research in the immediate post-war period in Britain. We shall consider three rather different attempts to develop the use of this concept within industrial sociology:

1 The work of W.H. Scott and his colleagues in the Department of Social Science, University of Liverpool, during the 1950s and 1960s which elaborated the idea of the factory as a social system with four main elements: formal structure, informal structure, occupational structure and tradition.
2 The work of Elliott Jaques and Wilfred Brown at the Glacier Metal Company analysing the company as comprising various systems of roles ('executive', 'representative', etc.), and developing a detailed prescriptive framework on this basis.
3 The work of members of the Tavistock Institute of Human Relations (Trist, Rice, Emery, Miller, Sofer and others) in developing and applying an 'open socio-technical systems' approach to the analysis of industrial, and other, situations in this country and abroad.

'Systems thinking' has been subjected to considerable criticism, against which none of these three groups of writers can be altogether satisfactorily defended. The use of the notion of 'system' has been seen as 'reifying' the organisation, that is treating it, spuriously, as a 'thing' with needs, goals and intentions, and the power to act and react, independent of the individuals and groups of which it is composed. As a result it can become difficult to account for conflict within organisations, and there is a danger that research will be biased in favour of management, the group which in practice does articulate the organisation's 'goals'. In contrast other researchers have emphasised the plurality of systems within any one industrial organisation; understanding and accounting for the changing structure of an enterprise requires an analysis of the processes of bargaining and negotiation between the claims of these different 'systems'. Further questions arise about the definition of the boundary to the organisation/system, and its relationship with its 'environment'. These are central to the second theme, discussed in Chapter 3.

In the course of comparative work a number of sociologists, notably Woodward and Burns, developed explanations of the structure of industrial organisations and the nature of social relations within them which drew attention to the differences in the 'context' or 'environment' within which the organisations operated. What has come to be known as 'contingency theory' attempts to provide an explanation of organisational structure and functioning as largely contingent upon such contextual factors as its factor and product markets, technology, ownership, and so on. The most ambitious attempt to pursue this line of argument in Britain was that of Pugh and his colleagues who were responsible for a programme of research, initially at the University of Aston, in the 1960s and early 1970s. Their large scale comparative studies of 'work organisations' of all sorts produced quantitative measures of contextual factors and aspects of organisational structure, and of the relationships between them, and went on to try to establish relationships between context and structure on the one hand, and organisational behaviour and performance on the other.

Most of the work in this tradition continued to conceptualise organisations as systems, though as 'open' rather than 'closed' systems, and to that extent it is subject to the sorts of criticisms which have been aimed at systems thinking more generally. The direction taken by the Aston team in particular has been more specifically criticised, both with regard to methodological detail and in its neglect of the scope for 'strategic choice' in structuring an organisation within the constraints set by context and environment. This criticism emphasises 'agency' as against 'structure', that is the role of actors – managers, workers, or whoever – in choosing to pursue certain goals and/or follow a certain line of action albeit within constraints set by the actions of others and the context within which they are placed.

In Chapter 4 we consider the 'social action approach' which argues that analysis of organisations should begin with the expectations and priorities, the 'orientations to work', of organisational members and see 'structural' features of organisations as the consequence of the resulting patterns of action. This approach was given particular prominence by the work of Goldthorpe and his colleagues in the 'Affluent Worker Project' in the 1960s, in the course of which a typology of orientations to work was developed and differences between these types explained largely in terms of actors' situations outside the workplace. Subsequently other writers have taken the 'action approach' in a phenomenological direction to develop a 'radically subjectivist' approach to organisational analysis, one which would limit the sociological task to exploring the ways in which people use notions like 'organisation', rather than analysing organisations seen as features of the world 'out there'.

Both the original 'social action approach' and these later developments have been extensively criticised. Most critics would accept that there can be no *a priori* statement of human 'needs' but only exploration of socially constructed and variable orientations to work; and that it is important to take the actor's 'definition of the situation' into account. They would be much more critical of the explanatory significance accorded to these factors in accounting for industrial attitudes and behaviour, and more generally in providing an understanding of the organisation as a whole. Constraints on action, and in particular the differential distributions of power and resources within society and within organisations, also need to be taken fully into account.

From the beginnings of industrial sociology in Britain some writers advocated and used a Marxist perspective in their work, particularly with regard to the explanation of industrial conflict and in relation to questions of ownership and control; but this use did not constitute an analysis of industrial organisations as such. From the late 1970s, however, perhaps the dominant form of analysis of organisations and of structures and processes within them became one which started with the 'capitalist labour process'. It is this which we consider in Chapter 5. The key publication in bringing about this transformation was Braverman's *Labor and Monopoly Capital* (1974) and much work in industrial sociology since the late 1970s has been framed within what can be called the labour process debate. This is concerned with the ways in which employers and/or managers ensure that the variable 'labour power' which their employees contract to make available to the organisation is transformed into 'labour' and produces value; it focuses therefore on the means by which employers *control* their employees and sees organisations predominantly as control structures.

One particular argument within this perspective which has

attracted a lot of attention and criticism is Braverman's assertion that the control strategy under monopoly capitalism involves 'deskilling' work and retaining all the mental and conceptual elements in management's hands. Though such processes do take place the universal degradation of work postulated by Braverman must remain unproven. More generally historical and contemporary empirical studies have shown that managements have potentially available a range of possible means of controlling the labour force, allowing some choice of strategy; and that the degree and nature of worker resistance to control, something explicitly neglected by Braverman, can influence the choice which is made. Thus whilst the perspective derived from Marx and Braverman remains illuminating it cannot be seen as adequate on its own and without amendment as an approach to the sociological analysis of organisations.

The final chapter considers how far the debates discussed in this book constitute any sort of cumulative theoretical advance in our understanding of industrial organisations and our ability to explain variations in their structure and operation. It then goes on to suggest that sociologists interested in 'industry' should pursue two related strategies of enquiry. On the one hand they should broaden the definition of their field to include work of all sorts; on the other, and within such a broader framework, they should take the employment relationship as the starting point for analysis. This relationship would provide a more satisfactory point of reference in defining the more specific field of enquiry and for the analysis of 'employing organisations'. Some of the crucial features of employment would be highlighted by comparison with other forms of and contexts for work. The broader focus of a sociology of work would make it easier to identify the interconnections and interdependencies between the social institutions of employment and the wider society in which they exist.

Chapter 2

Systems thinking

> In a general way it may be said that to think in terms of systems
> seems the most appropriate conceptual response so far avail-
> able when the phenomena under study – at any level and in any
> domain – display the character of being organized, and when
> understanding the nature of the interdependencies constitutes
> the research task.
>
> (Emery and Trist 1965, 21)

The notion of 'system' has played and continues to play a prominent part in attempts to understand and explain industrial organisations. As the quotation indicates there appears to be an
inherent appropriateness about using some sort of systems
concept or model to try to characterise industrial enterprises: their
fundamental quality is that they are 'organized'; they represent the
bringing together of a variety of resources for the achievement of
a purpose or purposes. The potential of the systems concept was
appreciated very early in the development of industrial sociology
as a distinctive area of study within sociology. The final part of
Management and the Worker (Roethlisberger and Dickson 1939)
opens with an account of 'an industrial organization as a social
system'. This and other accounts of the Hawthorne Experiments
have been enormously influential within industrial sociology; they
demonstrated what was possible in terms of both methods and
findings, set the agenda for a range of subsequent studies, and
generated a considerable secondary literature (see, for example,
Landsberger 1958; Smith 1987; and Parker *et al.* 1981, 85–91).
These writings also provided explicit links to the more general
development of systems thinking within social theory. Even without the example and influence of *Management and the Worker,*

however, the systems notion would surely have been applied to the study of industrial organisations because of the dominant position of structural functionalist theorising within sociology during the late 1940s and most of the 1950s.

In this chapter we shall explore some of the ways in which the notion of 'system' has been used within industrial sociology in Britain in research on industrial organisations. Systems approaches certainly have been, and probably still remain, the most common framework for organisational analysis, though their use is often largely implicit. I shall discuss three main examples of analyses of industrial enterprises as 'social systems': the work of the Department of Social Science, University of Liverpool in the 1950s and early 1960s under the leadership of W.H. Scott; the writings of Elliott Jaques and Wilfred (later Lord) Brown associated with the Glacier Metal Company enquiries from the late 1940s to the 1970s; and the contributions of members of the Tavistock Institute of Human Relations since the beginning of the 1950s in developing the notion of a 'socio-technical system'. Each of these groups attempted to use their own case study research in organisations to develop an explicit generally valid understanding of industrial organisations as systems. Their formulations are rather different and indicate something of the range of possibilities within a systems framework. They all made well-respected contributions to the sociology of industry through the reports of their empirical investigations and for that reason alone their theoretical work was not without influence. The 'socio-technical system' concept, however, has been of the greatest significance. In addition to their specific strengths and weaknesses all these approaches are subject to some of the more general criticisms of systems theorising which developed from the 1960s onwards.

The elaborations of a systems approach to attempt to meet these criticisms and take account of the findings of empirical research have led to formulations which seem at times to transform it altogether. The questions which remain are whether the concept of 'system' retains any significance in such a severely modified form, or conversely whether such a concept in at least a minimal sense is unavoidable in sociology. Alternative conceptions of the industrial enterprise will be considered in this light.

SOME GENERAL CONSIDERATIONS

The main theoretical framework for systems approaches to the sociological analysis of industrial organisations was to be found in 'functionalism'. Functionalism drew particularly on the contributions to sociology of Durkheim and Pareto, and was also strongly influenced by the writings of social anthropologists such as Malinowski and Radcliffe-Brown. The dominant figure in functionalist sociology in the 1950s was the American social theorist, Talcott Parsons (see, for example, Hamilton 1983, esp. 44), though there are relatively few explicit references to Parsons's writings in the analyses of industrial organisations discussed in this chapter. Accounts of the core elements of functionalist theory in sociology, of its development and diversity, and strengths and weaknesses, are available elsewhere (see, for example, Rex 1961; Cohen 1968; Moore 1979; Burrell and Morgan 1979, 41–117). Use of a functionalist framework clearly implied, indeed required, a systems approach to the analysis of the industrial enterprise.

Functionalism involves a 'holistic' approach to social phenomena, tending to 'treat societies or social wholes as having characteristics similar to those of organic matter or of organisms' (Cohen 1968, 14). It is anti-reductionist, and emphasises the 'systemic' properties of social wholes. These social aggregates are seen as involving differentiated units which are interdependent, and this 'combination of differentiation and interdependence permits asking two related questions: how is the interdependence of units effected? What contribution do the parts make to the whole?' (Moore 1979, 323–4). Explanation is therefore sought through the exploration of the 'functions' of the parts for the maintenance of the whole and showing how form is appropriate for such functions. Two important emphases in Parsons's contributions to this body of social theory are on the role of a common system of values in securing the integration of the social whole, and on the way in which the same explanatory strategy can be pursued at different levels of analysis so that the parts of the overall whole, whether it be a society or an organisation, can be treated as sub-systems of the total system. Each level of analysis has relative autonomy but at each level too the system or sub-system is analysed by exploring how its parts meet the 'functional requirements' of the larger whole (see, for example, the discussion in Mouzelis 1975, 149–57).

From the 1950s the parallel development of 'general systems

theory' reinforced this advocacy of a systems approach to the analysis of the industrial enterprise which was derived from functionalist social theory. General systems theory aimed to show how the same framework of concepts and assumptions could be used to analyse phenomena in a wide range of fields of scientific enquiry, to develop 'a new scientific doctrine, concerned with the principles which apply to systems in general' (Von Bertalanffy 1950, 28; see also Boulding 1956). General systems theory has been seen as of relevance for the whole range of physical, biological and social sciences but it draws heavily on the organismic analogy. Systems are conceived as 'open' with the connotation that they continue to exist because they exchange materials with their environment. A system can reorganise towards states of greater heterogeneity and complexity, and not maximum homogeneity of parts as is implied in the 'closed' system model. It has the property of 'equi-finality', being able to achieve a steady state, or homeostasis, from different initial conditions and in different ways, so that the system as a whole remains constant despite a considerable range of external changes. Attention focuses particularly on the exchanges across the boundaries of the system and the 'input–throughput–output' process by which the system maintains itself within its environment; and also on the feedback mechanisms by which homeostasis can be secured. As with Parsonian functionalism the overall system can be analysed into constituent sub-systems to which the same theoretical considerations apply (see the discussion in Burrell and Morgan 1979, 57–68).

As is clear from these brief accounts of theoretical sources, to refer to an industrial organisation as a 'system' is to make a number of assumptions about it: that it comprises a set of interdependent 'parts' such that a change in one part will affect some or all of the others, but that the whole system is more than just an aggregation of these parts; that there is some relatively clear continuity about this set of interdependent parts so that it can be considered the same organisation despite the changes which may take place; and that it has a relatively clear boundary which separates it from a wider 'environment'. In addition most conceptions of organisations as systems assume that there is an over-arching set of values and/or goals which secures the integration of the system; and, in open system models, that the maintenance of the system (and the achievement of its goals) are secured by exchanges between the system and its environment.

As any reading of the general literature on organisations as systems will reveal, such a list of assumptions is very much an essential minimum; most attempts to specify the systemic nature of industrial organisations are more complex and sophisticated (see, for example, Buckley 1967, 47–56; Burrell and Morgan 1979, esp. 118–60, 217–26; Clegg and Dunkerley 1980, 171–212; Silverman 1968, 26–38). Each of these characteristics raises questions, to which different systems approaches would give varying answers, some of which will be discussed below; at this stage it might be helpful to outline more explicitly certain key distinctions between types of system approach.

In the first place approaches vary in the degree of 'openness' attributed to the organisation/system: that is in the extent to which what happens within it is seen as explicable without refer- ence to anything outside it. Conceptions of organisations as completely closed are rare but some approaches place far more emphasis on organisation–environment transactions than others. This difference is related to two others: the model or analogy which is most likely to be referred to or implied in characterising organisations as systems; and the nature of the equilibrium which the organisation maintains so long as it survives. Closed system models imply a mechanical analogy with relatively static equilibrium maintaining a stable relationship between the parts. Open system models tend to draw on a biological analogy, though this may be with a single organism or with a species. Such systems survive by securing inputs of 'energy' from the environment and they are capable of adaptation, development or growth, thus achieving a dynamic equilibrium or homeostasis.

A further possibility is the use of a cybernetic model based on flows of information such as can be observed in (self-regulating) machines as well as in organisms (see Buckley 1967, 38–40, 58–80; Burrell and Morgan 1979, 65–8, 99–102). This approach uses the notion of system to characterise the ways in which the intended and the unintended consequences of social action feed back into the ongoing pattern of social relations; as such it appears to be emphasising the systemic nature of social life more generally rather than just that organisations should be seen as systems. The ways in which this system is structured are by processes of transmitting, receiving and interpreting information, meanings and decisions, and in this respect too it is clearly different from other approaches (Burrell and Morgan 1979, 99–102; see also Buckley 1967).

Even if what Buckley (1967, e.g. 17–23) terms a 'socio-cultural' system model based on cybernetics is left out of account, however, other models of organisations as systems differ markedly in terms of the conceptualisation of the parts of the system. A distinction used by Moore (1979, 338–9) in his discussion of functionalism is useful in this context, between 'concrete' and 'analytic' structures; the former 'constitute membership groups . . . or aggregates', the latter are 'identified by their functions'. Such a distinction is not always so clear cut; nevertheless, as we shall see, models of organisation can be placed on a continuum which ranges from those which are clearly concerned with relations of interdependence between sets of roles occupied by members of the organisation, to those which focus on patterns of activity which can be distinguished analytically but do not necessarily have a straightforward reference to some group, section or department within the organisation. Both types of formulation may be useful, but problems can arise if they are confused (see, for example, the discussion in Mouzelis 1975, xiv–xvi).

Management and the worker

Perhaps the earliest attempt to characterise an industrial organisation as a system was contained in the principal record of the Hawthorne Experiments (Roethlisberger and Dickson 1939, esp. 551–68). These 'experiments' took place at the Hawthorne Works of the Western Electric Company in Chicago between 1927 and 1932. They involved an, ultimately inconclusive, attempt to relate output in small work groups to variations in hours of work and rest pauses, and to changes in the payment system, over a period of two and a half years; an extensive interviewing programme using increasingly non-directive methods; and non-participant observation of a group of men for a period of six months focusing on the 'informal' organisation of the group and its controls over levels of output and other forms of behaviour.

The identification of the 'informal' organisation of an industrial enterprise became one of the most enduring legacies of the Hawthorne Experiments. It played a central part in the model which was developed of the industrial organisation as a social system. This conceived the organisation as having two major functions: producing a product and satisfying its members. The first function was economic and raised problems of external balance; the second had no readily accepted label and raised problems of internal equilibrium; but the two sets of problems were seen as interrelated and interdependent. The human organisation of an industrial plant can be distinguished from its technical organisation (the arrangement of machinery, materials, etc.). The human organisation can be seen as consisting of individuals, each with their own experiences, needs and sentiments, but also of the social organisation, the patterns of relations between the individuals and groups who constitute the organisation. These social relations give rise to and are influenced by processes of social valuation which assign status and create social distance; material objects, physical events, conditions of employment 'have to be interpreted as carriers of social value'; and 'the behaviour of no one person in an industrial organization . . . can be regarded as motivated by strictly economic or logical considerations' (Roethlisberger and Dickson 1939, 557).

It is on these lines that the social organisation is seen as divided into the formal and the informal organisation. The former comprises the systems, policies, rules and regulations of the plant and the patterns of human interrelations which are supposed to exist in order to secure cooperative effort and to achieve the economic goals of the enterprise. The informal organisation is all those social relations and social evaluations and distinctions which are not formally created and recognised; it may facilitate the functioning of the formal organisation and/or develop in opposition to it. Both the formal and the informal organisation of the enterprise have systems of ideas and beliefs. Three such systems were distinguished: the logic of costs and the logic of efficiency which express the values of the formal organisation; and the logic of sentiments, which expresses the values of the informal organisation. Because all these parts of the overall system may change at different rates there are possibilities of 'imbalance' in the system which may manifest itself in various ways. In particular the technical organisation can be changed more rapidly than the social, and the formal more rapidly than the informal, leading to the possibility of resistance to change.

It will already be apparent from the earlier brief discussion of the sources of systems approaches in industrial sociology that more recent conceptualisations of the industrial organisation as a system have become more complex than this fairly straightforward model. The development of such accounts is indeed in part a response to the inadequacies perceived in Roethlisberger and Dickson's formulations. Many of the criticisms to which it has been subject, however, such as questioning the possibility and/or desirability of consensus and harmony, or the difficulty of applying the 'formal/informal' dichotomy, are also applicable to some of its successors. Such arguments will be explored further below. The outline here of the ideas formulated in *Management and the Worker* serves as an example of an at-the-time relatively sophisticated attempt to conceptualise the industrial organisation as a social system. It was a major source on which industrial sociologists in Britain, and elsewhere, could and did draw as research developed after the Second World War.

THE FACTORY AS A SOCIAL SYSTEM

The most important and influential university-based group of industrial sociologists in Britain from the beginning of the 1950s until the early 1960s was that working in the Department of Social Science, University of Liverpool, under the leadership of W.H. Scott. Their researches included studies of joint consultation and industrial participation, of technical change in the steel industry and the introduction of computers in offices, and of industrial conflict and industrial relations in the docks and in coal mining. Much of this work involved very detailed empirical investigation of particular enterprises without any very great attempt to generalise beyond the particular case. As such it will not be described in detail here (for a review see Brown 1965). Nevertheless the group's research was also intended to 'develop basic knowledge of industrial institutions and behaviour' (Scott *et al.* 1956, 3). As the group's work was concentrated on case studies of one, or at the most a small number of enterprises, it was to the analysis of the industrial organisation that their main theoretical contribution was directed.

This contribution took the form of the development of an analytical framework around the notion of a factory as a social system (for the most important formulations see Scott *et al.* 1956, 263–81; Scott 1958, 18–42). The initial basic concept which formed the starting point for this framework was the notion of *social structure* – 'the observed tendency for social relations to be structured or patterned, that is, to assume a definite and recognisable form, which tends to persist and to be found widely in many situations'. Three main aspects of social structure were distinguished: formal structure, occupational structure and informal structure; they are abstractions, representing only a partial description of social structure; must be treated separately for purposes of description and analysis; but are interrelated and constitute an interdependent system (Scott *et al.* 1956, 13).

Though they do not always give it the most emphasis it can be suggested that for these authors the notion of 'occupational structure' was perhaps the most significant. It is just because 'a highly specialised division of labour is probably the most distinctive and important structural characteristic of industrial society' (Scott *et al.* 1956, 263) that formal structures are needed to achieve effective coordination or cooperation for the attainment of common purpose. 'Occupational structure is the division of a labour force into categories on the basis of differences of function and skill.' It is closely associated with the system of rewards, material and social; and it may give rise to the formation of occupational groups of greater or lesser cohesiveness, with shared values and attitudes, and greater or lesser awareness of common interests, and to the growth of occupational associations, such as trade unions, to further those interests (14–15).

The defining characteristics of the 'formal structure' are that it comprises those elements in social relations which are explicit, though not necessarily embodied in written documents, and intentionally created to serve particular purposes which are recognised in common by the persons involved, though not necessarily mutually accepted by them (Scott *et al.* 1956, 13–14; Scott 1958, 29–31). In conventional terms it includes the formal organisation of management, the allocations of responsibility and authority, conditions of employment, working arrangements on the shop floor, and the organisation of trade unions within the plant and the machinery of management–union relations. The idea that the 'formal structure' is intentional and purposive is somewhat weakened, however, by the comment that it 'may crystallise out gradually, as it were, from relationships which were previously informal and spontaneous' (Scott 1958, 30).

The *informal structure* of the plant comprises those aspects of face-to-face relations which are structured or patterned but which are not regarded by the participants as, nor preconceived for the purpose of, achieving a particular or limited objective. They are relations based on congeniality or friendship.

(Scott *et al.* 1956, 275)

Such relations will tend to reflect divisions and groupings created by the occupational structure and the formal structure, but are not determined by them; indeed social ties established outside the plant may influence the informal structure, and the norms and patterns of behaviour and of communication influenced and maintained by the informal structure may conflict with the demands of the formal structure (Scott 1958, 31).

All three elements – occupational structure, formal and informal structures – will influence the values and attitudes of members of the organisation. In addition, however, there may be values, attitudes and behaviour which are not the outcome of existing social structure but are influenced by 'tradition', which becomes the fourth main category in this framework of analysis. Some of these traditional values, ideas and ideologies may be characteristic of society in general, such as beliefs in 'fairness' and 'justice', or in 'a free market' and 'freedom of competition'; others may be specific to a particular plant, such as the 'family ideology' which can still be found in firms which have since grown to be large public companies (Scott *et al.* 1956, 15–16, and see summary 249; Scott 1958, 32–3).

There are clearly some similarities between this set of concepts and those outlined by Roethlisberger and Dickson, particularly the dichotomy between formal and informal organisation/structure, but also in the clear separation of social structural features from individual characteristics or personalities (see Scott *et al.* 1956, 270–1); and, as we shall see, in the assessment of the influence of technology. As was the case with the scheme developed in *Management and the Worker*, however, what Scott and his colleagues really provided was a taxonomy in terms of which to order and categorise observations, rather than a model of the factory as an organisation. The interdependence between the various elements of the framework is *ad hoc*, and the interrelations between them are fairly indeterminate. It does not pack much explanatory punch. There is, however, a somewhat weakly formulated expectation that the various aspects of the social structure of the plant will tend to be compatible with each other: informal structure 'may promote stability and satisfaction at work' (Scott 1958, 31–2), 'is important for the maintenance of lateral communication in a plant' but 'will supplement and modify the formal structure' (Scott *et al.* 1956, 275).

The authors' careful acknowledgement that the common *recognition* of the purposes served by the formal structure does not necessarily imply mutual *acceptance* of them leaves room for conflicts of interest within the organisation. It frees their approach from the criticism to which Roethlisberger and Dickson, and many others, are properly subject that their models imply an overriding consensus of interests within the industrial firm. That there is this room, conceptually, for conflict is not surprising given the stress on the way occupational differentiation gives rise to differences in attitudes, values and interests, and to the likelihood of collective organisation to pursue such interests. Inevitably, however, it weakens the sense in which the plant can be seen as a 'system' (see also Scott *et al.* 1963, 10–11).

The Liverpool approach can be classified as partially open:

> although for certain purposes a factory may be considered as if it were an isolated unit, immune to external influences, in reality it does not exist *in vacuo* but is closely related to, and moulded by, the wider society of which it is a part.
>
> (Scott *et al.* 1956, 263)

Certain external influences on the pattern of social relations inside the organisation are clearly identified: the fact, for example, that the occupational structure is in part at least determined on a society-wide basis and has to be taken as a given in formally structuring the organisation; and traditional societal values and informal structures in the community influence social relations at work. Nevertheless such influences are treated in an *ad hoc* way and in the research studies the search for explanation of differences in attitudes and behaviour tends to concentrate on factors internal to the organisations being studied. The 'parts' of the system are 'concrete' in that they are clearly seen as sets of roles which individuals fill (Scott *et al.* 1956, 16). The question of where to draw the boundary is not discussed explicitly; there is a strong sense – reinforced by references to the social system of the *plant,* rather than enterprise or organisation – that the notion of boundary would be interpreted literally, though equally there are frequent examples of practical recognition of the interpenetration of 'internal' and 'external' elements, for example in the discussions of trade unions and collective bargaining arrangements.

The account of a factory as a social system first appeared in the report of the study of technical change in the steel industry published in 1956. By this time studies of joint consultation (Scott 1952) and of industrial relations in the docks (University of Liverpool 1954) had already appeared, and the concepts could only be applied retrospectively (see Scott *et al.* 1956, 4). It was explicitly taken as the basis for the analysis and explanation of findings in the studies of mining (Scott *et al.* 1963) and of industrial participation (Banks 1963). By the time one of the last pieces of research by members of this group was completed and published (Mumford and Banks 1967), however, the framework had been quietly dropped, though it might be thought to be quite appropriate for a study of the impact of computers on clerical work.

In the studies where it was used the framework did allow some findings to be conceptualised so as to form a basis for generalisations. The dissatisfaction reflected in the attitudes and behaviour of the craftsmen in the steel plant was attributed to the discrepancies which had arisen between the occupational importance and the status and rewards of craftsmen in the industry, and to the absence of an effective formal structure for relations between management and the craft unions. In contrast the introduction of new technology without much conflict between management and process workers was explained as due to effective formal structures for negotiation, the support of shared traditional values, and the absence of any radical changes in the occupational and informal structures. Problems in management were attributed to the failure to elaborate the formal structure to match the changes in occupations brought about by technical changes, and to modify traditional values (see Scott *et al.* 1956, 105–7, 250–1).

In the mining study attention was focused particularly on the ways in which occupational interests had become more differentiated, leading to a situation where higher status and more highly rewarded production workers were the most likely to engage in 'organised' conflict (e.g. use of the disputes procedure) but also had higher morale and were less likely to engage in 'unorganised' conflict (e.g. absence). The notion of informal structure played no part in the analysis, but the formal structure of the disputes machinery was seen as adequate to contain but as inadequate to resolve the basic conflicts (Scott *et al.* 1963, esp. 186–90).

The coal industry study, therefore, reinforced the emphasis on the occupational structure as the key to an understanding of attitudes and behaviour, but this was questioned in the study of attitudes to industrial participation. The most important factor in explaining such attitudes appeared to be not workers' occupational categories but their work or task groups:

> In describing the plant as a social system, therefore, it is unsatisfactory to stop at the occupational structure as organized by the formal structure. It would seem to be more important to describe it as a *technological* structure organized formally into work groups for administrative and technical purposes, and to add that such a structure may at some levels coincide with the cruder divisions of a work force along occupational lines, but that for some purposes, such as the one with which we have been concerned here, this cruder division is unsatisfactory.
>
> (Banks 1963, 131)

In the context of this study occupational categories were seen as relevant for patterns of recruitment of personnel, and for the organisation of unions and collective bargaining, but it was suggested that 'for an understanding of what goes on in a plant beyond these two features of industrial organization, the technical divisions are probably more important than the occupational as such' (132).

The emphasis in these passages on the influence of technology was rather stronger than in most of the writings of this group, and it may have reflected the increased interest in the relationship between technology and social relations which was a feature of industrial sociology in the 1960s. Generalising about this relationship, Scott (1958, 36–7) repudiated the idea 'that technical organization is a rigid determinant of the social structure of the factory', and suggested that it might have greater influence on the occupational and the informal structure than on the formal structure. He concluded:

> Technical changes, therefore, will tend to lead to changes in social structure, but other factors must be taken into account if

we wish to understand the nature of a particular structure . . . .
Technical organization and social structure are interdependent, and in reality they interact. Thus whilst technical change
does lead to social change, technical change is itself conditioned by the social structure, both of the factory and of the
wider society.

(37)

These judgements are very general and difficult to quarrel with. In
the thirty or more years since this passage was published there have
been strong arguments advanced for the existence of both a
tighter link and a weaker link between 'technology' and 'social
structure', and attempts to specify in some detail what characteristics of the technical organisation of an enterprise constrain
or determine what features of its social organisation. Some of these
arguments will be examined in subsequent chapters.

The formal/informal dichotomy

The distinction between 'formal' and 'informal' structure or
organisation is a notable feature of the work of both the Liverpool
group and Roethlisberger and Dickson. This dichotomy, in one
form or another, has featured prominently in sociological
accounts of industry (see, for example, Brown 1954; Schneider
1957, 93–5, 184–203; Faunce 1967, Pt IV) and has probably
become part of common-sense understandings of social relations
in industrial organisations. Though the notion of an 'informal
organization' was clearly articulated in the report of the
Hawthorne Experiments, emphasis on this aspect of industrial and
other organisations was certainly increased by a series of studies of
'bureaucracy' in the 1940s and 1950s which took Weber's ideal
type as their starting point (for example, see Blau 1955; 1956,
45–67). The characteristics outlined in the ideal type were seen as
designed to ensure rational and efficient administration of complex organisations, and social relations and social groupings not so
prescribed were therefore labelled 'informal'. As is often the case
with social scientific notions which approach the status of ortho-
doxy, the dichotomy very soon came under attack. Mouzelis, for
example, suggested that the 'informal' had been variously defined
as 'deviation from expectations', as 'irrelevant to organizational
goals', as 'unanticipated', and as 'real or concrete', and dismissed

the pair of concepts as 'not adequate to deal with the complexities of organizational behaviour and structure' (1967, 147–9). Similarly Silverman (1968, 7), referring to papers by Gouldner (1959a) and Etzioni (1960), described the dichotomy as 'largely discredited'.

Two main lines of criticism can be distinguished: they concern, firstly, the confusion and ambiguity in the definition of the terms themselves, and, secondly, the associated difficulty of applying them in the analysis of organisations. The simplest definition is to equate the 'formal' with the 'official' so that everything not officially prescribed or provided for becomes the 'informal organisation'. This appears to be the usage of 'formal' and 'informal' proposed by Roethlisberger and Dickson (1939, 558–9), and in some of the studies of bureaucracy, and it raises the obvious question as to the need for any terms other than 'official' and 'unofficial'. The distinction is hard to apply in practice in organisations where very few relationships and procedures may be clearly articulated and officially proposed, and unless one asserts that what those who have power in organisations decide should happen has some special status, the distinction in these terms contributes little to any analysis. It is for these reasons that the definition used by Scott and his colleagues was drawn more broadly.

They tried to distinguish relationships and activities which were defined, explicit, recognised and purposive – the 'formal structure' – from an 'informal structure' characterised by spontaneity and diffuseness, and based on affinity and congeniality. There is no assumption that only top management can define the formal structure; it may be 'modified and extended as the cohesiveness and power of other groups develop' (Scott *et al.* 1956, 272). This comment, however, and the reference, already quoted, to the ways in which the formal structure 'may crystallize out gradually', indicate that the formal–informal distinction may be hard to make in practice because of a constantly changing, fluid situation. At best we are dealing with a continuum rather than a dichotomy. The same could be said of the distinction between instrumental and expressive action (action as a means to an end and action for its own sake), which closely parallels the Liverpool researchers' definitions of formal and informal. Purely instrumental or purely expressive actions represent two polar positions with most cases falling somewhere on the range of possibilities between them.

A further possible definition would see the 'formal' as

'functional' and the 'informal' as 'dysfunctional' or, at best, 'non-functional'. Such a distinction has its place, and its problems, within functionalist analysis, but Roethlisberger and Dickson, Scott and his colleagues, and writers like Blau in their analyses of bureaucracy, all reject it explicitly. They are aware of and want to stress the ways in which non-official, 'informal' relationships and activities can assist an organisation achieve its stated goals, as well as the ways in which they may hinder that achievement. The dual nature of both the formal and the informal (each may be both 'functional' and 'dysfunctional') also makes it impossible to equate the 'informal' with the deviant or pathological.

Even as a continuum rather than as a dichotomy, however, the formal–informal distinction can be difficult to apply. Its use pre-supposes the existence of a publicly recognised body of rules and procedures, of definitions of roles and relationships, and of allocations of authority and responsibility, rationally intended to secure certain ends, which can be contrasted with activities and relationships which are officially unrecognised and without such a purpose. The extent to which industrial organisations are so char-acterised varies empirically quite considerably.

Two examples may be given. Woodward (1958, 17) suggested that duties and responsibilities were most clearly defined, and written communication most frequent, in large batch and mass production firms in manufacturing industry; there was less formal specification of structure and greater flexibility in those firms in unit and small batch production with the least complex tech-nology, and in those with process production plants and the most complex technology. Secondly, Burns and Stalker (1961, esp. 96–125) suggested that firms operating in changing conditions needed an 'organic' form because they were constantly faced with 'fresh problems and unforeseen requirements for action which cannot be broken down or distributed automatically' (121). The formal–informal dichotomy implies an omniscience on the part of the directorate of an enterprise such that 'no functions are left wholly or partly undischarged'; such omniscience is impossible in conditions of change and innovation; instead much greater commitment to the overall goals of the concern is demanded from all members, with the consequence that 'it becomes far less feasible to distinguish "informal" from "formal" organization' (123, 122). Subsequently Burns (1962, 206) suggested that 'the distinction between the rational formal organization, uniformly bureaucratic in structure, and the largely irrational informal organization partly or wholly at odds with it has been discarded', and stressed the value of studying enterprises as 'working communities . . . with a large number of interrelated institutions and a generalised, organic, function of keeping itself in being on the best possible terms'. Much of the more recent research has developed along these lines.

The Liverpool studies demonstrated the value, and the limitations, of detailed empirical investigations of industrial organisations; their findings were carefully and precisely presented but carried limited implications for situations beyond those directly observed. The main attempt by this group of researchers to provide a more general framework for the analysis of industrial enterprises was the account of the factory as a social system. This provided little more than a set of fairly concrete categories to guide investigation and help organise observations, and even in this role it had certain limitations. It made little use of the explanatory potential of the systems notion. It is therefore not surprising that it was not developed much beyond its initial formulation and was more or less completely superseded by later and rather different conceptualisations.

THE GLACIER PROJECT

The Tavistock Institute of Human Relations was set up in 1947 by psychologists and others who had worked together during the Second World War, with the aim of undertaking research, consultancy and teaching in the field of the social sciences. It was felt that the techniques used on war-time problems such as officer selection and training in the Army, and the civil resettlement of prisoners of war, could be further developed and applied in industry and elsewhere. These origins gave the work of members of the Institute a distinctive character related especially to the theoretical sources on which they drew and the methods they used in pursuing their enquiries. Their theoretical sources included psychoanalysis, including the group psychoanalytic work of Bion (1961), and certain social-psychological research and writing such as that of Lewin and Moreno. Their methods normally combined research with consultancy, though in varying proportions. Typically the intention was to carry out social analysis in a way analogous to individual psychoanalysis: the researcher/consultant 'works through' problems with those who have raised them; tries to draw out and articulate the underlying features of the situation in question; and hopes in this way to be able to initiate action to resolve the problem (see Brown and Jaques 1965, 29–47; Sofer 1972, 194–215).

The first major project undertaken by the Institute was one of three sponsored by the Human Factors Panel of the Committee on Industrial Productivity to investigate joint consultation in industry. It involved work in one enterprise, the Glacier Metal Company, for two and a half years between 1948 and 1950, and deliberately ranged more widely than reference to 'joint consultation' might suggest to produce a study of 'the factory and the forces affecting it as a total community', within which specific events and patterns of social relations could be located and understood (Jaques 1951, 4). Elliott Jaques, director of the study and author of the main report, *The Changing Culture of a Factory* (1951), returned to the firm as social analyst. During the next three decades he and Wilfred Brown, the firm's managing director until 1965 when he became Lord Brown and, for five years, Minister of State in the Board of Trade, produced a series of publications, individually or jointly, developing the ideas first outlined in the original book.

It is some elements of these 'Glacier Theories of Organization and Management' which will be the subject of this section. The experience and research of both authors, however, is no longer largely confined to one enterprise but includes 'industrial, commercial, civil service, local government, hospital, social service, educational, university and church' organisations (Jaques 1976, xi). The later work of Jaques's colleagues in the original Glacier project team, and of other members of the Tavistock Institute of Human Relations, will be discussed in the next section.

The extensive work and writings of Brown and Jaques fall into two main categories only the first of which will be considered in any detail here. The initial generalisations about the nature of social relations in industrial enterprises with which *The Changing Culture of a Factory* concluded have been amplified and developed in a series of books on what was successively labelled 'management' (W. Brown 1965), 'organization' (W. Brown 1974) and 'bureaucracy' (Jaques 1976). Secondly, in articles and books both authors have argued for a more scientific and equitable determination of relative pay, within organisations and within society at large, based on the analysis of the 'time-span of discretion' of the work being done (see, for example, W. Brown 1962 and 1973; Jaques 1956 and 1967). (Work on the pricing of products [Brown and Jaques 1964] has been additional to these areas of work.)

In *The Changing Culture of a Factory* the pattern of social activity in the Glacier Metal Company was seen as the outcome of the interaction of the firm's 'social structure' ('more or less recognisable and stable organizational pattern'), 'culture' ('customary and traditional way of thinking and doing things') and members' 'personalities' ('total psychological make-up') (Jaques 1951, 249–52). The social structure comprised the formal relations between roles, to which were attached responsibility and authority, and status related to where these roles came in the horizontal strata into which the firm could be divided. Much of the detailed analysis reported in the book was concerned with clarifying the nature of various role-relationships, and especially those of superior and subordinate, and between colleagues; and with the ways in which the authority attached to a role was 'sanctioned' from both outside and inside the firm. All members of the organisation filled roles in the 'executive system' through which the day-to-day work tasks were assigned and carried out. Some individuals occupied more than one role in the executive system, for example as Managing Director and as General Manager of the London factory, or also had roles in the consultative machinery; confusion and conflict could result if this was not clearly recognised.

In subsequent writings a considerably more complex and detailed account of organisations in general has been developed, building on the core of a system or systems of roles. Four such systems have been distinguished: an executive system; a representative system ('constituents, constituencies, representatives, and elected committees') through which the opinions of a group or category of employees can be communicated by a representative they have elected; a legislative or policy making system in which representatives meet together with the overall manager of the enterprise, or of the relevant part of it, to agree policy; and an appeals system or machinery through which subordinates can challenge their managers' judgements (see W. Brown 1965 and 1974).

A major preoccupation of both authors has been with clarifying and clearly specifying the roles and role relationships, and the allocations of responsibility and authority, in these systems. As

Kelly (1968, 263–75) among others pointed out the accounts given of the Glacier Metal Company's organisation had close parallels with Weber's ideal type bureaucracy. It is interesting, but not surprising, that in his most recent discussion Jaques himself turned to the term 'bureaucracy' to conceptualise the executive system. Individuals are seen as entering such a bureaucracy by taking up a contract of employment, and 'bureaucracies are work systems in which people are responsible for using their judgement and discretion in carrying out tasks on behalf of a manager who is accountable for their work' (Jaques 1976, 62). The representative and legislative systems, and the appeals procedure, still have a place in this more recent account.

The analysis of the executive system or bureaucracy has proceeded in two main ways. On the one hand there has been the development of a set of categories which is designed to accommodate all aspects of the work of an industrial or other enterprise. Its operational work (that which it was set up to do) is divided between the design and development of products and/or services, their manufacture or provision, and their marketing or selling. The carrying out of these operational tasks involves the performance of specialist work, or support tasks, with regard to personnel matters, programming of activities, and using the appropriate technology. In addition there is necessarily a rather separate accounting system (W. Brown 1974, esp. 88–94, 148–87; Jaques 1976, esp. 245–52, 266–7). Secondly, a lot of attention has been devoted to conceptualising the vertical and horizontal role relationships which develop in executive systems, or bureaucracies, where tasks are allocated between those in operational and those in specialist roles. In this connection the second main body of work mentioned above becomes important, the attempt to conceptualise and measure levels of work.

The starting point for such measurement is a distinction between the 'prescribed' and 'discretionary' demands of work roles. Prescribed demands can be precisely and specifically stated, and it is objectively and unambiguously clear whether or not they have been met. The discretionary elements are those which involve the exercise of judgement, and where a decision as to the adequacy of performance, as to whether it has achieved an appropriate balance of pace of work and quality, can only be made by a superior. Jaques argued that the level of discretion or responsibility in a work role can be measured in terms of its time-span of discretion, the maximum period of time during which marginally sub-standard exercise of discretion can pass without review by a superior (Jaques 1967, esp. 75–99). This measurement is regarded as providing a basis both for determining 'fair pay', and for organising work roles hierarchically into a number of strata, distinguished by qualitative breaks in the nature of the discretion which is required for their satisfactory performance (Jaques 1976, esp. 127–60).

The development of these concepts and the descriptions of these relationships have drawn very considerably on the experience of the Glacier Metal Company. Though they have been explored in a wide variety of other organisations there is no sense in which they have been 'tested' in a representative sample of such bodies. It is, however, an important part of the argument of these authors that the concepts and the relationships they discuss are of universal applicability, though some important distinctions are made between commercial ('earned income') and non-commercial ('grant income') organisations (see W. Brown 1974, 251; Jaques 1976, 58–9). Even if it is not recognised as such, the authors argue, organisations which employ people will contain a system of representative roles, for example, however embryonic; and they will have to undertake the (specialist) tasks of recruiting, selecting, appointing and grading personnel, programming the flow of tasks and the allocation of resources, and determining, adopting and updating the appropriate techniques.

This argument is related to a further set of distinctions. In all organisations there is a structure which is 'manifest' in that it is formally described and displayed. This may or may not be consistent with the situation as it is 'assumed' to be by individuals in the organisation. Both manifest and assumed organisation may differ from the 'extant' organisation, the situation as revealed by systematic exploration and analysis (though it can never be completely known). 'Requisite' organisation is 'the situation as it would have to be to accord with the real properties of the field in which it exists' (W. Brown 1965, 47–8). The conceptual framework developed by Brown and Jaques represents both an attempt to provide a basis for analysing extant organisation and an attempt to suggest many of the general characteristics of requisite organisation. It is used both descriptively and prescriptively. The prescriptions draw on a number of sources: certain basic, largely psychological, assumptions about individuals and their capacities, and about the nature of work; certain explicitly stated values, for example regarding employee rights (see esp. Jaques 1976, Pts 3 and 4); and the previously mentioned quest for certainty and clarity regarding roles and role relationships.

Commentary

There are many aspects of this work which could be discussed in detail, but in the present context we are most concerned with the contribution Jaques and Brown make to the conceptualisation of industrial enterprises as systems. The formulations which they developed are considerably more detailed than the Liverpool approach discussed in the last section. The parts of the system remain relatively concrete, referring to sets of roles and role relationships, though there is some elaboration of the executive or work system in terms of rather more abstractly defined activities. The concepts have proved useful in making possible generalisable accounts of problems and conflicts occurring within organisations, particularly with reference to relationships between managers and their subordinates (see, for example, Jaques 1976, 245–57), though this potential has not, on the whole, been exploited by others. Although, especially in his more recent work, Jaques has emphasised that organisations are open systems involved in exchanges with their environments, the theoretical possibilities this raises have not been developed (Jaques 1976, 249–52; see also Jaques 1951, 258–61). Where to draw the boundary between the system and its environment is not seen as a problem.

The main interest has been in the structures and processes internal to the enterprise, and in the sources of change which may arise there. In the light of this it is surprising that there is a very limited sense in which the dynamic possibilities of the systems concept are in any way exploited. The main preoccupations are in spelling out the relationships which can, and/or should, exist between different types of roles within the various systems within the organisation, and with arguing that certain sorts of relationship are 'requisite' in terms of the tasks which have to be achieved. There is no systematic evidence in terms of which such claims as to the requisiteness of the advocated patterns can be tested, and in perhaps the most important independent investigation of a Glacier Metal Company plant, admittedly a not altogether satisfactory one, the author concluded that 'in the light of the present researches, the correspondence between theory and fact is limited and incomplete' (Kelly 1968, 289).

Given the forceful advocacy they have had over the past forty years, it is surprising that these ideas have not been more influential either in industrial sociology or within management (see, for example, Gray 1976). This may, of course, reflect the conservatism of academics or managers rather than the (in)adequacy of the ideas. The most widely used concept has probably been Jaques's distinction between the 'prescribed' and 'discretionary' elements in a work role (see, for example, Fox 1974). However, the arguments about the measurement of responsibility, equitable payment and the nature of bureaucratic hierarchies which Jaques has built upon this distinction remain highly controversial.

The assertions about the possibility of 'equitable payment' are, however, crucial for Jaques and Brown's presumption that there need be no irresolvable conflicts of interest within industrial organisations. Sociologists frequently distinguish two major sources of such conflicts: the distribution of the income of the enterprise as between wages, salaries, dividends and reinvestment; and the exercise of authority by those in superordinate positions with the consequent constraints on subordinates. If, as Jaques and Brown claim, levels of responsibility can be measured precisely; if levels of pay which are felt to be fair can be objectively determined for each level of responsibility; if individuals have innate capacities which determine the level of work (i.e. the responsibility) with which they can cope effectively and without undue anxiety; and if individuals can be allocated to jobs appropriate to these capacities; then there is a basis for resolving conflicts about wages and salaries. Similarly, Jaques and Brown would claim that the sort of structure and procedures for an enterprise which they advocate would largely remove or provide the means to resolve conflicts about the exercise of managerial authority. These structures and procedures include the joint agreed determination of policy through the representative and legislative systems (the latter operating a unanimity rule to prevent minorities being arbitrarily overruled [or ignored]), and an appeals procedure as a check on the managers' applications of such policy in particular cases.

These arguments, however, are not without problems. The claim to be able to measure responsibility and to determine 'fair' pay objectively has been widely criticised and was never accepted by all employees within the Glacier Metal Company itself. Many of these criticisms have considerable force (see Fox 1966; Child 1969, 198–203; Hyman and Brough 1975, esp. Chs 2 and 3; Whittington and Bellaby 1979). Alternative interpretations exist as to the meaning of claims that pay is 'fair' which have quite different implications for industrial conflict (see Baldamus 1961; Hyman and Brough 1975). 'Fairness' is a socially constructed, not to say ideological, notion and one which may, to some extent, be imposed by the more powerful on those in subordinate positions. It could be argued that the claim to have removed conflicts about the exercise of managerial authority is stronger, though the conditions which Brown and Jaques advocate in order to bring this about would be very difficult to realise in practice. The claim, however, ignores two considerations: the extent to which taking up a contract of employment in a society with considerable inequalities of condition and opportunity may be coerced, so that the employee cannot really be said to have voluntarily accepted the conditions of employment offered; and the possibility that the powers claimed on the basis of ownership of the means of production may be contested. On both counts the legitimacy of managerial authority is in question. The structures and procedures advocated by Jaques and Brown may be highly desirable in many respects, but they cannot be seen as removing such conflicts of interest altogether.

More generally, though much of this writing is stimulating and impressive, its deductive and prescriptive nature makes it difficult to assess other than by means of an examination and critique of its basic assumptions. For the most part the reader is not presented with conventional research findings against which the analysis offered can be assessed (see Child 1969, 197–8). The interpretations offered of actual patterns of action in organisations which give rise to problems are ones which are based on a presumption that solutions ('requisite' organisation) could be found. There is no place for inherent contradictions or conflicts of interest. The discrepancies between 'formal' organisation and the 'informal' patterns of action which are such a prominent feature of most sociological accounts of bureaucracy have no place in this account; they are seen as resolvable by means of further analysis and rational action. These writers' belief in the potential of rational administration appears to be even stronger than that shown by Weber himself!

Jaques's and Brown's developments of the systems notion have been unexceptionable and largely descriptive. Indeed in his more recent work Jaques placed relatively little emphasis on it and developed the older notion of bureaucracy. It is among Jaques' former colleagues in the Tavistock Institute of Human Relations that the concept of the industrial organisation as a social system received further development; and others have drawn rather different implications from the idea that organisations are comprised of a multiplicity of 'systems'.

OPEN SOCIO-TECHNICAL SYSTEMS

In 1951 two of Jaques's colleagues in the original Glacier project published a paper in the journal, *Human Relations*, entitled 'Some social and psychological consequences of the longwall method of coal getting' (Trist and Bamforth 1951). As a contribution to social science at that date the article was innovative and unusual in two main respects: it gave very detailed attention to the technical characteristics of the partially mechanised coal mining situations with which it was concerned, a level and type of attention to technology which was both greater and more elaborately theorised than was customary in industrial sociology at the time (or, with some exceptions, since then); and it stressed the interrelationship between technology and social relations in contrast to the usual contemporaneous view that 'human relations' were very little affected by technical considerations. In the words of one of its authors introducing the later book reporting the studies of mining, the article could be seen as arguing that 'socio-psychological factors are in-built characterisations of work systems rather than additional – and possibly optional – features to do with "human relations"' (Trist *et al.* 1963, xii). Trist and Bamforth's paper is seen as introducing the concept of a production system as a 'socio-technical system', although they do not use the term itself (see Rice 1958, 3; Trist *et al.* 1963, 5).

Trist and Bamforth (1951, 5) stated their approach in the following terms:

> the longwall method will be regarded as a technological system expressive of the prevailing outlook of mass-production engin-eering and as a social structure consisting of the occupational roles that have been institutionalised in its use. These inter-active technological and sociological patterns will be assumed to

exist as forces having psychological effects in the life space of the face-worker, who must either take a role and perform a task in the system they compose or abandon his attempt to work at the coal-face. His own contribution to the field of determinants arises from the nature and quality of the attitudes and relationships he develops in performing one of these tasks and in taking one of these roles. Together, the forces and their effects constitute the psycho-social whole which is the object of study.

For the next two decades members of the Tavistock Institute of Human Relations followed the lead offered by this initial paper to develop the notion of an 'open socio-technical system' as the appropriate framework for the study of organisations whether at the level of the whole enterprise, divisions and departments within it, or the primary work group. The most important empirical studies during this period were those in coal-mining (Trist *et al.* 1963) and in the textile industry in India (Rice 1958, 1963). The concept has also been used in a wide range of other studies both in industry, for example with reference to wholesale and retail distribution, dry cleaning, the steel industry and an airline (see Miller and Rice 1967), and outside, for example as applied to universities (Rice 1970).

Commenting on this development Trist (1960, 1) has noted that he and his colleagues have 'come to believe that open system and socio-technical thinking imply each other in the study of the enterprise'. The notion of an 'open system' was derived from the general systems theory of Von Bertalanffy and others, outlined above. It was regarded as more satisfactory than the more nearly closed system model of organisations, characteristic of most empirical studies, including the early reports of the Glacier project, because it provides a more satisfactory basis for dealing with questions of growth and change. In addition, although the concept of dysfunction can provide closed system theorising with an analytical approach to the study of dynamics and change by drawing 'attention to sources of imbalance within an organization', such an approach 'does not conceptually reflect the mutual permeation of an organization and its environment that is the cause of such imbalance' (Emery and Trist 1960, 84–5).

The open systems concept focuses attention on the exchanges which take place between the organisation or system and its environment, on the 'import–conversion–export process'; and it implies the property of 'equi-finality', being able to achieve a steady state from different initial conditions and in different ways. Variation in both input and output markets may be tolerated without structural changes (for example by substituting different materials or types of labour, or by producing a different 'product mix'). The degree to which this is possible, however, is limited very considerably by a variety of constraints in the environment, of which the technology of the enterprise, an 'internalized environment', is perhaps the most important. The technological component is seen as playing a key mediating role in the process of defining the boundary conditions under which a steady state can be achieved and thus the system should be seen as an 'open socio-technical system' (Emery and Trist 1960): 'the technological component not only sets limits upon what can be done, but also in the process of accommodation creates demands that must be reflected in the internal organization and ends of the enterprise' (87). As 'open socio-technical systems' enterprises must be seen as both influenced by and able to act back on their environments. Internal elaboration and differentiation of the enterprise's structure may make it independent of an increasing range of predictable fluctuations in its supplies and outlets, but in tying down resources they simultaneously make it less able to cope with newly emergent and unpredicted changes (94). The optimisation of the whole system may require a less than optimum state for each separate dimension (Trist *et al.* 1963, 7). This idea of 'joint optimization' – that 'an organization will function optimally only if the social and technological systems of organization are designed to fit the demands of each other and the environment' (Pasmore *et al.* 1982, 1182) – has been a key feature of socio-technical systems thinking.

The most notable applications of the open socio-technical systems concept have been in the analysis of work groups, but it has also been applied to analyses of the supervisory and management systems which control and coordinate such groups, and of enterprises as wholes with particular reference to their structures of management. A key concept in such analyses has been the 'primary task'. The identification of the primary task of an organisation, or of some part of it, is the starting point for investigating and judging the appropriateness of the organisation's structure in the light of the technological, economic and socio-psychological resources and constraints within which it operates. An enterprise may have a multiplicity of tasks which are performed simultaneously, but so far as possible any organisation or part of an organisation is seen as having one which is primary. Initially Rice (1958, 32) defined the enterprise's primary task as 'the task which it is created to perform'. Because of the 'once and for all' connotation of that definition (which is also open to the same objections as the analysis of organisations in terms of their stated goals – see Silverman 1970, 9–11), he subsequently modified it to be 'the task [the institution] must perform to survive': in the case of industrial and commercial enterprises, and in the most general terms, to make profits. Some organisations (e.g. teaching hospitals, universities) have multiple tasks, no one of which has primacy; as a result their structure and functioning may have to be a compromise between at least partially incompatible demands. The primary task is seen as more limited than the enterprise's 'mission', its overall objective (Rice 1963, 13, 185–94).

Primary tasks can be defined with varying precision, and the more precise the definition, it is argued, the greater the constraints on task performance – thus the decision to produce certain goods for a certain market sets limits to the form of organisation and technology which must be adopted. The organisation of an enterprise should be that which is most appropriate to the achievement of its primary tasks, and the function of enterprise leadership is to control both the internal conditions and the boundary conditions, the form of exchange between the enterprise and its environment. The latter task will be easier if the enterprise has developed what Selznick (1957) has termed a 'distinctive competence' in its chosen field vis-à-vis competitors.

The 'primary task' notion can equally be applied to the parts, or sub-systems, of which the organisation as a whole is composed. The identification of these sub-systems may not be entirely straightforward; Miller (1959) suggested that production systems can normally be differentiated along one or more of the dimensions of technology, territory and time; and it has been argued too that each sub-system should contain a 'whole task'. In Rice's studies of a group of textile and other manufacturing enterprises in India, for example, he drew on the open socio-technical systems framework to distinguish three basic 'operating systems' concerned respectively with imports (purchasing), conversion (production) and exports (sales). Each had a specific primary task, and a boundary across which exchanges took place, and each required leadership (management) to control internal and boundary conditions. Once any enterprise has grown large enough to be so divided into constituent operating systems (and sub-systems) an overall 'managing system' is also required to control them in order to ensure achievement of the primary task of the enterprise as a whole and to provide appropriate services such as finance and personnel. In a manner typical of 'systems thinking' this process of differentiation of managing and operating systems can be continued to lower levels until 'primary production systems' are reached (Rice 1963, 15–25).

In an important unpublished discussion of socio-technical systems Emery (1959, 8–9) pointed out that 'the first function of the concept of a socio-technical system is to serve as a frame of reference', and 'in its second function' it 'invokes a body of subordinate concepts and hypotheses to describe and explain the behaviour of enterprises and their members. This function is not strictly dependent upon the first. There is no single body of concepts that can claim on grounds of common usage or exhaustiveness to be *the* theory of socio-technical systems.' Such caution would be even more appropriate now, when the notion has been used, and misused, so much more widely. Indeed, in his more recent review Miller has referred to the concept as 'exploratory' rather than 'explanatory', and as generating a set of useful (in a practical sense) concepts and working hypotheses (Miller 1975a, 54–5; see also Trist 1981; Hackman 1981).

Rice's usage of the socio-technical systems concept clearly followed this pattern. As a consultant-researcher, he had to make explicit certain assumptions in order to have grounds on which to assess existing patterns of organisation and suggest alternatives. For example:

> an ideal organization is one that is sufficiently flexible to allow the enterprise to respond to short-term environmental change within the existing framework, and to adapt, without major disturbance, to long-term change. Maximum flexibility . . . is obtained when, consistent with overall integration: (a) control of parts is by results rather than detailed inspection; (b) parts have both 'whole' tasks and maximum autonomy; (c) communications are selective, rapid and undistorted.
>
> (Rice 1963, 17)

Using the open socio-technical systems framework *and* these and similar additional assumptions Rice was able to analyse the existing management structure of the Indian enterprises with which he was concerned and to propose alternative patterns of management based on the desirability of 'any grouping for command purpose ... having a discrete primary task that differentiates it from other groups of the same order of differentiation and from groups at higher or lower orders of differentiation' (Rice 1963, 225).

As is the case with the Glacier studies of management the open socio-technical systems framework does not suggest that there is one ideal pattern of organisation based on universal 'principles'; rather it provides a way of analysing organisational structures in order to establish their appropriateness for their primary task. In order to do this, however, certain additional assumptions are necessary, assumptions which explicitly or implicitly reflect (possibly contentious) hypotheses about social relations and individual motivation and performance.

The same analytical and prescriptive pattern characterised the Tavistock studies of work groups, perhaps the most widely influential of their contributions to applied industrial sociology. In this case the starting point was a critique of the conventional assumptions which had guided the introduction of mechanisation into mining and the organisation of tasks in an automatic weaving shed. These assumptions included the desirability of 'maximum job breakdown and work role specialization', often with the number of workers required in particular roles being determined by work study; that no attention need be given to the social relations of workers, who could be treated as isolated individuals, nor to their culture and traditions; and that planning, coordination and control could and should be specialised functions divorced from the work group (see Trist et al. 1963, 43–7; Rice 1958, 55–8, 231–3).

In contrast to these conventional assumptions of production engineering, derived from 'Scientific Management', the Tavistock researchers made explicit their own assumptions: for example, that a work group is capable of 'responsible autonomy' – acceptance of responsibility for the entire cycle of operations, recognition of the interdependence of one person or group on another – for effective progress of the production cycle, and self-regulation by the whole team and its constituent groups (Trist et al. 1963, 21); or, similarly, the desirability of providing individuals and/or work groups with the satisfaction of completing a whole task, of being able to control their own activities, and of having related tasks so organised that those performing them can have satisfactory relationships (Rice 1958, 34–5, also 36–9).

In their early studies Trist and Bamforth argued that when longwall systems were introduced to allow the mechanisation of coal getting, the formal and elaborate division of labour destroyed the quality of 'responsible autonomy' and the 'social balance' which had previously characterised the miner's role, and led to a situation where task groups were segregated from each other and bound by their own field of interest. The highly specialised work roles meant that forty men were distributed between three shifts and seven distinct roles, with five methods of payment. This organisation of work made for conflict within and between groups rather than the sense of interdependence which was needed if the system was to function smoothly. Control and coordination had to be provided by management, and by the wages system, with all the difficulties and uncertainties of the underground situation, and with a production system where failure to maintain the cycle of activities was likely to cause considerable disruption. In the circumstance there was a

> tendency to develop a norm of low productivity, as the only adaptive method of handling, in the contingencies of the underground situation, a complicated, rigid, and large scale work system, borrowed with too little modification from an engineering culture appropriate to the radically different situation of the factory.
>
> (Trist and Bamforth 1951, 23)

The writers also argued that 'the persistence of socially ineffective structures at the coal face is likely to be a major factor in preventing a rise of morale, in discouraging recruitment, and in increasing labour turnover' (37–8).

In later studies of mining in north-west Durham there was the opportunity to observe both the conventional longwall system and what is termed the composite longwall system. Comparisons of the two, and some intermediate forms, working with the same technology and in very similar underground conditions, showed that 'composite organization was found to possess characteristics more conducive than conventional to productive effectiveness, low cost, work satisfaction, good relations and social health'. Fully developed composite organisation 'removes the difficulties which stem from overspecialized work roles, segregated task groups, and lack of cohesion in the face team as a whole' (Trist *et al.* 1963, 291). It was based on a recognition that, in addition to specific, relatively easily learnt production task skills, there was 'a common fund of underground skill shared alike by all experienced faceworkers' of being able 'to contend with interferences emanating from the underground situation' and 'developed only after a number of years at the face' (47). In the place of the formal division of labour of the conventional organisation the team of about forty miners allocated men to shifts and tasks; miners had experience of different roles and utilised several skills; task groups were interchangeable in membership; there was continuity of working so that men carried on with the next activity in the sequence when their own was complete; and there was a common pay note based on a fixed rate plus a bonus according to the amount of coal produced. The group was self-regulating so that management no longer had to provide all control and coordination. This mode of working was also seen as a more appropriate basis for 'higher mechanisation' in mining.

Similarly Rice (1958) described how in the automatic weaving shed the process had been broken down into component tasks and a number of workers allocated to each task on the basis of work studies. This resulted in an aggregate of individuals with confused task and role relationships, even though their tasks were interdependent. For example,

> each weaver had on average the services of one quarter of a pair consisting of a jobber and his assistant, five-eighths of a battery filler, three-eighths of a smash-hand and so on. But any change of sort [type of cloth] altered these proportions.
>
> (Rice 1963, 56–7)

Although morale in the shed appeared good, efficiency was lower and damage higher than the target figures. In the non-automatic weaving sheds the problem was different: each of the weavers still had a 'whole task' but was formally socially isolated from the ancillary workers who assisted her or him.

In these situations the changes were introduced by Rice himself. In the automatic weaving shed he identified the primary task as keeping the looms running and reorganised work so that a small internally structured and internally led group of seven workers could be collectively responsible for sixty-four looms, and between them carry out the ancillary tasks as well. He reported that this reorganisation was spontaneously and enthusiastically accepted by the workers and, despite some setbacks, led to an increase in efficiency and less damaged cloth. In addition management of the shed was considerably simplified by the existence of team leaders responsible to the supervisor (Rice 1958, 49–110). In the case of non-automatic weaving an experimental shed was set up. In place of the formal social isolation of the individual weavers, internally structured work groups of eleven workers in four grades were formed to perform the tasks of weaving and maintenance on a group of forty looms and to receive, at their own request, a group bonus. The experimental system established new norms of performance and earnings for non-automatic weaving and subsequently spread to other parts of the mill. As in the previous case minimum rates of pay were fixed that were higher than had been previously paid, but there was also a reduction in the numbers employed. The structure of supervision in the shed was also clarified and simplified (Rice 1958, 114–66).

These changes succeeded, it was claimed, because they led to the adoption of work organisation appropriate to the tasks to be done. In addition, in all cases, workers derived considerable satisfaction from the effective performance of the primary task, and from having responsibility for a 'whole' task. The increased autonomy of the work group freed management for more effective performance of planning and other functions relating the system to its environment. Membership of stable work groups was also important, particularly in the Indian situation, but friendship on the job was not in itself what had desirable psychological consequences, but rather 'a system of work roles such that workers are primarily related to each other by way of the requirements of task performance and task interdependence' (Emery and Trist 1960, 91). Conventional Human Relations 'wisdom' was also questioned in the mining case by the discovery that groups of forty or more workers, without formal leaders, could be self regulating, though the persistence of appropriate traditions and practices from pre-mechanised systems in mining made an important contribution to this outcome.

In mining the partially mechanised longwall system of coal production was fairly rapidly replaced in most pits by full mechanisation (machines which both cut and loaded coal, etc.) and the particular composite system of working observed by Trist and his colleagues was superseded. In the Indian textile factory technical change was less rapid and in addition to Rice's own follow-up of his original intervention (see Rice 1963), Miller was able to review the situation some seventeen years after group working had initially been introduced (Miller 1975b). His report showed mixed success: 'By 1970, the so-called "group system" encompassed widely different methods of working' (377). The experimental non-automatic weaving shed had remained closest to Rice's original socio-technical system design, and had maintained the improved standards of efficiency and quality. Elsewhere, to a greater or lesser degree, there had been regression to more individualistic modes of working. Miller argued that this was primarily due to the failure of management and supervisory sub-systems to contain 'disturbances' from the environment caused by pressure for higher quality and increased output, and by the scarcity of spare parts and supplies of an appropriate standard. He concluded that 'the assumptions on which Rice worked have been largely substantiated' but that perhaps 'Rice's innovations were more radical than was recognised at the time' (385, 383).

The Tavistock researchers' contributions to the study of work groups have been extremely influential in this country and perhaps even more abroad. (For example, Pasmore and his colleagues reviewed 134 separate socio-technical system interventions in the USA [Pasmore *et al.* 1982].) They have provided support for the ideas that there can be alternative forms of work organisation, or 'organisational choice', within the same technological framework, and that there are advantages (technical, economic, and/or social-psychological) in structuring social relations at work so far as possible in the form of 'autonomous work groups' (for a detailed discussion of the diffusion, use and misuse of the notion of 'autonomous work group', see Mackay 1982). During the 1970s movements developed in the USA, Britain and continental Europe concerned with the development of new forms of work organisation, and with the quality of working life, which derived much of their inspiration from the work of the Tavistock researchers (see, for example, Davis and Taylor 1972; Wilson 1973; Klein 1976).

In a valuable review of socio-technical systems theory Kelly has argued that the theoretical work of the 'school' developed into two divergent trends: one, associated with the work of Miller and of Rice, 'characterized by its stronger emphasis on the significance of the group, and its relative down-grading of individual job design'; the second, associated with the work of Emery, Trist and Thorsrud (see, for example, Emery and Thorsrud 1976), focusing more on individual job design in a group context and attaching less significance to the group as such (Kelly 1978, 1095–6). This second strand can be associated particularly with the influential 'quality of working life' movement, whose work did not greatly develop socio-technical systems theory as an approach to an overall understanding of organisations, although it continued to claim reliance on socio-technical systems thinking.

Somewhat paradoxically, later work by members of the Tavistock Institute suggested that the social and psychological benefits derived from the reorganisation of work in the textile and coal mining studies might not be easily attainable elsewhere. In the mining and textile situations the new patterns of organisation were appropriate both for task performance and for meeting human needs for satisfaction and for 'defence against anxiety'. Miller and Rice distinguished the concepts of 'task group' (the human resources required for an activity system) and 'sentient group' (the group to which individuals are prepared to commit themselves and on which they depend for emotional support), a distinction reminiscent of earlier discussion of formal and informal organisation (see Silverman 1970, 109–25). They suggested, in the light of a number of studies in different organisations, that the boundaries of task and sentient groups quite commonly may not coincide, and that it may not be possible to bring them into coincidence. Some task groups involve members of more than one organisation, or are necessarily temporary, whilst other tasks are necessarily performed by isolated individuals. In such situations the analysis of patterns of social relations and the identification of sentient groups may prove more complex and involve consideration of the functions of other organisations such as trade unions and professional associations. Further, the coincidence of task and sentient group boundaries can even be a disadvantage in conditions of change as it may lead to too great an emotional investment in existing patterns of work organisation, and resistance to (necessary) changes (Miller and Rice 1967, esp. 29–32, 253–61). Trist (1981, 47–9) has suggested that larger 'primary work systems' may provide the opportunity for individuals to have multiple memberships which lessen this danger.

Though the openness of the systems they have been describing and analysing has been stressed by the Tavistock researchers they have devoted less attention to analysing the environments of the organisations with which they have been concerned. Emery and Trist (1965), however, proposed a typology of environments around the notion of their 'causal texture', the interconnections which develop in the environment independently of an enterprise and of any exchanges between it and the environment. Formulated at a fairly abstract level, the typology suggests a progression from a 'placid, randomised environment' (perfect competition) through two intermediate steps to 'turbulent fields' characterised by complex and continuous interconnected changes and great uncertainty. The authors emphasised that the development of new systems of values, and of an 'organizational matrix', may be necessary to meet this new and demanding situation. Though examples are given in this paper, these ideas do not appear to have been followed up in detail in subsequent research (but see Emery and Trist 1972; Trist 1981).

Commentary

The systems framework developed by Emery, Rice, Trist and their colleagues is clearly more complex and sophisticated than the others discussed so far. In addition to the more general criticisms of systems thinking, however, there are a number of specific comments to be made about it.

In the first place, despite its relative sophistication and some of the 'jargon' used, the parts of the system are defined in fairly concrete terms (as identifiable departments and groups, not abstract functions), though more recent formulations have been more abstract (e.g. Trist 1981). In the case of Rice's work the fundamental processes of import, conversion and export were seen in similarly concrete terms. This can be contrasted with examples of very much more abstract conceptualisations of systems and sub-systems, and of boundary interchanges between them, for example in the work of Parsons and Smelser (1956) and Katz and Kahn (1966).

This conception of the exchanges between enterprise and environment may be one reason why the nature of the environment is not investigated and analysed in greater detail. It tends to be seen either in narrowly economic terms as a number of markets, or as the source of certain traditions (mining) or of a culture (India), which may provide support for certain patterns of work organisation. In both cases it is notable how little attention is given to the wider society. This neglect of the environment contributes to a failure to acknowledge how far the specific characteristics of the Durham coalfield and Indian culture may have contributed to the outcome of the changes introduced into the mining and textile situations respectively (Eldridge 1971, 33–4; Kelly 1978, 1075–6). It also contributes to an unsatisfactory treatment (or absence of recognition) of actual or potential sources of conflict.

Though the word does not appear in the index of any of the main studies discussed in this section, there is some discussion of conflict in the texts themselves. It tends, however, to be concerned either with the the psychic stresses and conflicts experienced by individuals or with the intra-systemic conflicts which may arise from inappropriate patterns of work and management organisation. With the partial exception of Miller and Rice's work (1967), the assumption appears to be that thorough analysis of the tasks to be done and creation of a requisite structure of roles and relationships will enable the organisation to operate harmoniously. Conflicts between management and worker, which might arise from their respective positions in the wider social relations of production, are inadequately covered.

This sort of view of the enterprise is reflected in the discussion of its primary task; there is an implicit assumption that all strata within the organisation will be agreed about what it is, and indeed that commitment to it provides an important source of loyalty and solidarity. Defining organisational goals, or primary tasks, is more contentious and problematic than their discussion admits, and even if such goals are agreed there is generally still room for conflict over their interpretation and implications. This failure to acknowledge the inherent conflicts of interest of employer and employee in any system of employment may have contributed to the researchers' lack of emphasis on the possible effects of the changes made to patterns and levels of payment in the mining and textile mill cases; these changes were substantial and must be regarded as significant for an understanding of the workers' reactions to the new systems of working.

The Tavistock researchers' use of the systems notion for analysis and explanation depends on incorporating certain assumptions about what is possible and/or desirable for individuals and for management systems. These assumptions are made explicit – many of them were derived from psycho-analytic theory (see the discussion in Brown 1967) – and are framed cautiously but in universal terms; cultural variations in the sources of individual satisfaction and mental health, or of effective management structures, are not allowed for. Indeed the assumptions made about the intrinsic sources of individual work satisfaction (variety and challenge; continuous learning; discretion and autonomy; recognition and support; meaningful social contribution; desirable future (Trist 1981, 42)) bear a strong resemblance to those of more recent writers in the Human Relations tradition. In conjunction with these assumptions, and the central notion of the primary task, the systems approach is particularly useful for researchers who are also consultants because it emphasises the complex interrelations of phenomena, but provides an analytical starting point and an independent variable (the primary task), as well as criteria for assessing possible changes (see Gouldner 1959b; Miller 1975a).

The development of the concept of a socio-technical system was part of what came to be labelled the 'technological implications' approach in industrial sociology (see Goldthorpe et al. 1968, 44, 180–4; Rose 1988, 185–248; and further discussion in Chapters 3 and 4). Certainly the Tavistock work gave detailed attention to the technical characteristics of the production systems being investigated. In contrast to some writers in this tradition, however, they did not see technology as having direct effects on workers' attitudes or behaviour, nor as determining a particular set of work and social relations. The lesson of the mining and textile mill studies was that there was room for choice of work organisation, and that work organisation then mediated the social and psychological effects of technology.

Some critics have questioned this. Rose, for example, has argued that though the Tavistock work provided an important and valid critique of the 'prejudices' of production engineers, in so far as one pattern of work organisation (e.g. composite work organisation of longwall mining) was shown to be *both* more productive and profitable *and* more satisfactory for the workers involved the choice was a 'myth' (Rose 1975, 212–17; 1988, 237–48). Kelly also argues that 'perhaps there is "one best way" after all' . . . 'there is nothing in any of the socio-technical studies to suggest that *several* work organizations are *equally* effective, both economically and psychologically, for a given technology' (Kelly 1978, 1094–5). Certainly there is no doubt that the reorganised patterns of work in both the mining and textile mill studies are claimed to be superior on all counts. On the other hand the difficulties and delays which have been experienced over the last fifteen years in securing the adoption of new forms of work organisation, even when the economic and social case for them is strong, suggest that those in power in organisations, the 'dominant coalition', do have some real choices regarding work organisation within a given technical and economic framework, as for example Child (1972) has suggested.

It can also be argued that the Tavistock researchers have tended to accept uncritically the existing technology and an economic order based on market forces and the necessity of making a profit. In particular, although the idea of joint optimisation presupposes the possibility of changes in both technology and social organisation, almost all the work done on socio-technical systems has involved fitting social organisation to an existing technology (Pasmore *et al.* 1982, 1185, 1200). The most notable exception to this generalisation was the design of the Volvo car plant at Kalmar in the early 1970s, where the conventional assembly line was replaced by a radically new way of organising the production of cars (Jönsson 1978).

An 'open systems' approach to the analysis of industrial organisations has been the dominant approach within sociology for the past two decades, and some further developments of such an approach will be discussed in the next chapter. The Tavistock researchers have played a notable part in bringing this situation about, though their particular formulations have by no means always been adopted by others. In particular their arguments that the approach should be concerned with open *socio-technical* systems has been more controversial, sometimes because critics misunderstood and exaggerated the importance they attributed to technology as a determinant of social relations with industrial organisations. In fact, as the discussion of organisational choice reveals, technology was clearly seen as only one of the constraints to which the system had to respond. Though the work of the Tavistock researchers does not exhaust the possibilities inherent in an approach to industrial organisations as systems, it probably explores them more fully, systematically and self-consciously than any other writers in Britain have done. As such it is inevitably part of the target towards which more general criticisms of systems approaches have been directed.

A PLURALITY OF SYSTEMS

The three approaches discussed in the previous sections of this chapter do not, of course, constitute the only examples, even in Britain, of the use and development of the systems concept for the analysis of industrial organisations. Indeed, as Woodward commented, in the 1950s and early 1960s there was a virtual 'torrent' of literature on organisation, much of it American, from a variety of perspectives but 'all beginning to see themselves as concerned with systems' (Woodward 1965, 249–51). Despite the criticisms made of such an approach, which grew in number in the next decade, some sort of conception of the enterprise as a social, or socio-technical, system was characteristic of most sociological research and writing on industrial organisations between 1950 and the 1970s or later, and it would be impossible, as well as repetitive and unnecessary, to try to describe or comment on all such work. Two contributions, however, will provide examples of some of the ways in which the concept was further developed.

In 1955–6 a former member of the industrial sociology group in Liverpool, Tom Lupton, undertook an investigation into the social factors affecting production norms in factories. His open participant observation of the two workshops, each with an incentive payment system, revealed that whereas in one case workers regulated their output in terms of certain agreed norms as to what level was appropriate, in the other behaviour was much more individualistic and no such collective regulation occurred. In attempting to account for this contrast Lupton (1963, 187–201) was forced to consider not only factors 'internal' to the workshop but 'external' factors as well; 'the workshop as a system of social relationships [is] included within wider systems – the factory, the market for the product, and so on' (200). These 'external factors' could be seen as systematically related. Together with a colleague who had carried out a similar workshop study he wrote:

> We . . . feel justified in advancing the hypothesis that in industries characterised by clusters of factors such as a high degree of competition, easy entry of new units of production, high labour cost, and weak unionism, collective control over output by workers is less likely to be found than in industries where the reverse is true.
>
> (Lupton and Cunnison 1964, 124)

However, the familiar dichotomy of 'internal' and 'external' factors, or system and environment, was regarded as unsatisfactory; rather

> it seems to us that when we are dealing with workshop life we have to handle in analysis a number of *overlapping* systems . . . there are segments of different social systems which are latent in a single workshop. For instance, a man's role as a father, or as a member of a social class, may affect his behaviour in the workshop.
>
> (Lupton and Cunnison 1964, 125; see also Lupton 1963, 200)

The concept of latent social roles was not a new one (see Gouldner 1959a, 412), and the notion of *overlapping* social systems did not preclude descriptions of the workshops as *included* within wider systems of social relationships.

The need to explore both the wider systems of economic and social relationships within which a social system, such as a single workshop or a firm, is included, and these overlapping systems, has important consequences in terms of the research methods which became necessary, as Lupton and Cunnison (1964, 125) recognised. Indeed Eldridge (1971, 32) has argued that it makes the approach they advocated very close to the social action approach, which will be discussed further in Chapter 4, even though this has normally been seen as an alternative to systems thinking. (See also the discussion of Lupton's work and Cunnison's own study [1966] in Silverman [1970, 197–201] and in Elger [1975, 122–3].)

In more recent work Lupton and colleagues have utilised the open socio-technical systems concept. Their use of it appears to involve two rather different types of formulation. On the one hand they suggest that 'a manufacturing department or service area may be usefully conceived of as requiring a *technical organization* . . . and a *social organization* to carry out work', with 'a relationship of *mutual dependence* between the two' (Warmington *et al.* 1977, 52). After using the concept as a means of analysis and explanation of behaviour and events in three departments, however, they then focused on nine elements or variables and on the pattern of relationships between them; although the chapter is headed 'a generalised model of the socio-technical system', it outlines how certain constraints and actions, which may also be interrelated, have consequences for attitudes, behaviour and performance which also react back on some of the other variables; the emphasis is on processes and outcomes rather than on structure (155–68). In the light of the comments made already about the utility of systems models for action-research, it is significant that these authors were engaged in such a project. They are not alone in using the concept of organisations as open socio-technical systems in such a context, nor in subjecting it to criticism and modification (see, for example, Clark 1972).

In both phases of Lupton's work, though particularly in the earlier one, it becomes clear that those attempting to analyse organisations cannot assume that there is one system, or even one system with a coherent set of sub-systems, in terms of which social relations and social processes can be understood. To avoid a situation where actions and relations, which cannot be accounted for within a conception of an organisation as a social or socio-technical system, are regarded as residual (rather like 'informal organisation' in relation to 'formal organisation' or to bureaucratic structures) it may well be necessary to envisage a much more complex framework of a variety of overlapping 'systems'. Such a conclusion is indicated in Burns's discussion of his research findings.

Burns undertook research in the 1950s with the aim of explaining the relative failure of certain Scottish firms which were attempting to establish themselves in the rapidly developing electronics industry. Through comparison with firms which had been more successful he and his colleague were able to show that to be effective in a context where there were rapidly changing technical and/or commercial conditions it was necessary to adopt a much more flexible or 'organic' structure in place of the conventional bureaucratic or 'mechanistic' one. These arguments will be discussed in more detail in the next chapter. In trying to account for the failure of certain firms to adopt the appropriate structure the authors pointed out that a business concern is not only a working organisation but that 'the members of the working community which constitutes the concern are necessarily and unavoidably occupied (a) with the distribution and regulation of power in the concern, and (b) with their status in that community'. Any enterprise must therefore be seen as simultaneously a working organisation, a political system and a career or status structure; and 'they do not exist as isolated entities. Political and status considerations constantly influence the working organization, and influence it so as to reduce its effectiveness' (Burns and Stalker

1961, 144–6; Burns 1963, 1969). The inability to change from a mechanistic to an organic structure, and resistance to moves which might bring about such a change, were attributed to the commitments of members of the concern to sectional and/or career interests in addition to their commitment to the working organisation, commitments which might be upset by the change.

Burns's studies not only provided a rich vein of empirical materials which others could quarry but also necessitated some important rethinking of the use of a systems approach in investigating industrial organisations. The existing conceptions of the firm as a 'bureaucracy' or as a (single) 'system' proved inadequate as a framework within which to explain the social relations and behaviour which were actually observed. However, in taking account of members' commitments to internal political and to career considerations as well as to the working organisation, Burns and Stalker described organisations whose structure had to be seen not as some pre-given 'system' but as the outcome of on-going processes of interpretation and negotiation. Elger (1975, 109) has very effectively summarised the implications of their analysis:

> Though Burns and Stalker take the tradition of systems typologies as their point of departure . . . they develop, in relation to a rich array of empirical materials, a processual analysis which treats actors' allegiances, perspectives and strategies as problematic features of organizational action. In this context organizational structure and operative goals are seen as the outcome of negotiation and interpretation processes among organization members with differential resources.

This assessment encapsulates perhaps the most important source of criticism of systems thinking.

CONCLUDING DISCUSSION

Functionalist approaches in sociology were clearly dominant, though never unchallenged, during the 1950s, but no single theoretical standpoint could claim the same status, at least in Britain, from the mid-1960s onwards. The theoretical pluralism which developed alongside the growth of teaching and research in sociology in this country inevitably contributed to an increasing volume of criticism of systems approaches to the analysis of industrial organisations. As Burrell and Morgan (1979) have pointed out, some of these criticisms reflected different basic assumptions about the nature of social science, different philosophies of science, and different views and interpretations of the nature of society. In so far as this was the case – and these authors might be thought to base their arguments about mutually exclusive paradigms on over-exaggerated, and therefore possibly false, dichotomies – proponents and critics of systems approaches were talking past each other.

Much of the criticism, however, cannot be dismissed or bracketed off for these reasons and must be seen as constituting valid grounds for modification, or even abandonment, of a systems approach. There appears to have been greater reluctance to take such a step in relation to the study of the industrial enterprise than in other areas of sociology. This reflects the apparent suitability of the 'systems' notion for the study of organisations, and the utility of systems thinking to those concerned with action research or consultancy, as many are of those who write about the sociology of industrial organisations.

Perhaps the most basic criticism of systems approaches in the 'strong' form of socio-technical systems theory or functionalist sociology is that they 'reify' the organisation and do so in ways which are illegitimate and misleading. That is they treat it as a 'thing', an entity which can have aims and needs distinct from those of the individuals and groups which compose it, and can act on its own as it were independently of the decisions and instructions of (some of) its members. Such a conceptualisation can have undesirable consequences for analysis if it obscures the processes by which organisational goals and policy are determined and leads to the neglect of the conflicting interests which may exist as between groupings within the organisation. Some degree of apparent reification is probably almost unavoidable in thinking and writing about organisations (e.g. see the 'defence' by Donaldson 1985, 18–22); and it is legitimate if it remains a kind of 'shorthand'. As Mouzelis has argued statements such as 'the organization adopted a new policy' can quite properly be used and interpreted as referring to the complicated processes through which a new policy has been agreed (1975, xii–xvi); and though such processes can be studied, in the context of a particular research problem they may have to be taken for granted because the focus of attention is on other issues.

Some writing within a systems framework, however, clearly goes beyond such 'shorthand'. Rice, for example, has asserted 'open systems live by the exchange of materials with their environment and have the capacity to reach a time-independent steady state . . . once the steady state is disturbed for any reason, external or internal, the system will exert forces to restore it' and, even more starkly, 'any healthy system will resist change' (1963, 262). Such statements embody claims about inherent characteristics and behaviour of systems which are held regardless of the nature of the groups and individuals who compose them and must be considered at best dangerous and unwarranted simplification and generalisation (see also Clegg and Dunkerley 1980, 209). A contrast to this reification of organisations as self-regulating systems would be a view of them which stresses the ways in which organisational goals, and the rules, roles and order intended to achieve them, are continually negotiated and renegotiated in the interactions between organisational members. As Silverman put it: 'Our "system", unlike the almost metaphysical functionalist version, is only the present outcome of the ends sought by different groups and the actions which they have chosen to pursue in the light of the means available to them' (1968, 234).

The problem of 'reification' is linked to two further issues: the nature and specification of an organisation's goals, functions or primary tasks; and the nature and specification of the organisation's 'needs' as a system (see the discussion in Elger 1975, 94–6).

As we have seen, the type of analysis pursued by Jaques and Brown and by members of the Tavistock Institute depended on their being able to identify the objects or primary task of an enterprise, or some part of it, in order to postulate the arrangements most appropriate in the circumstances to meet it. Both Jaques and Brown suggest that the goals of an employing organisation can be identified in the form of the explicit intentions, often written, of the 'association' (board of directors, public authority, or whatever) which set it up. Donaldson (1985, 22–6) has stressed that 'goals' become organisational, rather than the interests of particular individuals or groups within an organisation, when they are authorised and institutionalised. The danger in such a position is that it may conceal the problematic nature of such organisational goals; such statements are unlikely to be endorsed by all members of the organisation; they are likely to need interpretation and cannot be read unproblematically. Further, goals may change, they may be 'displaced' (means may become ends), and even if the current goals of the governing association can be accurately identified this does not mean that they are endorsed by all members of the organisation (see Silverman 1970, 9–11; Elliott 1974, 84–6).

Miller and Rice tried to avoid these difficulties with the notion of 'primary task – the task it must perform if it is to survive' (1967, 25), but they recognise that this may have 'to be inferred from the behaviour of the various systems of activity, and from the criteria by which their performance is regulated' (27), which could make the analysis rather circular. Certainly the assertion that to make profits is the primary tasks of business enterprises is far from unproblematic if meeting that criterion is seen as necessary and/or sufficient for survival: unprofitable concerns have been kept in being for considerable periods of time, for example by government (Rolls-Royce, Upper Clyde Shipbuilders), or by their owners (some newspapers, many football clubs); and profitable ones have been closed. In such circumstances declaring that certain arrangements or activities are 'requisite' is fraught with difficulty.

The same sorts of problems are raised by attempts to define the functional 'needs' of an organisation. At a basic level there are some essential prerequisites of organisation, for example the need for some mechanisms for recruitment and socialisation of members. It may be possible to identify what is 'logically necessary' for organisations to exist at all (see Abrams 1982, 65). There may also be limits to the possible configurations of social relations which are possible within one organisation, because the consequences, intended and/or unintended, of one set of arrangements may render certain others impossible. As the notion of 'functional alternatives' implies, however, 'needs' can often be met in one of several ways, and this is even more likely to be so if 'needs' are defined in general and abstract terms. For the most part the theorists we have considered use conceptions of functional prerequisites or system needs only to provide a rather general account of organisational structure (Rice's three principal operating systems, for example); their more detailed criticisms and prescriptions depend on additional assumptions about human beings and human society, assumptions which are far from axiomatic and which must be open to empirical testing and possible modification or rejection.

The conceptualisation of an industrial organisation or business enterprise as a unified system with a clearly identifiable goal, or primary task, and with activities and relationships appropriately structured to accomplish the task, makes it difficult to provide a satisfactory account of conflict within the organisation. Those who operate with such a model tend to attribute the conflicts which do occur to causes which could be resolved. These may be structural or psychological. The structure of the organisation, it can be argued, is not yet fully as it 'requisitely' ought to be, and so, for example, communications are not fully effective, or roles and relationships are not yet appropriately defined. Or there is inadequate provision for helping those in positions of authority to work through the anxieties raised by their dependence on their subordinates and their subordinates' dependence on them.

Jaques and Brown both imply that any structural sources of conflict within organisations are removed by members' agreements to an employment contract, together with the provision of appropriate representative systems and appeals procedures, and the determination of pay by the objective means of time-span of discretion analysis. Neither they nor the Tavistock researchers adequately acknowledge that the inequalities of condition and opportunity which exist in all industrial societies mean that for most people entry into particular forms of employment is constrained and that it may, in effect, be coerced, resulting in the absence of anything other than a pragmatic acceptance of the goals and authority structure of the organisation, or of the terms of their employment in it. Once the commitment of organisational members to the goals laid down for the enterprise by those in power is seen as limited and conditional, then it is no longer legitimate to assume that it should always be possible to achieve consensus and harmony within the organisation. In addition, as the Liverpool researchers recognised, occupational differentiation creates groupings, in society and within industrial organisations, which share similar conditions of employment, similar situations in the labour market, similar rewards and similar status; recognition of a common situation, and collective organisation and action to further common interests, in opposition possibly to those of other groupings of employees, are inherent in the division of labour.

The implications to be drawn from our examination of the systems concept are that the stronger the sense in which the notion is used the less easy it is to account for structurally induced conflicts within organisations. Conversely those writers who recognise that social relations in employing organisations are inevitably characterised by conflict as well as cooperation, as the Liverpool researchers and Burns did in rather different ways, use the systems notion in a very much weaker sense, or see that organisations may have to be characterised as consisting of several systems 'any one of which may be invoked as the frame of reference for a particular action' (Silverman 1970, 41; Burns 1969). The use of a systems approach in this weaker but more appropriate sense necessarily leads to a focusing of attention on the reconciliation, at least temporarily, of the more or less incompatible ends of different groups and individuals within an organisation through processes of conflict, bargaining and negotiation within which differential power and resources are brought into play. In so far as the resulting organisation is an orderly system, it is a 'negotiated order' (see Strauss *et al.* 1971) and a highly contingent one, always likely to be upset by changes in the aims and orientations of organisational members and/or the resources available to them, as well as other changes in the environment of the enterprise.

The environment as a source of change is, of course, explicitly recognised in open systems approaches. Advocates of such an approach place considerable emphasis on the role of leadership in 'managing' the boundary conditions of the system. The notion of boundary is far from straightforward however. If a common-sense definition is used – like physical presence within a workplace, or having a contract of employment with a firm – there are often awkward anomalies: how to regard customers, or those employees whose work is outside the plant, for example, or those working, semi-permanently, as self-employed labour-only sub-contractors, or as part-time non-executive directors. If observable social relationships are the basis then, as Lupton and Cunnison found, the eventual picture is likely to be one of a partial overlap and interpenetration of several systems. Though some steps have been taken towards an adequate conceptualisation of the environment, this too is a not altogether satisfactory aspect of existing systems approaches. The emphasis has been on factor and product markets (the 'markets', respectively, from which supplies of raw materials, labour and capital are obtained, and in which goods and services are sold). These must be of central concern for an understanding of any enterprise attempting to produce and sell goods or services, but they do not exhaust the ways in which the 'environment' may influence structures and processes within an organisation. We shall return to this issue in the next chapter.

Problems of boundary definition and the conceptualisation of the environment also arise in relation to the account given of the values and priorities of members of an organisation. Within systems thinking this tends to be approached in two ways. On the one hand it is assumed that there are certain universal human 'needs' which influence the ways in which organisational members react to their situations within the organisation. On the other hand to occupy a position within a system of roles and relationships is to be subject to expectations, supported by positive and negative sanctions, as to how one should behave, and to be subject to processes of socialisation which may well lead to the internalisation of appropriate values and norms. Both approaches are inadequate. Beyond a very basic level the assertion of universal human needs is at best unproven; individuals may differ very considerably in terms of their expectations and priorities regarding employment. Such differences cannot be explained solely in terms of differences in their situations within organisations, and in the expectations and socialisation to which they may have been subject; they may result, at least in part, from influences and circumstances outside the organisation. These arguments will be discussed further in Chapter 4.

At various points in this chapter it has been emphasised that systems approaches are particularly appropriate for those engaged in action research or consultancy. A final criticism of them is that they tend to be biased towards a managerial point of view. The emphasis on consensus and integration, and the inadequate treatment of conflict, are possible signs of such a bias. More fundamentally Burrell and Morgan have argued that such a bias arises from an unthinking adoption of the analogy between organisation and organism:

> Insofar as [theorists] adopt organismic models which presume a functional unity of system parts, with certain imperative functions which must be satisfied if the organization is to survive, their analyses are constrained by the requirements characteristic of a managerial point of view. It is this consonance between the nature of the organismic analogy and the requirements of managerialism which underwrites the dominance of organismic models within the field of organization theory.
>
> (1979, 219–20)

The whole sociological endeavour implies a view of social life in which the whole is greater than the sum of its parts, and social entities – society, social institutions, organisations – have an existence in some sense independently of the individuals who constitute them. It is central to sociological enquiry, too, that one should explore the unintended as well as the intended consequences of social action and try to identify the ways in which such consequences react back on, reinforce and/or cause contradictions in the structures and processes which gave rise to them. It is therefore difficult and undesirable to avoid recognition of the 'systemic' qualities of organisations. In practice 'thinking in terms of systems' has clearly been very fruitful as a framework within which to organise and try to understand the patterns of social relations and social action which can be observed within organisations. When used cautiously to try to summarise and describe such patterns the approach raises few problems. It is when the systemic character of organisations is assumed, combined with very general assumptions about human 'needs', and used as a basis for explanation, prediction or prescription that it becomes questionable. These issues will be discussed further in the next two chapters.

Chapter 3

Context, contingency and choice

> We are concerned with the attempt to generalize and develop the study of work organization and behaviour into a consideration of the interdependence of three conceptually distinct levels of analysis of behaviour in organizations: (1) organizational structure and functioning, (2) group composition and interaction, and (3) individual personality and behaviour. We are also concerned to interrelate each of these levels. . . . We wish to undertake a factorial analysis to establish the significant variables at each level and their relationships, and then develop at each level a processual analysis within the framework thus established . . . . Furthermore the study of the structure and activities of an organization must be conducted in relation to its other characteristics and to the social and economic context in which it is found. In order to examine these relationships we have developed a list of contextual variables . . . . We use this list as a series of independent variables in order to relate them to the dependent variables of organizational structure and functioning.
>
> (Pugh *et al.* 1963, 292–3)

In 1963 the *Administrative Science Quarterly* published an article by six social scientists from the then College of Advanced Technology in Birmingham (later to become the University of Aston in Birmingham) entitled 'A conceptual scheme for organizational analysis'. It was the first major statement of a programme of research by the Industrial Administration Research Unit at Aston, which had commenced two years earlier with the ambitious intention (reflected in the above quotation) of carrying out a large-scale comparative study of 'work organisations' (defined as those whose members are all employed by the organisation Pugh [*et al.* 1963, 299]). Over the next two decades there appeared a steady stream of papers in journals, especially but not only the *Administrative Science Quarterly*, which reported the results of this research; more recently many of these papers have been reprinted, together with some additional material, in a series of four volumes which provide a comprehensive account of 'the Aston Programme' (Pugh and Hickson 1976; Pugh and Hinings 1976; Pugh and Payne 1977; and Hickson and McMillan 1981). This programme had its centre in the University of Aston itself only until 1968 when several leading members of the team moved to other institutions, including the London Business School which for a number of years became the home of the main attempts in Britain to follow up and develop these ideas. During the 1970s, however, research using 'Aston' concepts and methods spread internationally to include projects in the USA, Canada, West Germany, Sweden, Poland, Jordan, Egypt, India and Japan. In Britain alone nearly thirty individuals are mentioned as having contributed to these projects (excluding secretarial and support staff) and at least eighteen of them have been involved as authors of papers.

By any standards this represents a very considerable achievement providing a real possibility of cumulative findings based on the sort of large-scale long-term research effort which has been all too rare in the social sciences. That it has occurred at all is a tribute to the vision, leadership, persistence and entrepreneurial and administrative skills of those primarily responsible, especially Derek Pugh. Indeed notable features of this programme of research, especially but not only in the early years, were the enthusiasm of the leading researchers, the conscious and carefully fostered awareness of themselves as an innovatory team, and the active and highly effective propagation of their ideas and findings, all of which contributed to the programme's continuation and its growth to include international comparisons. It deserves attention, however, not solely or primarily on these quantitative grounds but because it represents a major attempt at a particular approach to the study of work organisations.

As Burns (1967, 113–14) has rightly argued 'comparative study is the fundamental sociological method' even, if implicitly, in single case studies, where findings must be reported using terms and concepts which permit comparison with the research, and the everyday experience, of others. The Aston team regarded such implicit comparisons as inadequate however; what was needed was not just qualitative descriptions of organisations, nor even verbal comparative statements of quantity in the form of 'more' or 'less', but the use of quantitative measures which would make possible precise comparisons between organisations in terms of concepts which have been clearly 'operationalised'. The success of the Aston programme has been built on their initial achievement in devising, testing and applying means of measuring organisational 'structures' and 'contexts', means which have proved reliable and, in so far as this can be judged and in their own terms, valid with little or no amendment when used on further samples of organisations in this country and abroad. This achievement has been dependent on the use of a highly 'objectivist' or 'positivist' methodology, one which assumes that 'organisations are hard, concrete, empirical phenomena which can be measured', and is characterised by an 'extremely high degree of commitment to the models and methods of the natural sciences' (Burrell and Morgan 1979, 162–4; see also Clegg and Dunkerley 1980, Chapter 6, and esp. 216–18). In our consideration of these studies, therefore, we will necessarily be concerned with some of these theoretical and methodological issues as well as with the substantive 'findings' of the research.

In many ways the initiation of the Aston programme can be regarded as something of an accident. It grew out of the workshop studies by Lupton, Cunnison and Wilson at the University of Manchester which were concerned with the explanation of shopfloor behaviour especially in situations where workers were subject to incentive payment schemes (Cunnison 1982; Emmett and Morgan 1982). As was outlined in Chapter 2 these researchers were forced to consider a range of factors outside the workshop, some 'internal' and some 'external' to the factory itself, in order to account adequately for the different patterns of behaviour they had observed. In order to follow up these studies of shopfloor behaviour in British factories Lupton obtained a large research grant from the Department of Scientific and Industrial Research, which he took with him when appointed head of the Industrial Administration Department at Aston. As 'he had no time himself to launch the research' this task fell to Pugh, a psychologist, and the colleagues who joined him in the original research team. In considering the potential factors which might influence workers' performance they realised that the 'organisation with a management control structure' must be one such, crucial, factor, and that they had no means at that time of comparing 'the structure of one organisation with that of another'. As a result 'structure itself became something to be explained, and in the end more effort was devoted to this than could be spared for the group and individual level work which came later' (Pugh and Hickson 1976, viii–x). Pugh's disciplinary background in psychology and his familiarity with factorial project designs and quantitative measurement clearly had an important influence on the methods and techniques which were adopted.

In other respects, however, as is carefully acknowledged in the 1963 paper, the programme grew out of and built on a developing body of research in Britain, in the USA, and elsewhere concerned with exploring the relationships between organisations and the contexts within which they operate, and/or with developing typologies of organisations in terms of differences in their structure (Pugh *et al.* 1963; Pugh and Hickson 1976, 17–29). It also drew on the sociological studies of bureaucratic organisation stemming from the work of Max Weber. Many of these studies are of importance in their own right and for that reason, as well as to provide an introduction to the Aston studies, we shall consider some of this earlier work in a little more detail before turning to an examination of the Aston programme itself. Indeed that programme should be seen as an example, though one which was very highly developed in particular ways, of the 'contingency theory' in organisational analysis which Burrell and Morgan (1979, 180, see also 164–81) have described as representing 'a synthesis of the concepts and ideas implicit in a great deal of contemporary organisation theory'.

FROM BUREAUCRACY TO TECHNOLOGY

Weber

Since the late 1940s the writings of Max Weber on bureaucracy have been a major source of ideas and insights for sociologists concerned with the analysis of organisations, especially but not only in the USA (Weber 1947, 328–41; Gerth and Mills 1948, 196–244). Weber's discussion of bureaucracy was part of his more general consideration of types of legitimate rule, or of authority, and in its most general sense could be seen as referring to 'an administrative body of appointed officials' (Albrow 1970, 42). His 'ideal type' of rational bureaucracy represented the identification and accentuation of the characteristics of the purest form of organisation based on legal-rational authority (that is authority legitimated on 'rational grounds – resting on a belief in the "legality" of enacted rules and the right of those elevated to authority under such rules to issue commands' [Weber 1968, 215]). Such an organisation would be staffed by 'officials' who were personally free, selected on the basis of qualifications, and appointed on the basis of a contract; they would receive salaries and (normally) pension rights, have no other (major) occupation, have the possibility of a career with promotion on the basis of seniority and/or merit, but have no personal rights in their post or the resources allocated to it. The tasks to be carried out by the organisation would be divided between functionally distinct 'offices', organised into a hierarchy with appropriate authority and sanctions, with a body of rules (including technical rules) governing the conduct of work; and the rules, activities and decisions of the organisation would be recorded in writing and preserved in the files. The growth of such forms of organisation, in industry and in a wide range of other spheres, was seen by Weber as inevitable in the modern world and as part of the more general process of the rationalisation of social life (see Albrow 1970, esp. 37–49).

As an aid to identifying and understanding important features of the industrialised world which distinguish it from 'traditional' societies Weber's ideas are very illuminating and present few difficulties. Some commentators have suggested that such 'macroscopic' comparisons are the only context in which they can properly be used (e.g. Mouzelis 1975, xviii–xxi). Certainly as a framework for the detailed analysis of modern organisations the ideal type has given rise to problems, especially if Weber's claim for the 'rationality' of bureaucratic organisation is taken to imply 'substantive' rationality (that is effectiveness or efficiency in achieving some goal) and not just 'formal' rationality (see Albrow 1970, 50–66). One source of problems has been the observation that a great deal of the behaviour and a great many relationships to be found in organisations were not officially prescribed and yet, in many cases, could be shown to contribute to the organisation's achievement of its tasks; the idea of a dichotomy between formal and informal organisation was one, not very satisfactory, response to such findings, with the ideal type being seen as an account only of the 'formal' organisation (see Chapter 2).

Other writers have perhaps been closer to Weber's own intentions and used the ideal type as a means of identifying changes within industry or society; one notable example was Bendix's discussion of the bureaucratisation of economic enterprises during industrialisation (Bendix 1956, Ch. 4). The difficulty with this approach is that the ideal type comprises a large number of characteristics of organisations which may not all develop in the same way or at the same rate. Bendix emphasised two indices of bureaucratisation: the growing proportion of administrative employees in industrial organisations, and the changes over time in the career patterns of top industrialists; but one cannot assume that movements in these two indices will necessarily coincide. We shall consider the Aston group's approach to this issue below. A third response to the finding that many organisations differ from the ideal type bureaucracy has been to create new types, and to try to account for their occurrence. Burns' development of the distinction between 'mechanistic' and 'organic' systems of management was one of the most important and influential contributions of this sort (Burns and Stalker 1961), and deserves more detailed attention.

Burns and Stalker

During a series of investigations in the 1950s, mostly in the electrical engineering and electronics industries, Burns and Stalker were able to identify firms which clearly approximated closely to the ideal type of bureaucratic organisation. In firms characterised by such 'mechanistic' systems of management there was a clear hierarchy of control, authority and communication; the tasks and problems facing the firm were broken down into specialisms and allocated to functionally differentiated roles each with defined methods, duties and powers; and the occupants of such roles could pursue their tasks as something distinct from those of the concern as a whole. This pattern of organisation was based on the assumption that the head of the concern knew what needed to be done, and could therefore make provision for all necessary activities to be carried out, and should have the exclusive power and responsibility to ensure the coordination of the tasks allocated to subordinates (Burns and Stalker 1961, 5, 120). In many situations such a machine-like organisation could work very effectively; it had the advantage for its members of specifying clearly and delimiting their obligations and responsibilities to the organisation.

Many of the enterprises investigated by these researchers, however, were facing situations of change and uncertainty. In some cases this arose from decisions to attempt to enter the rapidly developing field of electronics by introducing research and development departments which, they hoped, would introduce new products. In other cases the uncertainty came primarily from the product market as government contracts were cut back and attempts had to be made to meet rapidly changing consumer demand. In such circumstances the assumption that the head of the enterprise could be or should be omniscient and omnipotent was no longer tenable. A much more diffuse and pervasive commitment to the tasks of the concern as a whole was demanded from its members if the fresh problems and unforeseen requirements for action which constantly arose were to be met satisfactorily. The appropriate management system was 'organic', described by the authors in the following terms:

> Organic systems are adapted to unstable conditions, when problems and requirements for action arise which cannot be broken down and distributed among specialist roles within a clearly defined hierarchy. Individuals have to perform their special tasks in the light of their knowledge of the tasks of the firm as a whole. Jobs lose much of their formal definition in terms of methods, duties, and powers, which have to be redefined continually by interaction with others participating in a task. Interaction runs laterally as much as vertically. Communication between people of different ranks tends to resemble lateral consultation rather than vertical command. Omniscience can no longer be imputed to the head of the concern.
>
> (Burns and Stalker 1961, 5, see also 121)

Rates of change in technology and in product markets must be regarded as largely 'external' to the enterprise and thus Burns's work can be seen as contributing to debates about the relationship between industrial organisations and their environments. On the other hand the framework of explanation developed is far from a deterministic one. Indeed one of the main concerns of his work was to account for the failure of some of the organisations observed to adopt a management system appropriate to their circumstances, and in providing this Burns developed the ideas about 'the plurality of social systems' which were discussed in the previous chapter. 'The approximation of a working organization to mechanistic or to organic form' was seen as being 'determined by the operation of three "variables"'. Only the first of these was external to the concern: 'the rate of technical and market change'. The two internal factors were 'the strength of personal commitments to the improvement or defence of status or power', and 'the extent to which the managing director can interpret the technical and commercial situation, and can adapt the working organization and elicit the individual commitment to it for which the situation calls' (Burns and Stalker 1961, 209).

In *The Management of Innovation* Burns and Stalker provide ample evidence of the reality of the distinction between mechanistic and organic systems of management and of its implications for managerial relations and conduct. Its formulation and presentation nevertheless do pose certain problems. On the one hand the two systems represent 'ideal types', or perhaps more usefully 'polar types', and it is claimed:

> the two forms of system represent a polarity, not a dichotomy; there are, as we have tried to show, intermediate stages between the extremities empirically known to us. Also, the relation of one form to the other is elastic, so that a concern oscillating between relative stability and relative change may also oscillate between the two forms. A concern may (and frequently does) operate with a management system which includes both types.
> (Burns and Stalker 1961, 122)

On the other hand the examples, discussed elsewhere in the book, of organisations in intermediate positions on this range of possibilities appear mostly to be cases of failure to adapt fully to the requirements of their situation. Nor, given the internal coherence of the two types, is it easy to see what the intermediate stages might be like except as temporary points in transition between situations very much closer to one or other pole. Research in America, however, has lent support to the contention that an enterprise might require more than one type of management system; this can arise if its major operating divisions (research and development, production, sales) face rather different environments (see Lawrence and Lorsch 1967a, 1977b). In such circumstances the problem is to ensure that the parts of the organisation are both adequately differentiated (and not forced to adopt a uniform pattern) and fully integrated.

The subtle and probing style of research adopted by Burns does not permit of easy replication nor provide (nor see as possible or desirable) precise quantitative statements of differences between organisations. His findings represent, however, a major contribution to the study of organisations by establishing links between types of organisation and environmental circumstances and thus in showing that a non-bureaucratic system of management may be 'rational' in certain situations. As the authors pointed out:

> We have endeavoured to stress the appropriateness of each system to its own specific set of conditions. Equally, we desire to avoid the suggestion that either system is superior under all circumstances to the other . . . . The beginning of administrative wisdom is the awareness that there is no one optimum type of management system.
>
> (Burns and Stalker 1961, 125)

Woodward

The claim that there was 'one optimum type of management system' can be derived from a reading (and misunderstanding – see Albrow 1970) of Weber's work, but has been expressed much more clearly in the literature of management (see Child 1969). It was statements of such management 'principles' which provided the starting point for research by Joan Woodward which made a further influential contribution to the study of the relations between organisations and their environments. Woodward initiated research 'to discover whether the principles of organization laid down by an expanding body of management theory correlate with business success when put into practice' (Woodward 1958, 4). Her study between 1953 and 1957 covered 100 firms in manufacturing industry in south-east Essex, representing 91 per cent of all the firms in the area with over 100 employees. Starting with a focus on the relationship between line supervision and technical and advisory specialists the scope of the research quickly grew to include the whole structure of management and supervision. The researchers collected information from their sample of firms under four main headings: '(1) history, background, and objectives; (2) description of the manufacturing processes and methods; (3)

forms and routines through which the firm was organized and operated; (4) facts and figures that could be used to make an assessment of the firm's commercial success' (Woodward 1965, 11; and see 1958, 7–8). In the light of the procedures advocated and adopted later by the Aston researchers it should be noted that though Woodward and her colleagues used a standard schedule of information to be obtained, the process of acquiring and summarising data clearly involved judgements by the researchers and on some issues permitted the allocation of firms only to rather broadly defined categories (see Woodward 1965, 10–16).

This was the case with regard to 'commercial success' where, after consideration of a range of information, firms were classified merely as 'average', 'above average' and 'below average'. The researchers found, however, that there did not appear to be any relationship between the success, or lack of it, of a firm and its type of organisation, and in particular that those twenty firms which were 'above average' in success were not more likely to be organised according to the dictates of management theory. On the other hand neither were variations in the organisational structure of the firms related to the industry they were in nor to their size; some small firms, for example, had considerable specialisation within management, while some larger ones did not, and there was no apparent relation between size and 'the length of the command hierarchy' (Woodward 1965, 30–3). The relationship between technology and organisation proved, unexpectedly, much more illuminating:

> When, however, the firms were grouped according to similarity of objectives and techniques of production, and classified in order of the technical complexity of their production systems, each production system was found to be associated with a characteristic pattern of organization. It appeared that technical methods were the most important factor in determining organizational structure and in setting the tone of human relationships inside the firms.
>
> (Woodward 1958, 4)

Furthermore, 'when . . . firms were grouped on a basis of their production systems, the outstandingly successful ones had at least one feature in common. Many of their organizational characteristics approximated to the median of their production group' (20). The most important argument to arise from this research, therefore, was that the objectives of an enterprise and the methods and processes necessary to achieve these objectives (its technology or production system) were the most important, though not the only, determinant of its organisational structure.

The classification of firms according to the nature of their production system proved difficult, eight firms could not be categorised at all, and, indeed, there are minor differences between the distributions shown in the brief report published in 1958 and in the book published in 1965. By focusing on the objectives of the firm, the methods used to achieve those objectives and the nature of the product it was however possible to place the majority of the firms studied (92 out of 100) into one of 10 or 11 categories, which did not equate simply with industry or with production engineering classifications and were not related to size. Furthermore, the majority of those categories could be arranged in a scale of increasing technical complexity defined as 'the extent to which the production process is controllable and its results predictable' (Woodward 1958, 12; see also 1965, esp. 37–44). At one extreme were firms which produced individual units to customer orders; at the other were process production firms engaged in the continuous flow production of liquids, gases and/or solids. In between the range moved through small and large batch production, mass production and process production of batches as technical complexity and the predictability of production increased. For purposes of further analysis, however, Woodward concentrated on a three-fold division into unit and small batch production, large batch and mass production, and process production.

With the firms classified in these three main categories there appeared to be two main relationships between technology and organisational structure (Woodward 1958, 16–18; 1965, 50–67). On the one hand certain characteristics increased in direct relation to technical complexity: the number of levels in the management hierarchy; the span of control of the firm's chief executive; the proportion of graduates among supervisory staff engaged on production; and the ratios of managerial and supervisory staff to other personnel, of indirect to direct labour, and of administrative and clerical employees to hourly paid workers. However, labour costs as a proportion of total costs decreased. In other respects the two extremes of the scale of technical complexity, unit and small batch production and process production, seemed to resemble each other and be distinct from the large batch and mass production firms in the middle: specialisation between the functions of management, the amount of written as opposed to verbal communication, the span of control of the first-line supervisor and the extent to which the administration of production (its 'brainwork') was separated from its actual supervision were all greatest in the large batch and mass production firms. The firms at the two ends of the scale had higher proportions of skilled manual workers and were more 'flexible', less organisation conscious and more likely to have an 'organic' management system.

These findings made a considerable impact when first published, especially among teachers of management, but they have also been subject to considerable criticism because of the imprecise specification of certain key concepts like 'business success' and 'technical complexity' and the failure to use appropriate statistical analysis. One reviewer, for example, commented that 'the data analysis is hopelessly inadequate and provides virtually no support for the causal inferences that are made' (Hopkins 1966, 285)! On the other hand the findings had considerable coherence and plausibility and could claim support from case study evidence, for example in shipbuilding (which reflects Woodward's account of unit production), in the motor industry (mass production) and in oil refining and chemicals (process production).

Another source of contention was Woodward's argument that 'human relations' were on the whole better at the extremes of the technical complexity scale than in the middle primarily because of differences in the amount of pressure to which workers and supervisors were subject. In unit production little attempt was, or could be, made to control physical limitations of production and people were subject to relatively little pressure; it was traditional, for example, that engineers engaged on the development of a complicated piece of equipment 'were unlikely to work well "with a gun at their backs"'. Pressure on people was at a minimum also at the process production end of the scale because production was genuinely under mechanical control and predictable; 'people were hard pressed only when things went wrong'. It was greatest in large batch and mass production where the capacity of the production system was calculable in theory but output still depended on the amount of effort operators were prepared to put into the job (Woodward 1958, 18, 29–30). In addition to the more general criticisms of the apparent technological determinism of behaviour, which will be discussed in Chapter 4, it must be said that these generalisations do not accord so well with at least some case study evidence; for example research in shipbuilding (Brown *et al.* 1972) and in chemicals (Nichols and Beynon 1977) would lead to questioning of the claims made for 'human relations' in such industries.

In the light of later treatment of 'technology' as a variable it should be noted that Woodward's attempt to typify production systems emphasised the objectives being pursued by the enterprise which 'controlled and limited' the techniques of production which could be employed. This emphasis was pursued in the follow-up studies of a sub-sample of firms, which considered the 'situational demands' facing different types of concern and concluded that each type demanded a different sequence of the main functions of development, production and marketing and had a different 'most critical function' (Woodward 1965, 125–53; 1958, 22–9). In unit production (e.g. shipbuilding, bespoke tailoring) the cycle began with marketing, obtaining an order, proceeded with the most critical function of development and concluded with production. Mass production firms (e.g. motor cars, consumer durables) developed a product, produced it and then marketed it, and their success depended heavily 'on the efficient administration of production and the progressive reduction of unit costs'. Process production firms (e.g. detergents, pharmaceuticals) also developed products, and processes, first; an assured market was needed to justify the investment in new plant so that pilot production and trial marketing would precede full-scale production, and the efficiency of the marketing organisation was critical. These differences in the relative importance of the main organisational activities had further implications for the nature of managerial decisions and the relations between different management functions. In addition, in the studies made of firms undergoing technical changes it was found that it was those changes which involved adopting a different sort of production system, especially if it created new 'situational demands', which had major implications for management structure and functioning (Woodward 1958, 39–40; 1965, Chs 10 and 11).

Woodward's work, like Burns and Stalker's, was a major and influential contribution to 'contingency theory' in organisational analysis. Thus, though she reported that the 'principles' of management did reflect the requirements of large batch production firms fairly closely (not surprising, perhaps, as management theorists had mostly drawn on experience of such firms to formulate them), she too asserted 'there can be no one best way of organizing a business' (1958, 10). Her conclusions, however, were far from complete technological determinism. 'Organization appeared to grow in response to a number of stimuli' including organisation theory, fashion, and the 'empire building' activities of individual managers, past and present. Where the 'formal' organisation was out of line with situational demands, the 'informal' organisation often developed more appropriately (Woodward 1958, 38; 1965, 238–40). This recognition that the official (or 'formal') structure of organisations cannot be studied in isolation from the ways in which they actually operate, and that managerial ambitions and choices can affect structure, is not as prominent in Woodward's work as it is in Burns's account of the political system and status, or career, structure; it is, however, an important part of her argument which introduces an element of indeterminacy and also draws attention to processes of negotiation and choice within the organisation. Thus, though the 'technical implications' approach with which Woodward's work is so closely associated has been rightly described as 'a form of structural-functional analysis' (Goldthorpe *et al.* 1968, 181), and her own underlying framework was a systems one, the research as reported can also be seen as directing attention to processes of interpretation and bargaining within organisations, though not clearly enough to satisfy some critics (cf. Elger 1975, 105–6; Child 1971, 129).

As is often the case the relative certainties of Woodward's earlier findings became less clear-cut as a result of subsequent research. Between 1962 and the time of her death in 1971, she and her colleagues in the Industrial Sociology Unit at Imperial College concentrated their research on firms with large batch production systems which was where the earlier investigations had suggested that 'technology did not determine organization but merely defined the limits within which organization could be determined' (Woodward 1970, xi). In addition to attempts to develop more adequate ways of measuring technical variables, particular attention was given to the nature of the control system, which was seen as a crucial intervening variable in the relationship between technology and organisational structure and behaviour. It was suggested that control systems (activities concerned with objective setting, planning, execution and monitoring) could be classified as unitary or fragmented and as personal or impersonal, and that large batch production firms could have control systems falling within any of the four resulting categories, though they were predominantly fragmented rather than unitary (Woodward 1970, 43–56). In the light of the findings of a number of case studies in firms, however, 'it became increasingly clear that an additional and key variable to be taken into account was that of uncertainty' (Davies *et al.* 1973, 153). Though control systems may be intended to cope with the uncertainty arising from the nature of an organisation's technology (or 'tasks'), they can also create uncertainty; organisational structure and behaviour therefore came to be seen as the outcome of complex interrelations between technology, control system and uncertainty (Woodward 1970, esp. 234–43; Davies *et al.* 1973).

Other researchers have tried to utilise the ideas developed by Burns and/or by Woodward, with varying degrees of success and satisfaction (see, for example, Sadler and Barry 1970). Blain (1964), for example, investigated the organisation of management in twenty-four companies in a variety of industries. She expressed pessimism about the potential of such comparative studies because of the number of factors involved, and was herself reluctant to draw conclusions; her findings, however, appeared to indicate that managerial satisfaction with the effectiveness of their organisation's structure and communications was greatest where roles and relations were more highly formalised and clearly defined (27–30). In terms of Burns and Stalker's types, none of the companies was 'far towards the "organic end of the scale"', but the typology was difficult to use (partly due to the absence in her study of data on changes over time); four of the companies, for example, had both written job descriptions (mechanistic?) and complex authority networks (organic?) (35). Woodward's scale of technical complexity was equally difficult to utilise but there was some similarity in findings, for example, with regard to the relations between technology and number of levels of authority, proportion of managers to all employees and proportion of production managers with qualifications (36).

Blain's references to Burns and Stalker and to Woodward appear to have been introduced only after the conduct of her own enquiries. The study of systems of supervision in five firms reported by Thurley and Hamblin (1963; see also Thurley and

Wirdenius 1973), however, was deliberately designed to test Woodward's findings about the relationship between production systems and patterns of management by focusing on supervisory jobs. They concluded that there was 'no simple relationship between the "technology" and the nature of the supervisor's job' and that four factors were particularly important: the degree of planned variation in the operations (related to but not identical with type of production system); the degree of complexity of the operations supervised; the degree of mechanisation of the process; and the organisation of supervisory systems (Thurley and Hamblin 1963, 6–8). In one firm, engaged in mass production of electronics goods, it was possible to compare three shifts in the same department; although 'the behaviour of foremen on different shifts in the same department was much more similar than that of foremen in different departments and firms', the styles of supervision adopted by the three shift heads differed considerably and were associated with considerable differences in their respective subordinate supervisors' activity patterns. Thus, there were possibilities for choice of supervisory style and pattern of behaviour within a given production system.

The research by Burns and by Woodward, and their colleagues, made three notable contributions to the study of industrial organisations at the time when it was first reported. Both investigators undermined any idea that there was 'one best way' to organise a business; they demonstrated the value of and insights which could be gained from more extensive comparative studies of organisations; and they showed how organisations are influenced by the context or environment within which they have to operate. In addition Woodward drew further attention to the importance of technology, which had already been emphasised by the notion of 'socio-technical system' (Chapter 2) and in the writings of the French sociologist Touraine (1962) and was rapidly becoming prominent in the work of a number of Americans (for example, Sayles 1958; Udy 1959, 1965; Blauner 1964; Perrow 1970). Their work remains influential, but has been regarded as having two important limitations (no doubt, among others): the categories and concepts remained imprecise and difficult to apply, and explanations of variation in organisational structure in terms of variation in a single contextual or environmental factor were clearly inadequate. The Aston researchers promised to remedy both faults.

THE ASTON PROGRAMME

The central concern of the Aston researchers has been with the structure of organisations. The aims of the initial investigation were to compare work organisations in terms of the differences in their structure and to account for such differences, and this preoccupation has also dominated subsequent studies in this country and abroad. As a result the question of the wider consequences of 'structural' differences between organisations has not been pursued with any great persistence. This represents some reduction in the original research proposal, and periodic restatements of it. The proposal placed organisational structure at the centre of a 'paradigm' or 'scheme for organisational functioning' in which several sets of variables were seen as interdependent. The explanation of variations in the structure of organisations was to be sought in variations in their contexts. An organisation's context and structure together were expected to be related to, possibly even to enable prediction of, its performance, group and individual behaviour within it, and (in later writings) its 'climate' (Pugh and Hickson 1976, esp. Ch. 3 and 185–6; see also Payne and Pugh 1971). What made the proposed research particularly distinctive, however, was that all these variables were to be 'operationalised' in terms of numerical scales; organisational characteristics would be measured and relationships between variables, and comparisons between organisations, expressed in quantitative terms.

An organisation's structure was declared to be 'a construct derived from its activities' and Bakke's categorisation of organisational activities as concerned with processes of 'identification, perpetuation, workflow, control and homeostasis' (1950, 1959) was used as a guide, though this was not developed in any way. The specification of structural variables clearly drew on Weber's formulation of the ideal type bureaucracy, as well as on the researchers' own pilot studies. Thus, initially 'six primary dimensions of organizational structure' were distinguished (see Pugh *et al.* 1963; Pugh and Hickson 1976, esp. Chs 1, 3, 4 and 6):

1 specialisation of activities: the division of labour within the organisation, the distribution of official duties among a number of positions;
2 standardisation of procedures: the existence of rules purporting to cover all circumstances and applying invariably;
3 formalisation of documentation: the extent to which rules, pro-

cedures, instructions, and communications are written;
4 centralisation of authority: the locus of authority to make decisions;
5 configuration of positions: the shape of the role structure;
6 flexibility: the amount, speed and acceleration of changes in organisational structure.

The dimension of 'flexibility', which required data for more than one point in time, was not in fact developed any further or used in any of the empirical studies, thus making it difficult for the researchers to consider certain issues like Burns and Stalker's distinction between mechanistic and organic forms of organisation.

The contextual variables referred to aspects of the setting within which structure is developed and eight such variables were identified for analysis, on the basis of their postulated links with structure; they were not derived from a common conceptual base and were admitted to be 'heterogeneous' and 'disparate' (Pugh and Hickson 1976, 79, and Chs 3 and 5):

1 origin and history (age; 'personal' or 'impersonal' foundation; changes in location, product or service, pattern of ownership; etc.);
2 ownership and control (public accountability; concentration of voteholding; etc.);
3 size (number of employees; total net assets);
4 charter (purpose of the organisation and the ideology or value system present);
5 technology (for example, the rigidity, automaticity and interdependence of the workflow of the organisation);
6 location (e.g. number of operating sites);
7 resources (quality, quantity and range of human and ideational, and material and capital resources);
8 (inter)dependence (on parent organisation, and on suppliers, customers, trade unions, etc.).

In practice it was not possible to investigate the variable 'resources' adequately.

The empirical investigation of the characteristics of work organisations in terms of these variables was first carried out in fifty-two organisations in the Birmingham area, forty-six of which were a random sample of all such organisations with 250 or more employees, stratified by industry and by size. Thirty-one of the forty-six were engaged in manufacturing, and the remainder in a range of public and private sector services. The researchers collected data relating to a considerable number of items relevant to each of these dimensions of structure and context and applicable to all the organisations. They then used item analysis techniques to devise scales (and some sub-scales) for the various dimensions of structure and context. Subsequently principal components analysis was used to identify underlying factors which might summarise a number of the initial scales. This made it possible to study both the correlations between the original individual scales and subscales of structural and contextual variables, and the relationships between particular dimensions and the derived underlying factors.

As a result of their empirical investigation the researchers claimed that they had been successful in devising statistically reliable ways of measuring both the structure and the context of work organisations which were applicable across the whole range of such organisations. The principal components analysis of the scales of organisational structure suggested that there were four independent underlying dimensions, the first two of which were the most important in that they explained more of the overall variance. These factors were:

1 structuring of activities (encompassing standardisation, formalisation, specialisation, and vertical span);
2 concentration of authority (centralisation, and [lack of] autonomy from any owning organisation);
3 line (i.e. direct, personal rather than impersonal) control of workflow; and
4 relative size of the supportive component (e.g. percentage of clerks, and of non-workflow personnel).

It was possible to construct profiles for each of the organisations studied using either the original variables, or these dimensions. An important initial claim from this work was that, as the 'original primary dimensions of structure . . . were drawn from a literature saturated with the Weberian view of bureaucracy', and as the 'distinctive underlying dimensions of structure' were 'mutually independent', it was demonstrated 'that bureaucracy is not unitary, but that organisations may be bureaucratic in any of a number of ways . . . . The concept of the bureaucratic type is no longer useful' (Pugh and Hickson 1976, 60–1).

In place of a single view of bureaucracy the researchers outlined an empirical taxonomy of work organisations based on cross-classifying the three most significant underlying dimensions of organisational structure (structuring of activities, concentration of authority and line control of workflow) each of which their results showed to be independent of the others. The initial cross-classification of structuring of activities with concentration of authority revealed four clusters of organisations in terms of their scores on these two dimensions (Pugh and Hickson 1976, Ch. 6):

1 implicitly structured organisations – low on both structuring of activities and concentration of authority;
2 workflow bureaucracies – high on structuring, low on concentration;
3 personnel bureaucracies – low on structuring, high on concentration;
4 full bureaucracies – high on both dimensions.

The addition of the third dimension, line control of workflow (the extent to which the central work activities of the organisation were controlled by direct, personal, supervision), led to the identification of further sub-types: some organisations which had concentrated authority and impersonal (rather than line) control of workflow like 'full bureaucracies' had lower scores on the structuring of activities – they were labelled 'nascent full bureaucracies'; organisations with relatively unstructured or less structured activities but dispersed authority and impersonal control of workflow were labelled respectively 'pre-workflow bureaucracies' and 'nascent workflow bureaucracies'. As the use of these terms implies, developmental sequences were tentatively suggested by the researchers but the cross-sectional design of the research did not allow such ideas to be tested.

The 'implicitly structured' organisations were mostly small factories with operational control in the hands of the owners. The 'workflow bureaucracies' of various types were also found in manufacturing industry and had all developed impersonal means of controlling workflow; full workflow bureaucracies were large-scale manufacturing organisations with a high level of structuring of activities. 'Personnel bureaucracies' with centralised authority also tended to have standardised procedures for selection, promotion and so on; they were typically departments of local or central government or small branches of larger corporations. The only organisation to be categorised as a 'full bureaucracy' was a manufacturing branch factory of a central government department.

There were relationships between these types and certain contextual variables, especially size, external dependence, ownership and the extent to which technology was integrated. This reflected the findings of the researchers' more general exploration of the relationship between organisational structure and context using multi-variate methods, findings subsequently described as 'an encouragingly simple result' (Pugh and Hickson 1976). Size, and to a lesser extent 'workflow integration', were the contextual factors associated with structuring of activities; dependence, and to a lesser extent location on a number of sites, with concentration of authority; and operating variability with line control of workflow. Though the design of their study did not permit a stronger claim the researchers concluded that 'it is tempting to argue that these clear relationships are causal – in particular, that size, dependence, and the charter–technology–location nexus largely determine structure' (Pugh and Hickson 1976, 107).

In view of the arguments advanced by Woodward and others particular attention was given to the relationship between technology and organisational structure. As the Aston sample of organisations was not confined to manufacturing industry, scales for measuring variations in technology had to be developed which were also applicable in the service sector; the notion of 'operations technology' referred to techniques used in workflow activities (e.g. automation of equipment, rigidity of sequence of operations) (Pugh and Hickson 1976, Ch. 7). This represented a much narrower conceptualisation of technology than that suggested by Woodward; some of the features she considered would be categorised as aspects of the 'charter' of an organisation by the Aston researchers. In terms of the definition used, however, operations technology could not be shown to be associated with differences in organisational structure either in the total sample of forty-six organisations or in the sub-set of thirty-one manufacturing organisations. Nor could a scale of 'production continuity', developed to approximate to Woodward's notion of 'technical complexity', be shown to be significantly related to organisational structure; there were apparent relationships within the sample between technology and structure but they proved on closer examination to be due to differences in size. The only respect in which technology (as operationalised by the Aston researchers) was independently associated with structural variables was with respect to variables of structure centred on the workflow, for example the relative numbers of employees engaged on production-linked activities such as inspection. Woodward's sample included organisations with as few as 100 employees, however, whilst Aston's smallest organisations had 250, and in small organisations the structure of the whole organisation would be affected by such technological effects in a way not found in larger organisations. Thus it was claimed to be possible to make a partial reconciliation of these two sets of findings.

In the decade after the initial publication of these results in 1968 and 1969 a whole series of further studies were conducted to follow up the relationships identified in the initial project and to consider the interrelations of organisational structure and context with behavioural and performance variables. Only the most important of the conclusions of these investigations can be mentioned here. Many of the studies were primarily confirmatory of the original results and made small incremental contributions to the body of findings. Thus, Hinings and Lee showed that the basic relationships outlined above held for a sample of nine manufacturing organisations which included two with only just over 100 employees each (Pugh and Hinings 1976, Ch. 1). Inkson and colleagues were able to develop abbreviated versions of four of the more important scales (which have been used extensively in further research), and with a sample of forty organisations in the West Midlands confirmed the relationships between context and structure previously established. Fourteen of these organisations were being re-studied four to five years after the initial research: in general, structuring of activities had increased over this period, and concentration of authority declined; there was, however, evidence of at least a short-term 'ratchet effect' – structuring of activities did not decrease even if size did (Pugh and Hinings 1976, Ch. 2). Other authors have applied the same methods of research, using the same scales and/or additions and modifications of them to the comparative analysis of trade unions, local government departments, churches and educational institutions, in this country or abroad (Pugh and Hinings 1976, Pt 2).

The studies of manufacturing organisations overseas, using the Aston 'measures' or minor modifications of them, also appeared to justify a 'culture-free' hypothesis and a proposed 'focal paradigm' based on the 'empirical regularities of relationships between organization size and specialization and formalization, repeatedly positive, and between interorganizational dependence and centralization, also repeatedly positive' (Hickson and McMillan 1981, 193). 'Differences between organizations within nations are greater than the differences between nations' (191). Nevertheless some interesting cross-national differences were recorded. Formalisation was greater in organisations in the USA, and in Canada than in comparable organisations in Britain where, it was suggested, tradition could be relied upon instead. A possible 'late development effect' was observable in some societies in the adoption of more fully 'bureaucratic' modes of organisation for relatively smaller organisations. The existence of state planning in societies like Poland and Egypt increased the dependence and thus the centralisation of authority in organisations, though centralisation was greater in other countries too, like Sweden where it reflected the centralised pattern of industrial relations (Hickson and McMillan 1981).

The most substantial project to use the Aston approach was Child and his colleagues' study of a national sample, stratified by size, of eighty-two organisations in six industries – electronics, pharmaceuticals, chocolate and sweets, daily newspapers (editorial and production), advertising and insurance – selected to include both manufacturing and service industry, and organisations facing high and low variability in their environments. In interpreting his findings Child has suggested two important amendments to the pattern presented on the basis of the original Aston research, though these do not appear to have been completely accepted by other contributors to the Aston programme (Pugh and Hinings 1976, Chs 3, 4 and 10). Firstly, Child found a positive relationship between decentralisation of authority and the nexus of specialisation, standardisation and formalisation; this provided support for the view that managers may have a choice between two strategies of control: 'maintaining control directly by confining decisions to fairly senior levels', or 'maintaining control indirectly by relying on the use of procedures, paper records, and on the employment of expert specialists to take decisions at lower levels' (Child 1970, 378). Secondly, Child suggested a more complex pattern of relationships between contextual variables, such as size, and bureaucratic control variables, such as standardisation and formalisation, in which 'complexity' (specialisation of roles and functions) is an intervening variable. We shall return to these arguments below.

This national study also attempted to add to the investigation of relations between organisational structure and context some consideration of both organisational performance and managerial roles and behaviour (Pugh and Hinings 1976, Ch. 9; Pugh and Payne 1977, Chs 3 and 4). The research did 'not demonstrate very strong relationships between managerial or organizational variables and company performance' (Pugh and Hinings 1976, 159). However, it is interesting in the light of Burns's work to note that faster-growing (and more successful) companies in variable environments had lower levels of formalisation than low-growth companies, the opposite being true in stable environments. The studies of managerial roles focused on Hickson's identification of 'specificity of role prescription' as the key concept in a great deal of the writing by sociologists and management theorists (Pugh and Payne 1977, Ch. 1). Further studies led to the suggestion that this was in fact a multi-dimensional concept; the personal consequences of different strategies of administrative control for those managers subject to them, appeared to vary, sometimes in unexpected ways, for managers at different levels in the hierarchy. The studies also appeared to support the argument that the characteristics of a 'good manager' would vary depending on the wider organisational context (including, for example, industry and functional specialism) in which they were to work; stereotypes of 'bureaucratic man' or conceptions of managers as a homogeneous occupational group did not accord with the findings (Pugh and Payne 1977, Chs 3 and 4; Child and Ellis 1973). The studies of group functioning and of organisational climate (Pugh and Payne 1977, Pts 2 and 3) were restricted to two or three organisations; the findings were interesting but complex and tentative and they will not be considered further here. Some limited longitudinal studies of organisational decision processes have also been undertaken (Pugh 1981, 156–60).

THE ASTON PROGRAMME – COMMENTS AND CRITICISM

The Aston programme has, of course, given rise to a considerable body of writings reviewing and criticising their findings and the interpretations and arguments based on them. Much of this criticism comes from within the same research tradition – some of it, indeed, from contributors to the programme – but other critics raise more far-reaching questions about the possibilities and limitations of this sort of research altogether (see, for example, Clegg and Dunkerley 1980, Ch. 6, and esp. 251–62; Eldridge 1980, esp. 59–64; and esp. Starbuck 1981). We shall consider some of the more specific issues first before looking at the more general problems raised by the research and the contingency theory to which it contributes.

Data and measurement

Some consideration of the source and nature of the data utilised by these researchers is an essential preliminary to reviewing the arguments about substantive findings, yet such consideration also inevitably raises some of the more general issues to be discussed later. The information used to 'measure' organisational structure and context was obtained from chief executives and heads of departments. It therefore represents a 'top-down' view of the organisation, but this is not seen as a problem because the data are 'non-personal' and the senior managers are in the best position to provide the required answers. The researchers have been quite explicit that their concern was with the 'formal' (that is official) structure of the organisations they investigated; for example:

> The project deals with what is officially expected should be done, and what is in practice allowed to be done; it doesn't include what is actually done, that is, what 'really' happens in the sense of behaviour beyond that instituted in organisational forms.
>
> (Pugh and Hickson 1976, 45, see also 185)

The question of the meaning and significance of such data is met, in large part, by reference to the success in establishing scales and the high levels of correlation between some of the various aspects of structure, so defined, and between structure and context, and to the successful replications (see Pugh 1981, 149). Nevertheless in the light of the extensive literature on the discrepancies between 'formal' and 'informal' organisation, some of which was discussed in Chapter 2, it is difficult to be entirely happy with such a procedure. Two organisations might well have equally elaborate procedures for appointments and promotions, for example, but it would seem crucial to know whether they both used them. Gouldner (1955) identified what he termed 'mock bureaucracy', rules which were ignored and inoperative; how much of the information collected by the Aston researchers had the same quality? At the other extreme, rather than there being rules, procedures and job specifications which were ignored, many case studies of organisations have shown how the official organisational structure is supplemented in crucial ways by emergent 'informal' practices, but these too would not feature in the Aston researchers' data.

The Aston researchers concentrated on 'official' information because, among other reasons, of their concern to obtain standard measurements. They have expressed the view that 'there is a clear interacting effect from the formal variables' on informal organisational determinants of behaviour. This, in addition to introducing a difficult distinction between 'informal organisation' and 'behaviour', tends to pre-judge the answer to one of the questions behind the whole enterprise: the relationship between 'structure' and 'behaviour' (Inkson, Payne and Pugh 1967, 35–6).

In a formidable review, raising a number of detailed questions about the techniques used in the handling of the Aston data, Starbuck (1981, 180–8) has made the additional point that the procedures used to aggregate and analyse those aspects of organisations which were measured could themselves have created many of the associations which constitute the basic findings of the studies. He emphasised the importance of the influence of 'prior beliefs' on the ways in which variables were specified and inferences made.

The determination to measure what they studied and to study only what they could measure carried a further cost in that certain variables, which featured in the initial scheme, were abandoned at the data collection stage, notably the structural variable 'flexibility' and the contextual variable 'resources'. Loss of the former, for example, made it difficult to reassess Burns's notion of 'organic' management structures in relation to their findings. In addition the actual investigation of other dimensions was limited because of measurement problems; for example, it proved impossible to devise a satisfactory way of measuring the specialisation of workflow activities ('production' work) (Pugh and Hickson 1976, 48, 180). In the light of the debates about the 'de-skilling' of such work (see Chapter 5) this might be considered particularly unfortunate. It was due in part to the insistence on measures which applied to all work organisations equally, and this raises important questions about the Aston definition and conceptualisation of what they were studying.

The definition of work organisation

The aim of the Aston programme has been to study work organisations: those that pay their members. This broad definition of the scope of their enquiries was recognised as involving costs, in terms of the kinds of data that could be collected and the care needed to be sure of only comparing the comparable, as well as pay-off, in terms of the wider applicability of the findings. It is perhaps significant that much of the work done has been on samples of organisations in manufacturing industry, and that some investigators have appeared to see advantages in undertaking separate studies of different types of organisations: public bureaucracies, hospitals, educational institutions, trade unions and so on. It is not an adequate defence of the Aston definition of their field to declare 'So organizations are organizations whatever they do, and hence there can be organization theory. If not, we will have factory theory, hospital theory, local store theory, cafe theory . . .' (Pugh and Hickson 1976, 5, see also 180). There are various theoretically relevant ways of sub-dividing the whole range of employing organisations which offer alternatives to a false dichotomy between no sub-categories at all and ones based on common sense.

Indeed, it is a more important criticism of their work that the theoretical relevance of 'employing their members' as a criterion for distinguishing work organisations from other sorts of collectivity has not been developed by the Aston researchers. The fact that the entities studied were all based on social relations of employment has little apparent influence on the selection and conceptualisation of variables for investigation or on most of the subsequent analysis. For example, the central importance within employment relationships of 'control' activities (included in the list derived from Bakke but not emphasised) has not been realised, in contrast to their place in discussions of the labour process (see Chapter 5). The scope of the Aston programme would have allowed differences in the nature of employment within the different types of organisation to be explored. Jaques's distinction between an 'earned-income institution' and a 'grant-income institution' (Jaques 1976, 72) could have been used in this way. This certainly would have been a more appropriate way to proceed than the argument, put forward by Donaldson (1985, 159–61), that because the desire to establish democratic control in trade unions led to greater centralisation of authority this will necessarily follow in other types of organisations.

The question 'What is a (work) organisation?' raises other problems as well, ones which are given inadequate consideration in most of the Aston writings. The distinction between 'structure' and 'context' will be discussed further below, but there is another way in which drawing a boundary around an organisation should be seen as problematic. The world is increasingly dominated by big business and big government, with takeovers and mergers leading to complex structures of holding companies and multi-plant and multi-national corporations. The question must arise, therefore, of how far a particular factory, office or shop, which is a branch of such a larger organisation, can be studied as if it were on a par with an independent business, and of how to treat organisations which have any of a variety of statuses between subordinate branch and complete autonomy. The initial research project in Birmingham used Ministry of Labour lists as a basis for defining and selecting units for study (Pugh and Hickson 1976, 44–5); this also appears to have been the basis for the 1967–8 replication (Pugh and Hinings 1976, 14–15). The 'National' study was of 'whole units (organisations with a high level of functional autonomy and normally a separate legal identity)', and the small-scale replication in Coventry was predominantly of subsidiaries (4, 28). These later developments reflect a growing awareness of the importance of this question, but it has not really been resolved within the Aston programme. Such resolution may be impossible, but the confusion of units of different sorts clearly had important consequences for the whole discussion of centralisation and dependence.

The debate about bureaucracy

The results of the initial Aston investigation showed relatively small negative correlations between centralisation and specialisation, standardisation and formalisation. The principal components analysis of these and other scales produced two important underlying factors: 'structuring of activities' (highly loaded on specialisation, standardisation and formalisation) and 'concentration of authority' (centralised authority and low levels of organisational autonomy); and these factors were found to be mutually independent. As it had been argued that the Weberian tradition implied that specialisation, formalisation and centralisation would be highly correlated, these findings were seen as severely questioning the value of the ideal type of bureaucracy (Pugh and

Hickson 1976, 55–61). Child questioned both this interpretation of Weber and the significance of these results. He suggested that Weber's analysis of bureaucracy implied alternative means of maintaining control: directly (by centralising authority to take decisions) or indirectly (by relying on procedures, paper work and specialists). In the National sample the structuring of activities was more clearly inversely related to the centralisation of authority, and Child argued that the earlier results had been affected by the inclusion of a large proportion of branch plants, because the measurement of centralisation was sensitive to the status of the organisational unit (Pugh and Hinings 1976, 30–44).

No agreed view has emerged among contributors to the subsequent debate, except for the need to treat centralisation 'with care' (Greenwood and Hinings 1976, 155; Pugh and Hinings 1976, 169–72; Pugh 1981, 147). Mansfield (1973) rightly endorsed Child's interpretation of Weber, but was less conclusive on empirical findings. He made the important point that 'centralisation of authority' as measured by the Aston researchers was different from the other scales in that it was like an average of the locus of decision making for a number of different types of decisions; but after trying to disentangle the relations between bureaucratisation (standardisation and formalisation of procedures), centralisation and size in the National sample, he concluded 'the direct relationship between bureaucratization and the centralization of decision making is weak, but tends to be negative, and that organizational size affects both these variables' (Mansfield 1973, 487). Donaldson claimed to have shown that, contrary to Child's suggestion, the differences in the status of organisations studied did not account for the differences in the relationship between structuring of activities and centralisation in the Aston and National samples, but further examination of the same data led Aldrich to declare this conclusion 'premature' (Donaldson et al. 1975). It does seem, however, that care is needed to compare like with like. The doubts about the significance of the measurements of centralisation of decision making must also lead to a questioning of the relationship (apparently) established by the Aston team between 'dependence' and 'concentration of authority'. Indeed in so far as the specification of 'dependence' was largely in terms of intra-organisational dependence with the parent organisation this relationship must be questioned anyway as involving some tautological elements (see Mindlin and Aldrich 1975; also Pugh and Hinings 1976, 174–5).

Technology and organisation

Perhaps even more interest has been aroused by the Aston programme's findings regarding the relations between technology and organisational structure because these appeared to contradict Woodward's work and to question the whole 'technological implications' approach. Aldrich (1972, 40), for example, concluded on the basis of path analysis of the Aston data that 'rejection of technology as an important variable has been shown to be ill-advised and premature'. Though his own assumptions about organisational development appeared to assume that organisations always developed from scratch, he also argued that size, upon which the Aston group placed so much emphasis, is at least as much a dependent as an independent variable (i.e. that [growth in] size may result from organisational structure rather than the opposite); and he emphasised the need to adopt a wider conception of technology, for example to include 'operating variability' (i.e. the production of non-standard producer goods – a dimension of 'charter') as well as the degree of integration of the workflow. Child and Mansfield (1972) also developed more elaborate and differentiated measures of technology in their consideration of the findings of the original Aston and the National studies, but they questioned the appropriateness of path analysis for cross-sectional data (see also Pugh and Hinings 1976, 172–4). They reiterated the greater relationship between size and organisational structure, with the exception of the configuration (or shape) of the organisation; technology was more closely related to aspects of structure in smaller organisations, and to the organisation of functions closely tied to the main workflow.

These somewhat inconclusive discussions of centralisation and dependence, and size and technology, have been conducted within the basic framework used by the Aston researchers. They suggest that the at-first-sight highly precise quantitative findings of the various empirical studies must be approached with care and attention to the detailed procedures involved to ensure that unwarranted generalisations are not built on uncertain foundations. The confident tone of the early reports of the Aston studies has been slightly muted by the acceptance of the need for further research, but the approach to be adopted has been defined as more of the same. There are however important respects in which such a strategy might be mistaken.

Context and environment

A number of problems relate to the selection and specification of the contextual variables utilised in the Aston programme. Eldridge (1980, 60) has commented with justification that 'the term structure is used in a restricted and somewhat idiosyncratic way by the Aston researchers. Many of the contextual factors are understandably defined by others as structural.' It is not altogether clear why ownership and control, charter, size, intra-organisational dependence and even technology (an 'internalised environment') have been seen as 'independent variables', as aspects of the 'setting' within which the structure of an organisation functions, rather than as attributes of that structure. Such a view of organisations as being best characterised in terms of a configuration of a larger number and range of attributes and variables would demand a different approach to analysis and comparison but would eliminate the problem of dubious causal relationships between, for example, size and structure.

On the other hand as defined by the Aston researchers the 'structural' variables had a clear theoretical rationale in Weber's ideal type; it was a major weakness that no such rationale exists for the 'contextual' factors. This reflected, I think, the absence of any theory or theories, no matter how tentative or provisional, about how work organisations grow and develop and their relationship with the wider society. As a result the list of contextual factors was entirely *ad hoc*, contained certain weaknesses (limited conceptualisation of technology, confused notion of dependence) and omitted certain potentially important factors altogether.

Such theoretical rationales did exist and could have been used. Open systems approaches would have drawn attention to the importance of identifying the input–throughput–output processes, and should have led to a proper conceptualisation and consideration of the factor and product market situations of the organisations studied, especially but not only in the case of private sector organisations; the Aston measures of dependence were quite inadequate in this respect. Marxist approaches might have had a similar result, though for somewhat different reasons. In addition, a review of the more empirical studies of the growth of industrial bureaucracy would have indicated, for example, the need to consider more carefully the factors which increase the demand for predictability and accountability in organisations, such as the operations of various state agencies (taxation, health and safety inspection, etc.) and demands from trade unions.

Not only is the specification of 'context' *ad hoc* and its relationship to 'structure' more problematic than has been recognised but the definition and place of 'environment' in these studies is also more limited than might have been expected. Child's National Sample was selected with the aim of comparing organisations in stable and variable environments, but with that exception, environmental influences and differences have not really been made part of the framework in any systematic way. As Eldridge pointed out, the fact that the organisations in the original study were all in Birmingham (England) is neither seen as relevant nor apparent from the way the data are analysed and presented. Nor is any attention drawn to the specific features of the particular periods of time when the data were collected. A partial exception to this criticism of the location of these organisations in a geographical and historical limbo can be found in the cross-cultural studies. In these cases, however, probably unavoidably, the references to the influence of environmental (cultural) factors have involved tentative *post hoc* explanations of certain otherwise unexplained differences in the findings from different societies.

Strategic choice

The attitude of the Aston researchers to the question of whether 'context' causes 'structure' has been an ambivalent one (compare, for example, Pugh and Hickson 1976, 14, 107 and 186–9). Clearly, however, their work has been intended as a step towards causal explanation and the question arises of how deterministic this would, or could, be. In its strongest form contingency theory implies a high degree of determination of organisational structure by context (and/or environment) and of organisational behaviour by structure and context. In an important paper Child (1972) has pointed out that this argument assumes that environmental characteristics, such as variability or complexity, and/or contextual factors, such as size or technology, are constraints which 'have force because work organizations must achieve certain levels of performance in order to survive' (8). He argued in contrast to such a view that there exists a degree of 'organisational slack' with regard to performance standards which can permit some choice of structural arrangements. The influence of environmental constraints is mediated by the ways in which they are perceived and evaluated by relevant members of the organisation, and can be changed by decisions within the organisation as to where and how it will operate, and by action to manipulate the areas of the environment thought to be particularly important. Such considerations point to the critical importance of the 'strategic choices' taken by the 'dominant coalition' within an organisation with regard to the goals it will pursue, the environment(s) within which it will pursue them, the levels of performance to be regarded as satisfactory, and the organisational arrangements (scale of operations, technology, structure, human resources) to be adopted. Such choices will be influenced by both the prior ideology of members of the 'dominant coalition' and subsequently by information regarding the level of performance achieved.

In his *Defence of Organization Theory* Donaldson has dismissed 'the strategic choice thesis' because it is 'a programme of sociological explanation of extant structures rather than of developing design knowledge which can help change structure to better serve human purposes' (1985, 174; see also 135–52). This seems to miss the point of Child's argument that there can be and is room for 'choice' even when performance criteria are also taken into account, and that the political and ideological preferences of those with the power to influence organisational design will inevitably affect those choices. It also asserts that providing management with advice should have priority over the activity of understanding and accounting for organisations as they are, not an argument which would be accepted by everyone!

In more recent publications Child has argued that the structure of organisations may be affected by the need for 'consistency'. Different contingencies may have different, and conflicting, implications for organisational structure; some compromise may be necessary in which case what may matter for performance is the 'internal consistency' of structural arrangements rather than trying to match them to every contingency (Child 1977; 1984, 233–7). He has also suggested that an appropriate unit of analysis for organisation–environment relations might be 'organizations in their sectors'. Such sectors can be conceptualised as configurations of material and technical conditions, networks of actual and potential collaborators and cognitive fields; they should be seen as instrumental in shaping the modes of organisation which are adopted (Child 1988, 13–19). Both arguments imply an element of indeterminacy in the environment–structure–performance relationship.

The establishment of statistical correlations between features of the context (or the environment) of organisations and aspects of their structure leaves open the question of how and why such patterns occur. Child's 1972 paper emphasised what had largely been implicit in earlier discussions – in effect that the associations existed because they were functional for the survival of the organisation. This line of argument has been developed in the 'population-ecology' approach to organisation analysis, one which focuses on the survival, or failure, of species of organisations subject to 'natural selection' in changing environments; but this approach too tends to be very deterministic (Morgan 1986, esp. 66–71).

In contrast to such an approach, Child's 'conclusion that strategic choice is the critical variable in a theory of organizations' (1972, 15) introduced a welcome re-emphasis on the importance of human agency into an area of debate which had become preoccupied with statistical associations between organisational characteristics. Such associations, in so far as they can be established in any meaningful way, do not become unimportant but their significance must be carefully interpreted. All social action is constrained, and these patterns may indicate some of the constraints if the organisation is to achieve certain tasks in a specific context and environment, and (possibly) in competition with other organisations. Few situations, however, are completely constrained. As other members of the Aston group have argued, emphases on constraint and choice are not necessarily mutually incompatible; the strong correlations they established represented no more than half the variance (Pugh and Hickson 1976, 14, 187; Child 1970, 384, and 1972, 12). Thus contingency theory can survive in a modified and weakened form.

Child's arguments, however, do lead to the conclusion that it would be beneficial to pursue a different research strategy from that adopted in the Aston programme, one which is concerned with processes within organisations over time and enables 'structure' to be seen as the (possibly very temporary) manifestation of such processes. Indeed, in a detailed and useful elaboration of the elements of contingency theory Burrell and Morgan (1979, 167–81) have argued that 'the contingency model, based as it is upon an open systems approach, is essentially processual in nature' so that much of the research which has failed to recognise this has been 'an abstracted form of empiricism' (180).

The Aston programme was built on a deliberate separation of the study of organisational structure from the study of organisational processes. The separation was intended to be temporary, to be transcended in later stages of research, but with limited exceptions so far this has not in fact happened. In conversation the researchers did express the hope that those pursuing case studies of organisations might use the Aston measures to locate their case study organisation in the general population of work organisations, but so far as I am aware this has never been done. At the very least the separation of structure and process must be regarded as imposing considerable costs, which have to be set against the findings of the programme; more severe critics would argue that it vitiated the whole enterprise from the start (see Elger 1975, 138, fn. 72).

Considerable weaknesses have therefore been revealed in the Aston development of contingency theory. Their procedures reduced 'structure' to a number of measurable features of the 'official' organisation; their enumeration of 'contextual' factors was arbitrary and they were not adequately differentiated from structure; and the wider 'environment' was virtually lost to view. Indeed, Starbuck (1981, 180) has suggested that only two, not very original, general propositions regarding size and bureaucracy have been 'established beyond question' by the Aston studies. In the light of these and the other criticisms it would be possible to dismiss the findings of the Aston researches as lacking real significance, and to lament that so many resources have been devoted to such an enterprise. Even without accepting Donaldson's defence of contingency theory, to do this would be mistaken. The Aston work does contain important insights about some of the possibilities of and constraints on organisational design, and it represents a systematic not to say exhaustive exploration of one particular research strategy, one which has by no means been abandoned.

Sociological analysis of organisations must be at least implicitly comparative, but a different style and orientation of research effort is needed. As Burns's (1967) discussion of the comparative study of organisations demonstrated, there is a range of potentially fruitful possibilities none of which needs be less conceptually and methodologically rigorous than the Aston programme even if it does not use the same techniques. And for many sociologists the absence of supposedly universal generalisations about 'work organisations' at the conclusion of such research might be regarded as a strength rather than a weakness.

CONCLUDING COMMENT

An important part of the very considerable initial impact caused by Woodward's and Burns and Stalker's studies was due to the fact that, in drawing attention to the relationship between an organisation's structure and the context or environment within which it was operating, they each emphasised one factor as of importance – 'technology' and 'environmental uncertainty' respectively. As many case studies, and Lupton's comparison of two organisations, had suggested, however, such an apparent emphasis on a single factor was probably mistaken; it was more appropriate to explore a range of factors, though they might not be unrelated and could possibly be expected to cluster together into a number of distinctive patterns. It was such an approach that Pugh and his colleagues pursued, though as subsequent closer examination has revealed it was limited in its specification of 'contextual' factors and restricted in its possible findings by the researchers' methodological stance. 'Contingency theory' has moved in the direction of greater complexity with the recognition that the task is to show what, if any, relationship there is between a number of, possibly interrelated, aspects of an organisation's environment, and a number of aspects of its structure and functioning; and that different parts of the same organisation may be operating in significantly different environments. Burrell and Morgan (1979, 167–81) have usefully indicated what such a version of contingency theory might involve. Using such a framework might necessitate a comparative and multi-variate approach, but not one restricted to consideration on a cross-sectional basis of a number of quantitative measures of structure and context.

Indeed the need to reintroduce a processual perspective into such comparative studies is greatly strengthened by the emphasis on 'strategic choice', an argument which forces open what might otherwise become a closed and deterministic explanatory framework. To assert the scope for choice is to argue that action is not totally constrained by environmental demands or structural exigencies. To explain the exercise of choice directs attention to the sources of preferences in the objectives and values of the actors concerned. For many years there was relatively little research concerned with the values and ideologies of members of the 'dominant coalitions' which Child saw as having the power to determine how an organisation operates (but see Nichols 1969; Child 1969). In recent years, however, there has been increasing interest in the nature and role of management strategy. This can be found, for example, in the study of industrial relations policies (e.g. Thurley and Wood 1983; Purcell and Sisson 1983), and in the debates about the control of the labour process (Chapter 5). As those debates reveal, however, although the concept of management strategy does play an important part in attempts to explain organisational structures and processes, the notion is problematic and evidence for conscious and deliberate, and varied, strategies can be difficult to establish (see, for example, Hyman 1987). In contrast, there has been much more research on the values, objectives and 'orientations to action' of other, non-managerial, employees. It is with the debates about these, and the 'social action' approach to organisational analysis more generally, that the next chapter is concerned.

Chapter 4

Orientation and action

Consequently, in seeking to explain and understand attitudes, behaviour and social relationships within a particular work situation, analysis will more usefully begin with the orientations to work which are found to prevail, rather than with quite general assumptions about the needs which all workers have . . . .

The basic shortcoming of the 'technological implications' approach is that the attempt to provide explanations from the point of view of the 'system' entails the neglect of the point of view of the actors involved.

(J. H. Goldthorpe *et al.* 1968, 178, 183)

Systems approaches to the analysis of industrial organisations depend on certain basic psychological assumptions as to the needs and expectations of the managers and workers concerned. Developments within contingency theories of the notion of strategic choice also imply that the values and expectations of at least some members of an organisation must be regarded as of crucial explanatory importance. Until the 1960s discussion of these issues tended to focus on trying to identify supposedly *universal* patterns of needs and expectations. Under the influence of the Human Relations approach the emphasis was on the importance to employees of the non-economic rewards which could be derived from work. Variations in employees' attitudes and behaviour were therefore to be explained in terms of variations in the nature of their tasks and work roles and relationships. One can add that then, as now, these assumptions were often not extended to cover those in the more powerful and more highly rewarded positions in organisations!

In the mid-1960s the early papers and then the first book

reporting the findings of the Affluent Worker project, from which the quotations above have been taken, included a forceful and influential critique of such explanations of industrial attitudes and behaviour. They also included an alternative framework for explanation which gave central importance to 'orientations to work'. This 'action frame of reference' itself rapidly became a subject of controversy, though at the same time it provided the stimulus for a considerable amount of research. As a result of the criticisms and the questions which were provoked by the findings of the research, the emphasis on the importance of 'orientations to work' and their place in an explanation of attitudes and behaviour have been modified in important ways.

This chapter is primarily and mainly concerned with the debates about the action frame of reference and orientations to work, and with the research which attempted to use such a framework and to explore the origins, nature and consequences of different orientations. We shall start however with a brief consideration of the earlier patterns of explanation, and in particular with the two approaches which were the subjects of criticism by Goldthorpe and his colleagues – Human Relations and the 'technological implications' approach; and we conclude with a brief discussion of attempts to establish a 'social action' approach to the analysis of industrial organisations.

HUMAN RELATIONS AND TECHNOLOGY

There is no agreement as to precisely which research and writing should be considered part of the Human Relations movement. At times 'human relations' has been described as if it were coterminous with industrial sociology; at other times it has been defined much more narrowly as referring to a specific set of assumptions and theories, especially those to be found in the writings of Elton Mayo. Although Mayo's work (esp. 1933; 1949) was extremely influential it represented only one strand in the Human Relations movement, and some of the other research and writing was not only more modest in its claims but also, at times, suggested conclusions considerably at variance with those of Mayo himself (see, for example, Warner and Low 1947). Good accounts already exist of the main lines of enquiry and of the criticisms to which they have been subject (see Landsberger 1958; Baritz 1960, esp. Chs 5 and 6; Rose 1988, esp. Pt 3); here we will focus on the arguments and assumptions against which the 'social action approach' advocated by Goldthorpe and his colleagues was directed.

An important part of the impact of the Hawthorne Experiments, as they were reported by Roethlisberger and Dickson (1939) and popularised by Mayo (and, later, many others), derived from the fact that they claimed, apparently justifiably, to show the inadequacy of the then existing understandings of what influenced workers' behaviour. The assumption that workers were 'economic men', concerned to maximise their material rewards and minimise their costs, was challenged by the apparent ineffectiveness (or at best the limited effectiveness) of incentive payment systems within the Hawthorne works. The emphasis which industrial physiologists and psychologists had placed on environmental factors (heat, light, noise, etc.), and on physiological processes such as the development and relief of fatigue, appeared mistaken in view of the failures to establish any relationship between levels of lighting, or changes in hours of work and the introduction of rest pauses, and workers' 'efficiency' and productivity. In place of economic incentives and environmental conditions the reports of the Hawthorne Experiments stressed the importance of two 'social' factors: the influence of and the satisfactions gained from membership in cohesive work groups; and the role of leadership especially from foremen and supervisors.

Much of the research in the Human Relations tradition was concerned with trying to develop these findings. Thus, research by Whyte (1955) and others reinforced the view that economic incentives rarely have their intended straightforward influence on behaviour; and a whole series of investigations attempted to establish the relationship between some or all of small group cohesion, leadership style and practice, group participation in decision making, morale and/or job satisfaction, and productivity (for reviews see Schein 1965; Tannenbaum 1966). These studies accepted and reinforced a view of 'man' as having certain social needs at work: to belong to and be accepted by a small face-to-face group, to be treated with consideration and understanding by immediate superiors, and to have an opportunity to participate in and to influence the organisation and direction of work activities and conditions. In the hands of Mayo these ideas were placed in a broader context; he saw mid-twentieth century industrial societies as lacking in social solidarity, failing to provide their members with a sense of belonging, without adequate means of securing cooperation and in danger therefore of domination by an authoritarian state. Under the leadership of enlightened management industrial enterprises, properly organised, could fill these gaps and meet their members' needs for stable social relations with and acceptance by their fellows. 'Man's desire to be continuously associated in work with his fellows is a strong, if not the strongest, human characteristic' (Mayo 1949, 99).

By the time the results of the Affluent Worker project were being analysed in the mid-1960s there had developed a more complex and sophisticated 'model of man' than that proposed by Mayo, one which provided the cornerstone of 'Neo-Human Relations'. It contained two main components associated respectively with the work of two American psychologists, Maslow and Herzberg, though their basic ideas were adopted by a number of other influential management and organisational theorists. Maslow (1943) proposed that there was a hierarchy of human needs – physiological, safety, love, esteem, self-actualisation – and that as each lower need was satisfied the next in the hierarchy dominated consciousness and behaviour. Herzberg (1968) distinguished two sorts of influence on work-related behaviour: 'hygiene' factors, such as working conditions and pay, which could lead to dissatisfaction if they did not reach adequate standards but did not themselves create positive motivation; and 'motivators', such as achievement and recognition, which could provide satisfaction and motivate the individual to superior performance and effort. These two sets of ideas are compatible with each other (Warr and Wall 1975, Ch. 2), and carry the implication that work should be organised to provide the possibility of 'self-actualisation' and achievement, as well as satisfactory levels of pay, a sense of belonging, recognition and so on (see Schein 1965, 47–65).

At the same time as the ideas which have been labelled Neo-Human Relations were being developed and propagated other writers were publishing the results of research which led them to suggest that the constraints of technology prevented, or severely limited, the possibility of devising work organisations with such desirable characteristics. Though those who have been described as adopting a 'technological implications' approach to the explanation of industrial attitudes and behaviour were perhaps even more diverse than those associated with the Human Relations movement, their work did share certain common characteristics. In particular this research led to the suggestion that the technology, or production system, of an industrial enterprise determined, or strongly influenced, the structure of work roles and relationships within it, and these roles and relationships were a major determinant of attitudes and behaviour. For example, although Woodward's primary interest was in management organisation, as we saw in Chapter 3 she also identified what the results of her research suggested were the consequences for 'human relations' of particular production systems; and in an article in *New Society* (Woodward 1964) she stressed the extent to which behaviour could be seen as role-determined, and those roles shaped by technology. Earlier Goldthorpe himself had argued that certain forms of technical organisation in mining were far more conducive to conflict between supervisors and workers than others (Goldthorpe 1959). Sayles (1958) attempted to explain the bargaining and grievance behaviour of industrial work groups in the USA in terms of their place in the production system of their particular plant. In an influential study Blauner (1964) argued that industrial technology could be seen as having passed through several stages – craft, machine-tending, assembly-line and continuous-process – and that workers' 'alienation' (defined as powerlessness, meaninglessness, isolation and self-estrangement) was in general greatest in industries characterised by a machine-tending or (especially) an assembly-line technology.

What is clearest in Blauner's study, though it is not spelled out, is that the arguments of those pursuing the implications of technology for industrial attitudes, behaviour and social relations depended on certain implicit assumptions about human needs or about what motivates workers. In Blauner's case it is assumed that the opposite of 'alienation', as he defines it, that is autonomy and control, meaning, social cohesion and self-expression, are desired by workers; and that they will lead to satisfaction and commitment to the work and the occupation, and possibly to the employing organisation, if they are provided. As is readily apparent these characteristics of non-alienating, satisfying work are closely parallel to the sources of job satisfaction identified by the 'Neo-Human Relations' movement writers. However, whereas the emphasis in the human relations tradition is on inter-personal relations (e.g. supervisory style, informal organisation in small groups) as the means by which performance, job satisfaction, and social relations can be improved, the 'technological implications' approach emphasised the social structural sources of behaviour and the limitations derived from the technology itself on any possibility of changing roles and relationships.

Even before the findings of the Affluent Worker project were used to support a major critique of both these approaches a number of pieces of research had led to the suggestion that the explanations being provided were inadequate. For example, the differing reactions of workers to incentive payment systems, both in Britain and the USA, drew attention to the different expectations and priorities which workers from varying backgrounds might have; some were interested in maximising their economic returns from employment, whilst others placed greater value on the preservation of satisfying social relations at work (Collins *et al.* 1946, 1948; Lupton 1963). An American study which attempted to establish precise relationships between the attributes of particular tasks and the attitudes and behaviour of workers performing them was forced to conclude that the different 'motivational predispositions' of workers from town and from 'big city' backgrounds led to different preferences and reactions; the city workers did not like the more complex and intrinsically interesting jobs but sought the highest pay on the least demanding tasks (Turner and Lawrence 1966). Research in developing countries had revealed that workers attracted, or coerced, into plantations, mines and factories might well have very different sets of priorities and types and levels of commitment from those to which managers, and researchers, had grown accustomed in the industrialised world (Moore and Feldman 1960). The significance of the Affluent Worker study, however, is that it not only provided a very powerful critique of the human relations and the technological implications approaches but also proposed an alternative explanatory framework.

THE AFFLUENT WORKER

It was no part of the original intentions behind the Affluent Worker study to establish the centrality of 'orientations to work' for an understanding of industrial attitudes and behaviour. Such arguments were subsequently described by the authors as a 'by-product' of the main investigation (Goldthorpe *et al.* 1968, 1–2), though they were only possible because the research enquired about workers' attitudes and values in some detail. This element of 'discovery' about the claims made for the importance of 'orientations to work' gave the arguments considerable additional force. The design of the project, however, also imposed some limitations on the conclusions which could legitimately be drawn from it, limitations which appeared to be overlooked at times during the subsequent debates.

In initiating the research in 1962 Goldthorpe and Lockwood wished to investigate how far a process of 'embourgeoisement' had been taking place in post-war Britain, that is whether the increasing affluence being experienced by manual workers was resulting in their becoming 'middle class' in their attitudes and values, and in their patterns of behaviour and social relationships. Such a thesis had been put forward by a number of commentators, most notably in the aftermath of the third successive Conservative general election victory in 1959. Goldthorpe and Lockwood had considerable doubts about the soundness and empirical validity of the thesis (Lockwood 1960; Goldthorpe and Lockwood 1963; Goldthorpe et al. 1969, Ch. 1); they set out to test it by investigating a 'critical case', a situation where it was most likely that embourgeoisement would have occurred if the proponents of the thesis were correct. Though the discovery that embourgeoisement had taken place would not enable them to say very much about how general the process was, absence of evidence for such changes, in such a supposedly favourable situation for them, (which was what they expected to find) would indicate that it was highly unlikely that embourgeoisement was occurring at all.

The search for a locale with conditions which would provide a critical case led the researchers to Luton. This town with its immediate surroundings was relatively isolated from older industrial regions and had experienced considerable economic expansion in the post-war period so that there was a considerable population of relative newcomers living in socially heterogeneous residential areas. Within the town three major employers, Skefko (ball bearings), Vauxhall (cars and vans) and Laporte (chemicals) operated 'progressive' employment policies and had experienced harmonious industrial relations; only Laporte provided the process production technology which was thought most likely to favour embourgeoisement (Skefko and Vauxhall were in the 'intermediate' ranges of the technology scale – large batch and mass production); and none of the firms was small or of moderate size, as a preliminary paper had suggested would be desirable (Lockwood and Goldthorpe 1962, 31; cf. Goldthorpe et al. 1969,

39–41). This mix of technologies was in fact to prove important for later arguments. Within the three plants it was possible to sample populations of manual workers who were (relatively) affluent, economically secure and consumption minded, and many of whom had moved to Luton in search of better housing and well-paid and secure employment. Interviews were conducted with 229 men, all aged between 21 and 46, married and living with their wives in or very near Luton, and in work in a main area of production in one of the three firms, with regular earnings in October 1962 of at least £17 per week gross (Goldthorpe *et al.* 1969, 30–49).

On the basis of existing research findings at that time levels of job satisfaction were expected to be related to skill level and type of work; craftsmen and process production workers would be more satisfied than, respectively, less skilled workers, and machinists and assembly line workers. In fact, the relatively skilled setters were more satisfied with their work tasks than the highly skilled craftsmen, and although the process workers had no strong dislikes related to particular features of their job, neither did they experience any great degree of positive satisfaction. Furthermore, the authors argued, the question of task satisfaction (or dissatisfaction) has to be separated from the more general and important question of satisfaction with and attachment to the job as a whole. Thus, although

> overall . . . it could not be claimed that our affluent workers derived any very high degree of satisfaction immediately from the work-tasks and -roles which they performed . . . job satisfaction in terms of workers' experience of their immediate work-tasks and -roles cannot be associated in any direct way with job satisfaction in terms of workers' attachment to their present employment . . . the question of satisfaction from work cannot in the end be usefully considered except in relation to the more basic question of what we would term orientation towards work. Until one knows something of the way in which workers order their wants and expectations relative to their employment – until one knows what meaning work has for them – one is not in a position to understand what overall assessment of their job satisfaction may most appropriately be made in their case.
>
> (Goldthorpe *et al.* 1968, 25, 31, 36)

The differences in overall satisfaction with their jobs were therefore seen as explicable in terms of how far work-tasks and -roles, and the rewards and deprivations of their particular jobs, met the expectations these men brought to their employment. Thus, the machinists and assemblers had a relatively high degree of attachment to their employment, despite the deprivations of, for example, work 'on the line', because it met their first priority of high pay; many of them, and of the other respondents, had in fact left previous jobs which were intrinsically more rewarding and interesting for the sake of greater extrinsic rewards. The process workers were on average the lowest paid of these affluent workers, but were somewhat less strongly oriented towards extrinsic rewards and had fewer dissatisfactions with their tasks. Both the setters and the craftsmen were concerned with intrinsic as well as extrinsic rewards from work, but the more highly skilled craftsmen were the less satisfied because important expectations about non-economic aspects of their jobs were not met (Goldthorpe *et al.* 1968, 10–37, esp. 36–7; also Goldthorpe *et al.* 1969, 54–74).

The authors argued, however, that these differences should not be allowed to obscure the extent to which all the workers in their sample emphasised the 'instrumental' aspect of employment, its importance to them as a means of securing rewards, pay – especially – and security, extrinsic to the job itself. This instrumental 'orientation to work' was reflected in the other aspects of the men's situations and social relations at work which were investigated. For example, they had low levels of 'affective' involvement with their fellow workers and attached little importance to membership of solidary work groups (Goldthorpe *et al.* 1968, 49–63); relations with supervision were generally harmonious but largely because foremen and supervisors left them alone, not because they displayed 'human relations' skills (63–8); attitudes towards the firms were largely favourable, but reflected a 'calculative' involvement, one concerned with the terms of the employment contract; consequently both the operation of work study and the firms' ability to pay higher wages were contentious issues (72–89); and although levels of participation in work-based trade union activity were relatively high, the workers' view of trade unionism was also instrumental and restricted to local, predominantly economic issues (93–115).

It was the workers' 'instrumental' orientation to work which accounted for findings so much at variance with expectations based on either the human relations or the technological implications approach. Solidary work groups, sympathetic employee-centred supervision, and opportunities to participate in decisions about work were not important to workers whose prime interest in their jobs was with the level of material rewards it offered; and although technology influenced the tasks workers had to perform, it was not associated with variations in attitudes and behaviour towards the employing organisations more generally which in contrast reflected the fact that each of the firms largely satisfied their workers' economic priorities and expectations. Thus in place of attempts to specify a general 'range and structure of individual human needs' Goldthorpe and his colleagues were led by their findings to emphasise that

> wants and expectations are culturally determined *variables*, not psychological constants; and [that] from a sociological stand-point what is in fact of major interest *is* the variation in the ways in which groups differently located in the social structure actually experience and attempt to meet the needs which at a different level of analysis may be attributed to them all.
>
> (Goldthorpe *et al.*, 1968, 178)

Equally, in contrast to the (largely unspoken) assumptions of the technological implications approach, 'the orientation which workers have to their employment and the manner, thus, in which they define their work situation can be regarded as *mediating* between features of the work situation objectively considered and the nature of workers' response' (182).

The researchers accepted that in our sort of society 'all work activity tends to have a basically instrumental component'. They elaborated the notion of orientation to work by identifying four elements and emphasised the distinctiveness of the basic, ideal typical, instrumental orientation by comparing it explicitly with 'deviations' in a 'bureaucratic' and a 'solidaristic' direction, and implicitly with a 'deviation' in a 'professional' direction as well (Goldthorpe *et al.* 1968, 41). The elements were:

1 *the meaning of work*, and especially whether it is a means to an end or, at least in part, an end in itself;
2 *the nature of involvement in the employing organisation* in terms of intensity (low or high) and affect (positive, neutral or negative) leading to three types of involvement: moral, calculative and alienative (see Etzioni 1961);
3 the *ego-involvement* of workers in work – is it part of their 'central life interests'?; and

4 whether or not workers' lives are sharply divided into *work and non-work*.

In terms of these four elements the differences between an instrumental orientation to work and the other 'types' can be summarised in Table 4.1.

It was an important part of the argument of Goldthorpe and his colleagues that the orientations to work of the workers they interviewed were formed independently of their current employment and had led to the choice of that employment. In an early, unpublished, paper Goldthorpe set out their position (1965, 10–11):

1 That industrial workers do not enter diffcrent kinds of industrial employment in a quite random manner in terms of their social characteristics, but tend rather to form labour forces which are in some degree 'self-selected' and thus – in some respects – relatively homogeneous.
2 That this homogeneity will frequently be greater than could be explained in terms of limiting factors such as ability, training, skill-levels, etc.; it will also result, and in particular under conditions of full employment, from workers making *choices* between

Table 4.1 Orientations to work

| | | ORIENTATION | |
	Instrumental	Bureaucratic	Solidaristic
Meaning of work:	Labour for income	Service for career	Valued group activity
Involvement in firm:	Calculative	Moral (alienative*)	Alienative (moral+)
- Intensity	Low	High	High
- Affect	Neutral	Positive (negative*)	Negative (positive+)
Ego-involvement in work:	Weak	Strong	Strong
Work/non-work dichotomy:	Yes	No	No

* Involvement where career expectations are not realised
+ Involvement where the 'valued group' is the enterprise as a whole not just the work group
Source: Goldthorpe *et al.* 1968, 38–41

different kinds of employment available to them, according to their existing wants and aspirations relative to work.

3 That in this way, members of labour forces of particular enterprises, or more probably of sections of these, will tend, as collectivities, to have a distinctive orientation towards work and to inject a certain set of meanings into their work situation; these meanings will then play an important part in determining their behaviour within this situation.

4 That since the homogeneity in question results from individual choice of employment – that is, from a process of self-selection – the sources of the *specific content* of orientations to work and of definitions of work situations will to some significant extent be located externally to the industrial enterprise and pertain to non-work aspects of the individual's total life situation.

The approach derived from these propositions was seen as making the first step towards an 'action frame of reference' in industrial sociology.

In seeking to explain the content of the affluent workers' orientations to work Goldthorpe and his colleagues emphasised the family life-cycle, community and status positions of the workers concerned. All of them were married and aged 21–46, and 83 per cent of them had at least one dependent child; they were thus at the stage in their lives when financial pressures were greatest. They had typically experienced geographical mobility; less than a third had been brought up in the Luton area, and nearly half outside the South-East altogether; and for half of them their previous job had been outside the Luton area. This mobility was important directly in that the great majority had moved to Luton in search of better living conditions and higher incomes; and indirectly in that they were separated from their kin and living among others who were also geographically mobile, and who in response developed a 'privatised', home and family centred, style of life. Many of them had also experienced downward social mobility in comparison either with their father's occupation, or with their own previous highest occupational status, or with the occupations of their siblings. This 'relative deprivation', it was suggested, led to their seeking high paying work in order to support as high as possible a standard of living, and to their placing little value on their working lives which were sharply separated from their family and domestic situation (Goldthorpe et al. 1968, 147–59).

In a further related development of ideas about the sources of workers' social perspectives Lockwood, in a widely influential paper (Lockwood 1966; see also Goldthorpe *et al.* 1969, Ch. 5), outlined three types of working class 'image of society', all of them distinct from a middle class perspective. They were 'proletarian traditionalism' associated with solidary communities around industries such as mining, docking and shipbuilding; 'deferential traditionalism' associated with small towns and rural areas with smaller, paternalistic firms; and the 'pecuniary' model of society associated with workers with an instrumental attachment to work and privatised community relationships – like the affluent workers in Luton. The industrial and community situations which provided the experiences which led to both the proletarian and the deferential versions of traditionalism have been in decline in the post-war period, and for this and other reasons the researchers argued that the attitudes towards and behaviour at work of the affluent workers might be considered 'prototypical', 'revealing a pattern of industrial life which will in the fairly near future become far more widespread' (Goldthorpe *et al.* 1968, 174–8; see also 1969, 162–5).

The 'technological implications' approach, at its simplest, suggested that a given technology or production system gave rise to a structure of work roles which largely constrained workers' social relations and behaviour, and would be associated with certain attitudes understandable as reactions to such work roles and relationships. As we saw in previous chapters it has been convincingly argued that the link between technology and the structure of work roles is not as close as had been thought; both the Tavistock researchers and Child, for example, have made the case for a marked degree of organisational choice. The findings and arguments of the Affluent Worker study led to questioning of the second link between the structure of work roles and relationships (whether or not they were technologically determined) and workers' attitudes and behaviour. This, it was argued, should be seen as dependent on the workers' orientations to their work. These orientations, however, had their origins in workers' situations and experiences outside work, and influenced both the choice of a job (at least in conditions of full employment) and attitudes towards and behaviour in that job. Thus not only did Goldthorpe and his colleagues contribute in important ways to the criticism of the 'technological implications' approach; they put forward an alternative explanatory framework in its place, and in

place of the Neo-Human Relations approach. It is to the development and criticism of this 'social action' approach that we must
now turn.

DEVELOPMENTS AND CRITICISMS

Even before the full accounts of the Affluent Worker project had
been published a number of studies had been initiated which
included, as a major element, the investigation of the causes,
nature and/or consequences of employees' orientations to work.
It is neither necessary nor possible to give detailed consideration
to the very considerable body of research and writing on this topic
during the late 1960s and the 1970s. In this section we shall discuss
the main ways in which the approach advocated by Goldthorpe
and his colleagues has been developed and the main modifications
and criticisms which have been proposed. Many of those who
investigated or wrote about orientations to work also considered
the issue of the more general images of society held by the workers
in question, and brief reference will be made to these debates (see
Bulmer 1975). The question of the implications of increasing
affluence for the class structure and for political affiliations and
behaviour, however, will not be of direct concern to us though that
too has continued to be controversial (for early comments see
Westergaard 1970, Beynon and Nichols 1971, Mackenzie 1974;
and see also Platt 1984).

In addition to these specific issues the reports of the Affluent
Worker project, and especially those concerned with industrial
attitudes and behaviour, claimed to represent 'an action approach
to industrial sociology' (Goldthorpe 1965; see also 1970), or the
use of 'an action frame of reference . . . within which actors' own
definitions of the situations in which they are engaged are taken as
an initial basis for the explanation of their social behaviour and
relationships' (Goldthorpe *et al.* 1968, 184). Whereas for some
writers, including the authors of the Affluent Worker volumes,
such an approach represented primarily a change of emphasis
within conventional sociological theory and methodology, others
saw the priority given to the actor's definition of the situation as
necessarily implying a radically subjectivist sociology. We shall
consider these arguments, and the attempts to develop a 'social
action approach' to the analysis of industrial organisations, in the
final section.

Categorising orientations to work

Goldthorpe and his colleagues saw orientations to work as comprising a number of different elements which they suggested might typically cluster in certain ways so that it was logically possible and empirically plausible to postulate a number of 'ideal-typical' orientations to work. Though they also suggested that the 'instrumental' orientation to work was more basic than any of the others, because '*all* work activity, in industrial society at least, tends to have a basically instrumental component' (Goldthorpe *et al.* 1968, 41), they used the three (or four) types they had distinguished to identify and characterise the distinctive features of the orientations to work of the affluent workers. In the subsequent discussion by other researchers of the appropriate way to typify orientations to work a variety of rather different reformulations has been proposed. Some of these have involved primarily an attempt to tease out the further implications of the approach outlined by Goldthorpe and his colleagues; others have introduced new considerations and/or proposed a rather different approach to identifying such orientations. As a result the fairly straightforward typology used in the Affluent Worker studies, which was immediately appealing because it drew on a number of established stereotypes in sociology, came to seem much more questionable.

In an early study of the relationship between size of industrial organisation and worker behaviour (absence and labour turnover) Ingham developed the idea of orientations to work as an important intervening variable in three ways. He subdivided and relabelled the 'solidaristic' type of orientation to work by developing Goldthorpe and colleagues' distinction between a 'positive' orientation to the employing organisation and 'moral' involvement in it, and a 'negative' orientation and 'alienative' involvement (Ingham 1967; the terms are derived from Etzioni 1961). This resulted in the accurately but clumsily labelled 'instrumental–expressive (positive)' and 'instrumental–expressive (negative)' as well as the basic 'instrumental' orientation to work, types which were translated by Silverman (1970, 179) as 'Hawthorne Man', 'Marxian Man' and 'Economic Man' respectively. Secondly, he classified the major potential rewards which can be received from industrial work into the economic (security of employment; wages/fringe benefits) and the non-economic (activity [task]; social relations [with peers; with those in authority]) (Ingham 1970, 45). Thirdly, using this distinction between economic and non-economic rewards he argued that orientations could be classified 'in terms of the importance attached by the worker to economic and non-economic rewards of various kinds' leading to a fourfold classification around 'high' or 'low' requirements regarding 'economic' and/or 'non-economic' rewards from work (49). He focused particularly on two of these four possibilities, 'high economic, low non-economic requirements from work' (labelled 'economistic–instrumental') and 'low economic, high non-economic' (labelled 'non-economistic–expressive'). The distinction between economism (sensitivity to wage issues and the pursuit of high earnings) and instrumentalism was introduced because he argued 'instrumentalism may be used to describe the definition of work as a means to an end but it does not necessarily imply anything about what these ends are' (50).

Ingham was right to suggest that 'instrumentalism' does not necessarily imply 'economism', and that there may be some workers (craftsmen and/or professionals perhaps?) for whom work is primarily an end in itself, but he did not seem altogether consistent in his application of these distinctions. A worker with low economic and high non-economic requirements from work could well be labelled as having a 'non-economistic–instrumental' orientation if the non-economic rewards for which work was a means were social relations at work rather than the activity itself; and in his own research he slipped back into the conventional approach of regarding the 'end' for which employment is the means as primarily economic when he wrote 'the basis for all orientations to work is an instrumental one. If, in a situation of full employment, the level of earnings in a given plant fails to rise above a certain level, high rates of labour turnover will occur whatever the orientation to work' (52).

The type of work where an emphasis on the intrinsic value and importance of the work itself is most likely to occur is that of 'professional' occupations (see, for example, Salaman 1974, 65–75), and it is in connection with such occupations that a related distinction, between a 'local' and a 'cosmopolitan' orientation or 'identity' has frequently been introduced and developed (see Merton 1957; Gouldner 1957–8). In the context of employment, 'local' implies an emphasis on the employing organisation, its interests and problems, and the opportunities and rewards it offers, such as opportunities for promotion. 'Cosmopolitan' implies an emphasis on the world outside the organisation and the more general concerns of the occupation (or profession) and, at least in some cases, the value of occupational activities for their own sake. Thus, for example, Sheldrake (1971) distinguished 'organizational' and 'technical' orientations among computer programmers; those with the former orientation were concerned with administrative and commercial considerations in contrast to the others who stressed the creative aspects of their work as experts. In discussing the 'identities' of scientists Cotgrove and Box (1966, 1970) similarly argued that some had an 'instrumental' or 'organisational' orientation and used science as a means to pursue a career within an organisation; the others were committed to a career in science, valued scientific work for its own sake and wanted autonomy at work, but could be divided between those for whom publication ('disciplinary communism') was important – the 'public' scientists – and those for whom this was not important – the 'private' scientists. Both Sheldrake, and Cotgrove and Box were able to show relationships between such orientations (or identities) and behaviour within the organisation. In addition Cotgrove and Box demonstrated that the career preferences of the scientists they studied, as between academic research and work in industry, were strongly influenced by such differences in identity, though also by the perception of occupational opportunities.

Ingham's elaboration of the possible rewards obtainable from work has been developed further by others. Bennett (1974, 1978), for example, has suggested that orientations can be seen to vary according to the relative priority given to 'economic' rewards (pay, security of employment), 'personal' or 'intrinsic' rewards (job interest, possibilities for personal growth) and 'social' or 'relational' rewards (social relations, friendship). Other studies of the factors influencing job choice and/or satisfaction have added a fourth set of features which may be given priority; these can be termed 'convenience' factors (being near home, convenient hours of work) (see, for example, Brown et al. 1983, esp. 36–45). Such approaches certainly provide a more satisfactory framework than the simple dichotomy between more or less 'instrumentally' oriented workers, but they do so because they allow for a more complex range of possible orientations to work. Rather than a limited number of ideal type orientations clearly distinguished from each other it becomes necessary to conceive of a more complex pattern with differing degrees of priority being placed on different types of reward from work, with no one necessarily dominant. We shall consider below some of the implications of such an approach.

Some commentators have modified the notion of an orientation to work even further. Fox (1971, 8–10), for example, has distinguished 'substantive' from 'procedural' orientations to work. The Affluent Worker study and most subsequent work concentrated on the former: the various dimensions of work (pay, security, challenging tasks, etc.) which may be given priority. However, workers may well also seek the right to participate in the decision making procedures which determine the nature of work and its rewards; such a procedural orientation could be 'instrumental' or 'terminal', that is wanting the opportunity to participate for its own sake. Whereas Fox's contribution added something extra to the substance of an orientation to work, Wynn (1983, 53–77; see also 1980) has suggested that it is necessary to separate out and relate three elements within the notion of 'orientation': the actor's 'motivation to work' (their view or definition of work), which will influence the basis of their 'attachment to work' (categorised as 'moral', 'calculative' or 'alienative' – the familiar trichotomy from Etzioni [1961]), which in turn influences their 'motivation at work'. In effect this appears to be stressing the possible partial independence of the first two elements in Goldthorpe and colleagues' account of orientations to work – the meaning of work and the worker's involvement in the firm.

Clarity, strength and stability of orientations to work

Thus the categorisation or typification of orientations to work must clearly be seen as more complex than was implied by the original formulation in the Affluent Worker study. Indeed this complexity inevitably raises questions about the clarity, strength and stability of whatever orientations to work employees can be shown to have. With regard to clarity this is likely to be greatest where workers have one overriding objective such as maximising earnings. The evidence of many studies, however, is that such a single-stranded orientation to work is relatively unusual; workers typically look for a range of rewards from work, though some may be given greater priority than others (see the review of research in Brown et al. 1983, 14–28). If, for example, workers are looking not only for a high level of economic rewards from work but also for interesting work, autonomy on the job, and/or satisfying social relations, then the question of priorities is bound to arise. These various desiderata are, however, strictly incommensurable (they cannot be measured on the same scale); in assessing potential employment opportunities or evaluating a job workers may have to decide between higher pay or more interesting work, but it is much more difficult for an outside observer to establish, and even more so to predict, any clear relationship between orientations and such choices or evaluations.

The 'affluent workers' must be regarded as relatively unusual in the clarity and strength of their 'instrumental' orientation to work. Certainly this would be the conclusion to be drawn from Blackburn and Mann's study of the labour market situation of non-skilled manual workers in Peterborough. In addition to the strong sense of orientation to work, where 'one type of work reward dominates, to the exclusion of all others', they suggested that

> there is, however, a weaker sense in which we may speak of workers having orientations. Rather than a single dominant concern, the worker may have a whole set of expectations and relative priorities . . .
>
> This more complex version still allows for orientations to determine job choice, attitudes and so on, but only in the limiting case is the priority for one sort of work reward so great as to be completely dominant. More typically, job selection is a matter of balancing different combinations of rewards against the actor's relative preferences, and the optimal choice may not always be that maximising the top priority.
>
> (Blackburn and Mann 1979, 145)

In their own detailed investigations the clearest strong orientation was a preference for outdoor work, with wages (especially the rate per hour) being second clearest, and a concern with intrinsic job quality also important (242).

There were two respects in which the stability of the orientations to work of the affluent workers, or of other types of worker, might be seen to be threatened. In the short term the failure of an employer to meet expectations, which workers felt to be reasonable and legitimate, might lead to a change to a much more negative and alienative involvement in the organisation. This was

one of the main points made in Westergaard's critique: he pointed
out that an employment relationship dependent solely on a single-
stranded cash nexus was inherently fragile, liable to change rapidly
if workers' economic expectations were not met (Westergaard
1970, esp. 120–1). It is also, however, built into Goldthorpe and
colleagues' account of the 'bureaucratic' orientation to work
where 'involvement of workers with their organisation' is seen as
tending 'normally to be positive, where moral expectations are
being faithfully met, or perhaps strongly negative, if it is felt that
commitments of a moral kind are not being honoured' (Goldthorpe *et al.* 1968, 40). In the longer term the links postulated
between stages in the family life cycle and orientation to work
imply that orientations will change with age and with changes in
domestic situation and family status. What is missing from these
formulations, however, is any allowance for the changes in orientations to work which are likely to occur, possibly more gradually and
over the medium term, as a result of the experience of employment, and possibly also of unemployment.

Contexts for orientations to work

If orientations to work are likely to be more complex and less
stable than the types outlined in the Affluent Worker study, then
the contexts within which workers act and/or express attitudes are
of crucial importance; a change of context may evoke a different
response from the worker or workers concerned. This was one of
the main points made by Daniel in his critique of the initial
advocacy of the action approach, and of the explanatory importance of orientations to work (see Daniel 1969, 1971, 1973), and it
was perhaps not entirely met in Goldthorpe's replies (see Goldthorpe 1970, and especially 1972).

Daniel argued that there was

> strong evidence to the effect that the factors that attract a person
> to a job are very different from those that determine his satis-
> factions, performance and behaviour on the job. These in turn are
> often very different from those that predispose him to leave the job
> ... all the research on occupational motivation requires that very
> sharp distinctions be drawn between these three areas of job
> choice, intrinsic job satisfaction, and job quitting.
>
> (1969, 367)

In support of this position he referred to his own research in the petro-chemicals industry where, he claimed, pay, security and physical working conditions attracted people to the job and kept them in it; the opportunity to use mental ability and experience in problem resolution and learning was the main source of satisfaction in the job; and lack of promotion opportunities the main reason why a few workers left (367). Further, in a study of productivity bargaining in the same industry (Daniel 1970) the emphasis in the bargaining situation was on the relationship between the higher earnings offered for the greater volume of work. In contrast, some months later, when the agreement had been reluctantly accepted, it was viewed much more favourably because it had led to welcome improvements in job interest and satisfaction and day-to-day relationships at work, issues which had not appeared important in the bargaining situation, and the previously contentious levels of pay were accepted, more or less, as a given (see also Daniel 1971, 1973).

Goldthorpe argued in reply that this sort of evidence did not really constitute a criticism of the use of the concept of orientation to work. Workers who were strongly instrumentally oriented were not 'ipso facto entirely desensitized to all deprivations or satisfactions in work that are of an intrinsic kind'. Indeed 'there is nothing whatsoever surprising in such [instrumentally oriented] workers taking an active interest in all matters relating to the effort bargain and to the conditions of their work within the particular shops and plants in which they are employed' (Goldthorpe 1972, 269, 271). What would be needed to establish the importance of the context, he argued, would be evidence of changes in workers' priorities, for example ones leading them to leave a high-paying job to seek one offering more intrinsically interesting and satisfying work, or placing job interest and satisfaction on the agenda in any future productivity bargaining situation.

Despite the tone of these exchanges, the protagonists were not as far apart as might appear at first sight. Daniel's criticisms do not amount to grounds for rejecting altogether reference to orientations to work in an explanation of industrial attitudes and behaviour. Indeed his own criteria, which would justify an 'approach via orientation to work', appear to be ones which Goldthorpe would accept and feel that, at least in the second case, the Affluent Worker project had met: 'it must be convincingly shown that people with different orientations to work respond in different ways to the same work situation, and that people with similar orientations respond in similar ways to different work situations' (Daniel 1969, 368). Goldthorpe was quite right to draw attention to the need for evidence that orientations to work change as a result of experiences at work, if his critics were to establish that orientations were much less fixed than he had implied; we return to this question below. What the exchanges did suggest, however, was that the notion of an orientation to work and its use in accounting for actions at and opinions about work was more problematic than had originally been implied, and that these questions about its formulation and use had been obscured by the fact that in the Affluent Worker project the workers had unusually strong and single-stranded orientations to work.

The first and probably least important difficulty concerns the methods to be used to obtain evidence of any particular body of workers' orientations to work and how to interpret that evidence once acquired. The general difficulties this raises were recognised early (see Westergaard 1970, 118–25; Daniel 1969, 366–7). If orientations to work are complex, however, with multiple priorities, different questions, or gathering data in different contexts, during the research process itself, may provide very different pictures of workers' overall orientation to work, if one can be assumed to exist.

Secondly, in situations where workers have a number of priorities of roughly equal weight the context is likely to influence their order of importance, as appears to have happened in the situations studied by Daniel. The relationship between orientations to work and actions or attitudes is therefore inevitably less determinate than in the case of the strongly instrumentally oriented workers in Luton. The point here is not whether orientations have changed under the influence of work experience, or that workers' objectives in the work situation have been shown to be unimportant in explaining their attitudes and behaviour, but that different objectives may receive different priority in different circumstances.

Thirdly, the context has an important effect on the orientations to work, especially of those with multiple priorities, because it represents the conditions for action which can be seen as constraining the possible actions of the workers involved. As Fox (1971, 22–3) has argued, consideration must be given to the way the order of priorities may be influenced by the practical possibilities of realising them, as perceived by the actors themselves. Workers who would like to have interesting and responsible jobs and good pay may give low priority to the former objective because they realise that they are unlikely to find both; but this does not mean that interest and responsibility are necessarily abandoned as objectives altogether and have no influence over their behaviour. The order of priorities may change over the long term, or even – in the context of an unusual event like an industrial dispute – the short term. This sort of argument has been developed more generally by Prandy and his colleagues (1982, esp. 78–87) who have distinguished between 'wants' ('what individuals would want in some ideal sense'), 'expectations' ('what they realistically desire, given the situation in which they find themselves') and 'salience' ('the extent to which an individual is motivated to pursue an improvement in a particular reward'); they have argued that any exploration of orientations to work must consider both expectations and the relative salience of possible rewards.

Determinants

One of the issues which proved most controversial when the reports of the Affluent Worker project were first published was the determinants of orientations to work. It was an important part of the original argument of Goldthorpe and his colleagues (1968, e.g. 182–5) that orientations to work were largely formed outside the workplace and brought to it by the workers concerned. Similarly Ingham (1970, 57) asserted

> it is essential to the approach of this study that the independence of orientations to work is demonstrated: otherwise it could be assumed that *all* variations in orientations are the result of a process of socialization within the *immediate* socio-technical system or that industrial behaviour is best understood merely as a response to the exigencies of this formal organization.

Most subsequent commentators have not been happy with such claims. Indeed in this respect too the Luton workers appear to be a limiting case which forms a bad basis for generalisation: it is precisely instrumentally oriented workers, with no affective involvement in their jobs, employing organisations or social relations at work, who are unlikely to be influenced by their experience of work; workers with more complex orientations and greater involvement may well alter their priorities as a result of past and/or current work experience.

Thus, although a number of studies have also demonstrated a relationship between aspects of male and female workers' individual, family, community and class situations and their orientations to work (e.g. Ingham 1970, 129–37; Cotgrove and Box 1970, Ch. 3; Blackburn and Mann 1979, Ch. 8; Cunnison 1966, 83–5; Beynon and Blackburn 1972, 147–9), few if any researchers have considered orientations to work as solely or primarily determined or influenced by non-work factors. The influence of work experience, however, can be considered as occurring, potentially, in two ways.

Firstly, past work experience, in other workplaces than the current one, may be seen as an important factor in shaping current orientations to work; such influence might be ascribed particularly to experience during a worker's 'formative' years – their first job, apprenticeship, initial training and so on. This sort of position seems to be the one adopted by Ingham (1970, 137–40) in his tentative discussion of job socialisation as a source of variations in orientations to work.

Secondly, it can be argued that there is no reason to suppose that the influence of work experience suddenly ceases at a certain age or stage, even if workers' expectations and priorities do become more firmly set with greater experience. Any satisfactory explanatory schema must at the least allow for the possibility that the characteristics of the job, the employing organisation and social relations and events at work influence orientations to work even as the orientations of the actors involved influence those social relations and events. Recognition of such a two-way relationship between orientations to work and work situation, however, necessitates a substantial modification in the approach to understanding industrial attitudes and behaviour as compared with that advocated by Goldthorpe and his colleagues.

The arguments of the Affluent Worker study were built on the apparent lack of association 'between technologically conditioned experience within the work situation and attitudes and behaviour' (Goldthorpe et al. 1968, 182). Much subsequent research, however, has stressed the relationships between features of both the work and the non-work situations of workers and their orientations to work. Two studies can provide examples of such conclusions. Blackburn and Mann defined orientations to work as 'a central organising principle which underlies people's attempts to make sense of their lives' (Blackburn and Mann 1979, 16, quoted from Beynon and Blackburn 1972, 6). They reported that for the majority of their sample of Peterborough manual workers orientations to work were weak. They considered a wide range of non-work and work-related variables in the 'social backgrounds' of their respondents, including age, place of birth, education, family and life cycle situations, social mobility and religion, in the former category, and aspects of work history (e.g. range of experience in different occupations, industries and employing organisations; and unemployment) in the second; and they found relationships between most of them and at least some elements of orientations to work. Their examination of a complex body of data led them towards a more sophisticated conception of how the notion of orientations might be used:

> orientations relate to all aspects of people's lives, and we have seen how orientations to work are enmeshed in the totality of social experience, both at work and outside. A view of them as something brought into the work situation from outside is too static and fragmentary. Not only are they influenced by experience of work and market processes, but through their influence on job rewards they influence non-work life.
>
> (Blackburn and Mann 1979, 242)

In one respect, however, their findings were more clear-cut and again emphasised the influence of both work and non-work experience. They identified certain types of people as likely to have (stronger) orientations to work: 'people who are generally satisfied with their lives, well integrated socially in their family and the community, with relatively good jobs and successful careers ... whose experience leads them to believe that they can make effective choices and exercise some control over their lives' (1979: 239).

In a study of white-collar workers Prandy and his colleagues (1982, 87-9) argued that rather than investigating simple, direct relationships between background factors and orientations to work prior to the current work situation it was necessary to develop a more complex model including an individual's employment location, their rewards and perceptions of these rewards, their expectations and the priority given to those expectations, as well as background factors. After analysing their data in these terms they concluded that it was 'misleading to think of *prior* orientations ...

they derive from an individual's total experience'. However, their findings suggested that 'present work experience' was of crucial importance and that age had a 'marked effect' (1982: 112).

There are two more diffuse and general influences on the development and formulation of orientations to work which should be mentioned though they have not always been considered in the sorts of studies discussed so far. The first has primarily methodological implications. Any workers' expressions of their objectives in work will reflect the meanings of work which are culturally available; for manual workers these are likely to include a predominant emphasis on instrumental aspects of the job, whilst for some white-collar workers, such as professionals, it is these aspects which may be de-valued.

Secondly, as Fox (1980, esp. 172–80) has pointed out there are strong pressures on all of us, which operate well before entering work, to be 'realistic' in expectations concerning work, to adapt to the available opportunities (or, for the majority, to the lack of them), and to accommodate to the world as it is. The result of such processes can be the expression of a very limited range of priorities regarding work, perhaps leading to an 'alienated instrumentalism', an attempt to maximise income at minimum cost in terms of the time given to work (Blackburn and Mann 1979, 243). The result can also be apparent satisfaction with jobs which most people would regard as highly unrewarding. To take such satisfaction at face value is to ignore the 'latent aspirations' which may be revealed by asking people to 'speculate about the world as it might be – or might have been'; it can also lead to a justification by the observer of the existing organisation and allocation of jobs and the restriction of terms like 'alienation' to refer solely to expressed job dissatisfaction (Fox 1980, esp. 176).

Homogeneity of orientations to work

The significance of orientations to work for the explanation of industrial attitudes and behaviour was seen by Goldthorpe and his colleagues as being dependent on a considerable degree of homogeneity of such orientations within a particular labour force. Orientations will clearly have a particular significance when all members of an organisation, or of some department or section within it, share the same expectations and priorities. Nevertheless the explanatory importance of orientations to work may be at least as great in situations where a workforce is divided into two or more different groupings in terms of their predominant expectations, and these differences are associated with differences in attitudes and/or behaviour at work. The emphasis on homogeneity reflected the arguments that orientations to work existed prior to current work experience and influenced the choice of current job; and in conditions of full employment the key process bringing this about was seen as that of self-selection:

> Thus it is likely that there is a fairly general tendency in operation for the labour forces of particular enterprises to become to some degree homogeneous, in terms of their members' orientation to work, as a result simply of processes of self-selection.
>
> (Goldthorpe *et al.* 1968, 183)

In an unpublished discussion of these arguments Goldthorpe himself outlined two other possible ways in which homogeneity of orientations to work among labour forces or identifiable sections of them might occur, both of them involving socialisation rather than self-selection (see also Goldthorpe 1972, 267–8). On the one hand in localities where there are dominant shared orientations to work and at most a very limited range of choices of employment, homogeneity in orientations to work within the workplace will be brought about by socialisation within the community. Examples might include company towns, mining communities and towns or parts of them dominated by industries such as shipbuilding, the docks, steel and the railways. In all these cases the content of orientations to work will be influenced to a considerable extent by the character of the industry or employer in question and orientations cannot therefore be treated as straightforwardly independent of the work situation. On the other hand homogeneity may result from socialisation within the current workplace itself. Though there were good reasons for dismissing this possibility in the case of the Luton workers, as has been argued already one cannot generalise from this case.

Indeed in addition to the evidence already cited there are a number of studies which have observed the workplace socialisation process as it has occurred and have recorded how, in general, it produces acceptance of dominant definitions of the situation. Thus, for example, Lupton (1963, 147–8) described how a trainee was 'indoctrinated' with the appropriate norms for working on piecework, a process of 'secondary socialisation' which Baldamus

(1961, Ch. 9) has suggested on theoretical grounds is necessary if there is to be any stability in the employment contract (see also Turner 1971, Chs 5 and 6). A study of shipbuilding apprentices over a period of three and a half years recorded changes in attitudes and expectations on questions such as the most important characteristic of a job, promotion, and management and trade union functions, which showed moves towards attitudes similar to those held by adult shipbuilding workers (Brown 1974a).

Thus the process outlined on the basis of the Affluent Worker study whereby prior orientations to work lead to self-selection of a homogeneous workforce has to be seen as only one possibility among several, the others involving much less independence of orientations from the work situation in question. In addition, however, questions have been raised about the account given in *The Affluent Worker* of the ways in which the workforce were recruited. Grieco (1981) has shown how Vauxhall in particular deliberately recruited non-unionised labour from peripheral areas of high unemployment, as well as acquiring Londoners through an Industrial Selection Scheme which provided public sector housing to those who had been offered a job. Both categories of worker were under pressure to migrate and to take the job offered and neither had adequate information to assess their future employment. As a labour force they were 'highly selected' not 'highly selective', and even in the conditions of relatively full employment at that time, constraint rather than choice characterised their moves to Luton. In other regions and in the more recent period the conditions necessary for self-selection to operate have, of course, been found even less frequently and generally than was assumed in the Affluent Worker project.

These reservations about the extent to which workers are able to choose their employment should not be allowed to obscure the evidence which exists as to the importance of orientations to work for choice of job, either through initial application or by a process of selective 'winnowing-out' in the early weeks of employment (see, for example, Cotgrove and Box 1970, Ch. 4). This is one area where the influence of orientations to work has been clearly shown, even if such influence is less frequent and operating within more severe constraints than may initially have been allowed for by Goldthorpe and his colleagues. Thus in the case of the Affluent Worker project Grieco's arguments restrict the extent of such influence rather than eliminate it altogether; and Ingham (1970, esp. 97) showed that the engineering workers he studied made relatively well-informed choices between small and large plants in terms of their different priorities regarding work. Blackburn and Mann (1979) have stressed the difficulties facing manual workers in the labour market due to the scarcity of information, and the cost of acquiring it, the opaqueness of employers' selection procedures and the inaccessibility of many jobs because of the existence of internal labour markets. Nevertheless they concluded that workers were likely to be in jobs where the rewards met the priorities in their orientations, at least to some extent, and that such congruence appeared to be the result of job choice rather than socialisation (241–2, 281).

The influence of orientations to work

Arguments about the influence of orientations to work on attitudes and behaviour at work must be more cautious and complex. The influence is not all one way, and the place of orientations in an account of work situations cannot be that of either an independent or a sole causal factor. Two studies, both published in the wake of the Affluent Worker project, illustrate the sort of conclusions which can be expected (see also the helpful discussion by Bechhofer 1973). In an investigation of workers' attitudes and behaviour in a large chemical complex in the north-east of England Wedderburn and Crompton (1972; see also Wedderburn 1972) reported that all the semi-skilled workers had primarily instrumental attitudes to work. Variations in their levels of job satisfaction and in their militancy, however, could be explained in terms of the differences in the technology of the three works on the site, and in the management style and control system associated with them. Beynon and Blackburn (1972) studied a luxury food factory in north-west England where men on night-shift carried out the same work (i.e. experienced an identical production system) as women on days. The differences in their levels of satisfaction, in their collective organisation and ability to exercise some control over the work situation, and in their relationship to management and to the union, reflected differences in their expectations and priorities regarding work. In both cases it was true that 'the way in which work is experienced. . .depends neither on work factors nor orientations alone but on the interaction of the two' (Beynon and Blackburn 1972, 157).

Prototypicality

Goldthorpe and his colleagues attempted to locate their study within a more general understanding of the changes taking place in Britain (and possibly in other industrialised societies) at the time so that they could refer to the 'affluent', 'instrumentally oriented' workers as 'prototypical'. Important elements in this argument were the comparison with the ideal typical solidaristically oriented worker and the link between the typology of orientations to work and the broader notion of 'images of society' (Lockwood 1966; Goldthorpe *et al.* 1969, esp. Ch. 5). The use of this latter notion has given rise to extensive debates which in many ways parallel the discussion of 'orientations to work': there are the same methodological problems of how to investigate and discover such 'images', and how coherent, clear and stable they could or should be expected to be; and there are many of the same questions as to the sources of 'images of society' and what, if any, influence they have, what part they play for example in explanations of class consciousness or collective action or inaction (see Bulmer 1975; Roberts *et al.* 1977; Davis 1979).

The argument about the prototypicality of the 'instrumentally oriented' worker depends on two major assertions. First, there is a comparison with workers who are 'traditional' not only in some ideal-typical sense but also historically, in that their solidaristic (or deferential) orientations to work were more common in the past and are now being displaced by the instrumental orientations of the 'privatised' worker. In the second place the mechanism for this is seen to lie in changes in the industrial structure which led to the decline and eventual disappearance of those industries, and communities, which generated such orientations to work, and in the growth of new industries and localities – like Luton – where the conditions for such orientations are unlikely to be found or to develop. The changes in industrial structure and in the associated communities have certainly occurred, though much more unevenly than has often been supposed, but there are weaknesses in both these main assertions.

Instrumental orientations to work were much more common in the past, and solidaristic ones rarer and more ambivalent, than a straightforward assumption of a secular decline in traditionalism would lead one to suppose. Indeed an alternative cyclical view of the sorts of changes in orientations and images which have taken place over the past century or more could be suggested: the privatised and instrumental worker was, and is, a common phenomenon in new or rapidly expanding communities with new sources of employment, and can be expected to be followed by a more solidaristic (or deferential) worker as stability in employment and residence allow industrial and community social relations and culture to develop; the continuing processes of industrial restructuring, however, mean that this cycle constantly recurs. This cyclical process has, of course, taken place against an overall secular rise in the standard of living – an increase in affluence; but Goldthorpe and his colleagues themselves argued that 'affluence' in and of itself had limited effects on social relations and social consciousness.

The implied historical comparison in *The Affluent Worker* must therefore be questioned; and so must the assumed connections between particular industrial and community contexts and images of society. The pattern of influences on them has been shown to be complex and confused. Similarly attempts to trace the connections between workplace and community characteristics and images of society have produced findings which are far from straightforward. Most industries had or have patterns of social relations between workers, and between workers and management, which were or are ambivalent, including both shared and conflicting interests. In addition a multitude of other situations and influences, such as education and the mass media, provide experiences and present interpretations of their society to its members which may be strongly at variance with the interpretations dominant at work. No simple relationship can be expected between work situations and images of society, and generalisation about such relationships is made particularly hazardous if it depends on stereotyped views about 'traditional' industries or about the changes which have taken place in the recent past.

Important elements of the notion of orientation to work have clearly survived the detailed critical consideration to which these ideas have been subjected. In this respect the debate launched by Goldthorpe and his colleagues in the mid-1960s has established the limitations of the human relations tradition, with its assumption of universal human needs, and of the technological implications approach, with its neglect of the definition of the situation of the actor. It has also established the importance of considering the influence of factors which are external to the enterprise on the attitudes and actions of those within it, and of the effects of labour market processes. The place of orientations to work within attempts to account for and explain social relations, actions and attitudes to work, however, is much more complex than was implied in the early confident formulations of the Affluent Worker project. Orientations to work are frequently not formed independently of the work situation and brought to it; and not only is the action which may result from particular orientations constrained by various conditions of action effectively outside the individual's or the group's control, but the orientations themselves are influenced by such conditions, by limited opportunities and the need to accommodate to the world 'as it is'.

The question remains, however, as to whether the 'action approach' more generally represented a viable alternative theoretical framework for the analysis of industrial organisations, and, if so, what its characteristics might be; this issue will be considered in the concluding section of this chapter.

THE SOCIAL ACTION APPROACH

A 'social action approach' in industrial sociology was advocated by Goldthorpe and his colleagues as a result of their experience of investigating embourgeoisement among affluent manual workers. It was not, however, formulated in any complete or detailed way within the corpus of writings which derived from that study, nor, given the unexpected and unintended nature of this emphasis, could that project be taken as an example of the proper application of such an approach. Even in the subsequent debates the focus was on the use, or abuse, of the notion of 'orientation to work', and on the implications of the substantive findings of the study for our understanding of industry, politics and the class structure. The development of an action approach to the analysis of industrial organisations was therefore carried forward by other writers, and, in some cases, in directions neither intended nor welcomed by the authors of *The Affluent Worker*.

Perhaps the most influential contributions to this process were those of Silverman (1968, and especially 1970). He provided some powerful criticisms of the reification embodied in systems thinking (see Chapter 2) and advocated an alternative 'action analysis of organisations' based on a view of the structure of organisations as the product of human beings pursuing their own ends with the available means. This approach drew on the tradition in social theory derived primarily from the work of Weber, as developed by Schutz and, more recently, Berger and Luckmann, Cicourel, Cohen and others (Silverman 1970, 126). It involved looking at six inter-related areas in the following sequence (154):

1 The nature of the role system and pattern of interaction that has been built up in the organisation, in particular the way in which it has historically developed and the extent to which it represents the shared values of all or some or none of the actors.

2 The nature of involvement of ideal-typical actors . . . and the characteristic hierarchy of ends which they pursue . . . The way in which these derive from their biographies outside the organisations . . . and from their experience of the organisation itself.

3 The actors' present definitions of their situation within the organisation and their expectations of the likely behaviour of others with particular reference to the strategic resources they perceive to be at their disposal and at the disposal of others . . .

4 The typical actions of different actors and the meaning which they attach to their action.

5 The nature and source of the intended and unintended consequences of action, with special reference to its effects on the involvement of the various actors and on the institutionalisation of expectations in the role-system within which they interact.

6 Changes in the involvement and ends of the actors and in the role-system, and in their source both in the outcome of the interaction of the actors and in the changing stock of knowledge outside the organisation . . .

Silverman used this framework to reinterpret a number of published studies but with one partial exception did not offer an original analysis of an organisation in these terms. He described 'the action approach' as 'a method of analysis rather than a theory' (1970, 222). In his concluding discussion he argued that such a method would allow sociologists to tackle some issues, such as change within organisations or the origins of policy, which had not, or only inadequately, been dealt with by systems approaches; and to take seriously questions of meaning and the implications of the W. I. Thomas dictum: 'If men define situations as real, they are real in their consequences.' Whilst in his earlier paper Silverman had suggested that the action approach might produce an open 'system' model of industrial organisations, this possibility was not reiterated in the book, although he did suggest that it could lead to both 'substantive' and 'formal' theory (the terms are from Glaser and Strauss 1968).

Thus, there appears to be some ambiguity in these writings and those of Goldthorpe and his colleagues as to whether a 'social action approach' to the analysis of industrial organisations should be seen as a corrective to systems approaches, and in some ways complementary to them, or as an alternative; and if as an alternative the extent to which there is fundamental incompatibility between the two approaches. This parallels the debates about theories of social action which have occurred in sociological theory more generally (see, for example, Dawe 1970, and especially 1979). As it developed historically in Britain in the 1960s the action approach appeared initially as a corrective to the then conventional sociology of industrial organisations and of industrial attitudes and behaviour; Goldthorpe and his colleagues were attempting to deal with some fairly specific and limited problems arising in their research. At the same time, however, more general criticisms were being articulated about conventional sociology in its functionalist and systems theory versions. These criticisms included the neglect of actors' definitions of their situations both as this affects substantive findings and predictions and in its implications for methods of research (e.g. Cicourel's strictures on the 'measurement by fiat', where those formulating questions made no attempt to discover and understand respondents' views of the world and the language they used to describe it [Cicourel 1964]). They included too the danger of 'reifying' organisations and other institutionalised sets of social relations and failing to explore and emphasise continually the ways in which they are socially constructed, socially sustained and socially changed (see, for example, Berger and Luckmann 1967); and the familiar arguments regarding the inadequacy of systems thinking and functionalism generally in accounting for conflict and change.

Silverman's *The Theory of Organisations* can be seen against this background as an attempt to spell out the implications of the criticisms for the analysis of organisations: the need for greater sophistication in research methods; exploration of actors' definitions of their situations and their consequences; awareness that terms like 'organisation' and 'role system' were a sort of shorthand used to refer to the intended and unintended consequences of particular patterns of action, though ones which could become highly institutionalised and take on an objective, thing-like quality; a concern with process and meaning rather than structure and cause; and so on. Although Rose (1988, 273–80) labelled it 'phenomenological actionalism', Burrell and Morgan (1979, 195–201) were probably more accurate in regarding it as, in their terms, within, even if on the borders of, the functionalist paradigm: 'a different way of studying the same reality'.

Though there would be disagreement about this it can be argued that an altogether more radical development in sociological analysis is inherent in the action approach; this is exemplified in some of Silverman's subsequent work, which is clearly not just a different way of studying the same reality (see Silverman 1972, 1975; Silverman and Jones 1973, 1976). Whereas the approach adopted in the Affluent Worker volumes involved distinguishing actors' definitions of the situation (their expectations of and attitudes towards the employing organisation, for example) from observed features of that situation (the firms' employment policies and production systems), accounting for them, and exploring the consequences of the workers' understandings for their behaviour, the phenomenological approach as spelt out by Silverman rejected this objective–subjective dichotomy. Social phenomena were seen as different in kind from natural phenomena; their reification in everyday life becomes something to be studied, not taken for granted:

> A phenomenological consciousness leads to a suspension of belief in the reality of these objects and an analysis of the social processes through which human definitions are objectivated by members. A profession, an organization or an ability range, to take three examples, are no longer treated as 'real' things, or as objects which (in the case of the first two) take actions to meet their needs; they are viewed instead as labels which members use to make sense of their activities and as ideologies used to defend these activities to others.
>
> (Silverman 1972, 68)

Because much conventional sociology operates with conceptions of 'organisation', for example, which are reified and objectified, pre-given in common-sense usage, it, like common-sense, obscures the ways in which such terms are used. The task of sociology in this view is to see how people make sense of the world, how they account for the actions of others and account to others for their actions. Questions as to the 'real' nature of the social world are irrelevant. As Silverman (1972, 168) explains in a footnote: 'I am not suggesting, however, that people are "wrong" in treating the world as real. The subsequent analysis, then, does not seek to remedy this view but to see how it is sustained and the "work" that it does.' (See also Silverman 1975, 300.)

In accordance with this conception of what it is possible for sociology to achieve a great deal of attention is given to the analysis of participants' accounts, their use of language, the ways in which they show their activities to be 'rational', that is 'in-accord-with-a-rule', and have them recognised and accepted by others as having that quality. At the same time it is argued that the conventional sociologist's account will not be fundamentally different from nor necessarily superior to the accounts which participants themselves construct and use to make sense of their world. The concepts used in industrial sociology are also used by laymen and the sociologist can only investigate this use, not try to establish it as 'correct', 'scientific' usage; for example, with reference to 'bureaucracy':

> Rather than seeking clearer specifications of what bureaucracy 'really means' or attempting to formulate 'operational definitions', the object of investigation becomes the manner in which a concept of bureaucracy is called upon, usually as a tacit resource, to display and to acknowledge the 'sense' of actions . . . . In itself, then, bureaucracy has neither an intrinsic meaning nor is it the determinant of actions – it does not have this kind of ontological status. Rather the concept of bureaucracy exists in and through the socially sanctioned occasions of its use.
>
> (Silverman 1975, 296–7)

In his own empirical work within this frame of reference Silverman has investigated the ways in which selection is 'managed' and 'accounted for' in large organisations (see Silverman and Jones 1973, 1976). Though the detailed materials are fascinating it is not possible to discuss them here, nor to provide a full discussion of the phenomenological and/or ethnomethodological approach within industrial sociology. That would involve discussions of the nature of the social world, of social sciences, and of the methods of enquiry available to them, which are beyond the scope of this volume (but see, for example, Burrell and Morgan 1979, Pt 1 and Chs 6 and 7; Mennell 1980, esp. 131–41; Lassman 1974). However, the selection study does provide a basis for arguing that despite the validity of some of the strictures on conventional sociology, a thorough-going phenomenological approach is seriously inadequate. It was apparent through the accounts of the interviews that the conversations and decisions reflected or displayed differences in power and authority, both between interviewers and candidates, and amongst the interviewers. Silverman reported and commented on one instance of this as follows:

> Thus the two parties talk to each other as a 'senior' and a 'junior' by displaying through their utterances the features of hierarchies. It should be stressed that hierarchies are relevant socially *only* to the extent that members attend to their existence as a relevant means for bringing off interactions. This is not, however, to engage in a solipsistic denial of the factual character of hierarchies. Rather the author is pointing out that only in and through members' activities do hierarchies acquire their facticity.
>
> (1975, 298–9)

Whilst accepting the point embodied in the final sentence it is important to note that an important characteristic of unequal distributions of power and resources, such as hierarchies represent, is that subordinate participants are compelled to attend to their existence by sanctions which can be applied regardless of their will. Insofar as approaches to the understanding and analysis of social life, which emphasise the central importance of actors' definitions and understandings of the situation, ignore distributions of power and resources which may be unrecognised by the actors but nevertheless constrain their actions, they are seriously deficient. At least in some formulations this seems to be the case with phenomenological versions of the action approach. The interactions and accounting practices, which are at the centre of the stage in their analyses, take place within a context, and although that context is the result, wholly or in part, of the actions of others it has to be considered as a given set of constraints so far as the analyses in question are concerned. 'Men' can 'define situations as real' only up to a point.

It is significant that in developing the type of more conventional action approach to the analysis of organisations advocated in *The Theory of Organisations* these have been some of the areas which have received attention. One influential idea has been the notion that organisations represent a 'negotiated order' (Strauss *et al.* 1963). Even sympathetic critics, however, have stressed that 'negotiation' does not necessarily, nor normally, take place between parties with equal power and resources; nor does it take place in isolation from the wider society from which those resources may be derived (Day and Day 1977). The 'political' nature of organisations has been emphasised by Salaman (1979) in a general study of 'work organisations', which explores the exercise of control and the resistance to its exercise, and shows how, in particular, knowledge and ideologies are used as resources by the parties to these conflicts (see also Pettigrew's [1973] case study of the introduction of a computer). Such concerns with questions of power and resources (material and ideational) and with the environment have been given additional emphasis in the last decade by the revival of a Marxist approach to industrial sociology, following the publication of Braverman's *Labor and Monopoly Capital* (1974), which is discussed in the next chapter.

By the end of the 1970s, at the latest, the debates and arguments which had been aroused by the publication of *The Affluent Worker* study had largely petered out. Though some researchers continued to develop such ideas the 'social action frame of reference', which drew especially on the work of Weber, was no longer very prominent. Many mainstream sociological accounts of industrial organisations or of attitudes to work and/or behaviour at work included consideration of the actors' 'orientations', but few, if any, gave them the explanatory importance which had been suggested by Goldthorpe and his colleagues.

One of the positive features of the action approach, however, was that it allowed for the possibility of conflict within industrial organisations wherever the interests of different groupings of actors, as they perceived them, were opposed. Such a position represented a distinct improvement over systems approaches, though it did not satisfy those who asserted an inherent conflict of interest between management and worker, capital and labour, regardless of actors' views of the situation. This was the view to be found in the Marxist analysis of the 'capitalist labour process' which became the centre of attention from the late 1970s, and which appeared to be able to offer a more comprehensive framework. Labour process analysis focuses on processes of control and resistance, conflict and negotiation. The action approach could claim to be able to contribute to an understanding of these processes too, though this potential has not so far been fully developed nor widely recognised and used.

Chapter 5

Labour power and the labour process

Traditionally the academic study of work and work relations has been distributed among managerial studies and organization theory, industrial relations, the sociology of occupations, and something called industrial sociology. However, industrial sociology never amounted to an integrated subject . . . Braverman's major contribution was to smash through the academic barriers and offer the potential for the birth of a new, *integrated* approach to the study and history of work.

(Littler 1982, 25–6)

By the mid-1970s there was a sense that the sociology of industrial organisations was ready for a fresh input. This is apparent in Michael Rose's lively review (first published in 1975) of 'theoretical development since Taylor' in the study of what he termed 'industrial behaviour'.

But any new approach to industrial behaviour must begin from an altogether different standpoint from that adopted, consciously or otherwise, to date. Under prevailing conditions it would imply a study of the changing forms and consequences of socio-economic exploitation in the production of all goods and services, especially of those consequences which generate challenges to the principle of exploitation itself.

(Rose 1975, 277)

As is apparent in the second edition of Rose's book, published in 1988, where more than one hundred additional pages accompany the substantially revised original text, both new specifications of the problems and new ways of discussing them did appear on the scene very soon, and have by now generated a very considerable literature. At the centre of this intellectual activity have been the debates about 'the labour process'.

The term 'the labour process' is derived from Marx's discussion of the nature of capitalist society, notably in *Capital* itself (Vol. 1, Marx 1976, esp. 283 *et seq.*); its meaning and connotations are outlined later. Marx's ideas have been influential within industrial sociology for many years, especially with regard to attempts to understand the origins and manifestations of industrial conflict (and also in the discussion of 'alienation' and employees' attitudes to and satisfaction with their work). However, as Nichols (1980, 15–16) points out, Marx's writings on the labour process had been largely neglected until recently, even by writers who drew their inspiration from Marx. This was the case not only for those writers whose interests were too 'theoretical' (as Nichols suggests) but also for writers concerned to explain the practicalities of industrial conflict and industrial relations from a Marxist perspective. The term is given no prominence at all, for example, in influential writings on industrial conflict by Allen (1971, 1975) and Hyman (1975, 1977), both of whom explicitly adopted a Marxist per-spective. The single most important event which led to a change in this situation was the publication of Braverman's *Labor and Mono-poly Capital* in 1974. Although its limitations are better appreciated and more widely acknowledged now than they were in the early years after publication, Braverman's book remains the most appropriate point of reference for the labour process debate.

With hindsight it is possible to see that the importance of Braverman's work may initially have been exaggerated. He himself tended to dismiss most other work in industrial sociology as largely irrelevant to an understanding of management–worker relations in industrial organisations, and for a time such a claim was often accepted (see, for example, Thompson 1983, 11–34). The con-tinuing relevance and usefulness of much earlier research is now more widely recognised even by writers sympathetic to Braver-man's approach (see, for example, Burawoy 1978, esp. 267–8; and Thompson 1983, 34–7). Indeed, it has been rightly pointed out that not all of what Braverman had to say was as new as he appeared to claim; some of his concerns, such as the critique of Scientific Management and the discussion of 'de-skilling', can be found, to give one notable example, in the work of one of the founding fathers of French industrial sociology, Georges Fried-mann (1955, 1961; see Rose 1988, 285–6, 319–21), though not altogether in terms of which Braverman would have approved. Indeed there have always been industrial sociologists who were sceptical of the importance accorded to Braverman's book (see Eldridge 1983) or who saw 'the revived Marxist perspective' as one strand to be combined with others from quite different theoretical roots (Hill 1981, viii). It is also important to emphasise that from very early on Braverman's arguments gave rise to a debate with little agreement as to which parts of his thesis could be accepted unamended and which should be modified, or indeed rejected altogether, in the light of empirical, and especially historical, evidence or theoretical critique. As is the case with the other perspectives discussed in this book, the end result of more than a decade of discussion has been to leave an approach which is both less distinct from other approaches and more subject to reservations and uncertainties than was initially claimed.

Labor and Monopoly Capital was published in 1974. At that time there were a number of ongoing developments in the sociology of work and industry which provided particularly fertile soil for Braverman's contribution. Three of these – the debates about theoretical perspectives within industrial relations, the growing interest in labour market segmentation, and the concern with work organisation – will be considered briefly in the next section. Despite this favourable context, however, it was some years before the influence of Braverman's book was at all widespread, and only perhaps in the 1980s that the labour process debate came to dominate the sociology of industrial organisations. The Open University course, *People and Work* (DE351), for example, published in 1976, only referred to Braverman in one of the sixteen units, significantly one written by Nichols (1976). Some of the social scientists who were first to draw attention to his work were economists rather than sociologists (for example, Friedman 1977a, 1977b; Brighton Labour Process Group 1977). In Britain specifically sociological discussion came towards the end of the 1970s (see, for example, the brief references in Nichols and Armstrong 1976, 215; and Nichols and Beynon 1977, 108); and, more especially, in the 1980s, stimulated by books like Nichols's (1980) collection of readings and Thompson's (1983) review of the debate, and by the annual labour process conferences which have been organised at the Universities of Aston and Manchester since 1983. For most of the 1980s, however, the labour process debate dominated discussion in industrial sociology, and only very recently has its importance appeared to be on the wane. No new perspective has yet clearly taken its place, though there are a number of contenders such as concerns with modernism and post-modernism, and arguments about new forms of flexibility in organisations.

After outlining in the next section three areas in the study of work which were important for understanding the context in which *Labor and Monopoly Capital* was published, we shall turn in the following section to consider briefly the account of the labour process given by Marx himself; this provides an essential basis for understanding Braverman's arguments and the debates to which they have given rise, which are the main topic of this chapter.

PREPARING THE GROUND – INDUSTRIAL SOCIOLOGY IN THE 1970s

Industrial relations

In his Research Paper for the Royal Commission on Trade Unions and Employers' Associations, published in 1966, Alan Fox set out very clearly the view of employer–employee relations which was dominant among academic students of industrial relations at that time. In contrast to the 'unitary' view of the industrial enterprise held by many employers and managers he argued convincingly for a 'pluralist' perspective. The former, unitary, view assumes that all members of an enterprise share common interests; the enterprise is a team with 'one source of authority and one focus of loyalty'. Opposition to this authority (management) is either due to mis-understanding, to be met by improved communications, or is the action of malcontents or subversives who have no legitimacy and can and should be forcefully suppressed (see Fox 1966, and also 1973).

In contrast the pluralist view recognises that any enterprise is 'a coalition of individuals and groups'. They are mutually dependent but have different interests and priorities and the terms of their collaboration have to be set by bargaining. 'Conflict is endemic to industrial organization' (Fox 1966, 8). To advocate courses of action which are opposed to those proposed by management remains legitimate, and tensions and conflicts within the organ-isation have to be managed not suppressed. Disruptive levels of conflict indicate that the procedures for dealing with disputes need to be renegotiated. The pluralist position also implies that it is possible to achieve consensus on appropriate procedures, and that there are no differences which, with goodwill on both/all sides, cannot be settled satisfactorily and result in an acceptable and workable compromise. Despite the acknowledgement of inherent differences of interest it is implied that there is an underlying normative consensus, a position – as Fox points out – compatible with at least some versions of normative functionalism (Fox 1973, 214).

This pluralist perspective on industrial organisations and industrial conflict was the dominant viewpoint among industrial relations academics even before Fox produced his Research Paper. (As Fox noted, it had, for example, been clearly formulated in a paper published eight years earlier [Ross 1958].) It received powerful endorsement in the *Report* of the Royal Commission (1968). The unitary view, of course, continued to be reflected in the pronouncements and actions of some employers (and politicians), but initially among academic commentators the only serious criticisms of pluralism, and the liberal-reformist policy prescriptions associated with it, came from the few who pursued an avowedly Marxist analysis. They saw industrial conflict as one important manifestation of wider conflicts between classes whose differing interests could never be reconciled within the framework of a capitalist society.

In this context Fox's reconsideration of his earlier position, in a paper delivered to the British Universities Industrial Relations Association in 1972, proved something of a bombshell. As he records in his autobiography it aroused highly diverse reactions, ranging from 'and about time too', through a sense of intellectual liberation, to alarm and disapproval. The last was diminished by Fox's argument that 'the nature of one's analysis did not necessarily determine the nature of one's policy prescriptions' (i.e. a Marxist type of analysis did not necessarily lead to support for revolutionary change) (Fox 1990, 236–42).

What Fox argued was that the pluralist perspective was fundamentally deficient in its assumption of a rough balance of power among the various interest groups that make up capitalist society, and the capitalist industrial enterprise. This not only misrepresented but also helped to conceal the real power of the owners and controllers of property rights in economic resources. In that way pluralism is an ideology as much as is the unitary perspective. The bargaining which the pluralists saw as evidence of the negotiation of order within the enterprise is effective only at the margins, and can be considered to take place under duress; it does not include the possibility of challenging or changing the underlying and unequal distribution of power and resources in society.

Fox's alternative to pluralism, a radical perspective, involved an analysis of society, and of industrial enterprises, which recognised the fundamental inequalities of condition and opportunity inherent in capitalist society and the basic relationships of domination and subordination between classes. One might not see any acceptable way of changing this state of affairs, but it was important to analyse it properly. Other influential social theorists put forward similar analyses at much the same time (e.g. Goldthorpe 1977). As Fox acknowledged his analysis drew upon and closely followed those derived from Marxist bases, but, as already noted, he explicitly separated his analysis either from policy prescriptions – for example the desirability of reforms of property relations or of the management of industrial enterprises – or, still more, from prediction – the inevitability of a proletarian revolution. The later views of Fox, and those who argued along similar lines, were less widely accepted and less influential among experts and practitioners in industrial relations than his Research Paper for the Royal Commission had been, but they probably became the accepted position for most industrial sociologists. As such they provided a favourable context for the reception of Braverman's restatement of the Marxist analysis of the labour process.

Labour market segmentation

For many years the labour market was seen as an area of social life of interest primarily to economists, and their analyses focused especially on the ways in which such markets operate to determine the price of labour, wage and salary levels, and the level of economic activity, employment and unemployment. At least two developments in the 1960s led sociologists to give greater attention to labour market processes and to begin to develop specifically sociological analyses of them. In the first place Goldthorpe and his colleagues' accounts of the orientations to work of the affluent manual workers in Luton included an emphasis on the ways in which the workforces in the factories they studied were in effect 'self-selected'. Such an argument drew attention to the need to consider the operation of the relevant labour market(s) if one was to gain an adequate understanding of the determinants of the priorities and expectations of employees in any enterprise. A concern to follow up this lead was evident in two books which were clearly influenced by the Affluent Worker studies, though they also developed quite independent analyses of their own: Mann's (1973) study of the relocation of General Foods Ltd from central Birmingham to Banbury, and Blackburn and Mann's (1979) study of the Peterborough labour market for non-skilled male manual workers.

Secondly, research on poverty, deprivation and discrimination, both in the USA and in the UK (e.g. Townsend 1979), had revealed the persistence of disadvantaged groups in society (especially women and ethnic minorities) despite policies and programmes to reduce or eliminate such conditions. In many cases the disadvantages stemmed either from unemployment or from under- or sub-employment in a series of low paid and insecure jobs. Rather than such situations being attributable to the inadequacies of the disadvantaged (their lack of appropriate skills [human capital], experience and work motivation), analysts argued that such low quality employment opportunities were a permanent feature of labour market structures, and that discriminatory recruitment practices ensured that certain categories of employee were likely to fill them. Those who did so, of course, were unlikely if not unable to secure the skills, experience and motivation which would give them a realistic chance of obtaining higher paid and more secure employment in the future. The concepts of 'dual' and 'segmented' labour markets became widely accepted (see e.g. Doeringer and Piore 1971; Amsden 1980). The former notion, for example, was used in an influential paper by Barron and Norris (1976) to provide an explanation for the low pay and inferior employment opportunities for women workers in Britain.

Labour market processes are of interest and importance in their own right and the beginnings of a sociological analysis of them must be welcomed. In the present context, however, one aspect of this analysis is particularly important: the links between the structuring of the labour force through processes of segmentation and the possibilities open to employers to control the employees they subsequently recruit to these differentiated positions. Though it is important to recognise that not all segmentation can be attributed to employers' interests and actions – workers and their trade unions can play an important part too (see Rubery 1978) – the use of labour market segmentation by employers to 'divide and rule' their employees was an element in many analyses of industrial organisations from the 1970s onwards. Such tactics could be particularly effective when divisions on grounds of occupation and skill were made to coincide with differences in other social characteristics – ethnic origin, gender, language, religion, age and so on. As we shall see such an analysis proved highly compatible with many of the developments after 1974 in the analysis of the control of the labour process.

Work organisation

The third topic of enquiry which contributed to preparing the ground for the labour process debate was the study of work organisation. There were a number of reasons for a growing interest in work organisation from the 1960s onwards. The overall effect was to direct attention to the details of the ways in which tasks were specified and jobs designed, allocated and controlled. Though the orientation of much of this work was very different from that of labour process analysis it did draw attention to the importance of the same issues.

One starting point can be traced in the easier availability of Marx's early writings, and especially his 'Economic and Philosophical Manuscripts' (see Bottomore 1963). This gave wider currency to the notion of alienation and to the alienating consequences of the ways in which much industrial work was organised. Although he used it in a way which gave it a much more narrowly psychological emphasis than can be found in Marx's own formulations, alienation provided writers like Blauner (1964) with an essential link between the characterisation of industrial situations in terms of their technology and the exploration of the consequences for the worker which followed from working in each type of production system. Within the technological implications approach the structure of work tasks and roles were taken largely as determined by the technology. The notion of a degree of 'organisational choice', however, as advocated by the socio-technical systems theorists, made it relevant to analyse the organisation of work to see whether less alienating/more satisfying arrangements could be devised. Whilst socio-technical systems theorists did not generally refer to 'alienation' as such, Neo-Human Relations ideas which informed some of their thinking, such as the desirability of 'self-actualisation' in work, were not incompatible with the usage of the term by Blauner and others.

From the late 1960s there was considerable activity on both sides of the Atlantic to improve the quality of working life by, among other things, discovering and securing the adoption of new forms of work organisation (see Davis and Taylor 1972; Littler and Salaman 1984, esp. Ch. 5). Some of the changes proposed were relatively trivial – for example, much job rotation, job enlargement and job enrichment (see Nichols and Beynon 1977, 16). In other cases there were more thoroughgoing attempts to redesign work to give workers greater autonomy and more possibility of deriving some sense of satisfaction and achievement from their labours. In the 1970s Swedish industry gained a reputation for being at the forefront of such developments (they had been influenced by the ideas of the Tavistock researchers, which had subsequently been applied to work organisation in Norway and from there had been introduced into Sweden). In 1974 the then Social Science Research Council organised a conference in London to publicise the Swedish experience (Gregory 1978). One consequence of the interest this aroused was the establishment of a Working Party by the Management and Industrial Relations Committee of the SSRC to consider research needs in work organisation. The Working Party's report (SSRC 1978) advocated a considerable increase in research funding in this area, a recommendation which was accepted, though only in part. At much the same time the government supported Work Research Unit was established to provide advice and assistance to managers and trade unionists in firms undertaking work reorganisation.

The late 1960s and the 1970s were a period of considerable industrial unrest (see Crouch and Pizzorno 1977; Crouch 1977). Though in most analyses it would only be one factor, the nature of the work manual and routine white collar employees were required to do came to be seen as both contributing to this dissatisfaction and something which could, in principle, be improved by drawing on the lessons of social science research. The ways in which work was organised, and the assumptions which underlay the design of many jobs, were seen as issues of practical importance as well as of theoretical interest. ('Industrial democracy' and greater opportunities for worker participation in decision making were also advocated as solutions to the 'crisis' during this period – see Ramsay 1977.) In both areas further research tended to show both that the actual changes which could be observed were fewer and less radical than had sometimes been believed and that their consequences for the degree of 'alienation', worker satisfaction, or whatever were somewhat less than had been hoped for. An emphasis on the labour process was congruent with these developments in that it too focused attention on the organisation of work at the point of production; the analysis offered by Braverman, however, had the advantage in this context of appearing also to offer an explanation of why changes in work organisation in capitalist industrial societies were always likely to be limited in scope and in their effects.

MARX

Marx defined the labour process 'in its simple and abstract elements' as 'purposeful activity aimed at the production of use-values' (Marx 1976, 290). Considered in its most general sense, that is 'independently of any specific social formation', the labour process refers to man's (*sic*) efforts to 'appropriate the materials of nature in a form adapted to his own needs' (283); to the activities of changing the form of natural materials to achieve certain purposes which the worker already has in mind before starting work (and in the process also changing his own nature). 'The simple elements of the labour process are (1) purposeful activity, that is work itself, (2) the object on which that work is performed, and (3) the instruments of that work' (284). The product of the labour process is a 'use-value, a piece of natural material adapted to human needs by means of a change in its form', and in the process of producing this product labour becomes 'bound up in its object' or 'objectified' (287). Some use-values, products of previous labour, are not consumed directly but are either the raw materials or the instruments of labour of subsequent labour processes.

For Marx the value of any commodity was determined by the amount of labour socially necessary for its production (Marx 1976, 129). This labour includes both that required in the immediate labour process which gave rise to the product, and also an appropriate proportion of the labour necessary to produce the raw materials (i.e. any natural materials which have been worked on) and the other means of production (tools, machinery, etc.) which have been used – and to a degree used up – in the process of production. 'Use-values' defined in this way, have to be distinguished from 'exchange-values', the prices or relative values at which commodities may be exchanged in the market.

The specifically capitalist labour process is one in which the purpose of the activity is laid down by the capitalist, and the means of production, both the objects on which work is to be carried out and the instruments to be used in performing the work, are the property of the capitalist. The essential preconditions for the development of the capitalist labour process are therefore twofold: the existence of a category or class of persons who have accumulated sufficient resources to be able to employ workers and to provide the raw materials and buildings, tools, machinery, etc. necessary for production to take place; and the existence of a category or class of persons who lack the means of production themselves and therefore have no other commodities to sell than their own capacity to work. This they must be both *free* to sell (i.e. they must not be legally prevented from doing so as, for example, slaves would be), and *forced* to sell in order to provide themselves with the means of subsistence. In many societies during the world's history, of course, such conditions have not existed, and the ways in which such a situation developed, initially in Britain and subsequently in many parts of the world, are too complex to discuss here (but for Marx's discussion of 'so-called primitive accumulation' in the British case see Marx 1976, Pt 8).

What workers bring to the market to sell, however, is not their labour but their labour power.

> 'As soon as his labour actually begins,' says Marx, 'it has already ceased to belong to him; it can therefore no longer be sold by him'. At the most, he might sell his future labour, that is, undertake to perform a certain amount of work in a definite time. In so doing, however, he does not sell labour (which would first have to be performed) but puts his labour power at the disposal of the capitalist for a definite time (in the case of time-work) or for the purpose of a definite output (in the case of piece-work) in return for a definite payment: he hires out, or sells, his *labour power*. But this labour power is intergrown with his person and inseparable from it.
>
> (Engels 1958, 75)

Workers make available their capacity to work for a given period of time. This capacity can only be realised (labour power can only be transformed into labour) over time in the course of the working day, week or year. This involves the worker entering into a continuing relationship with the capitalist employer and working under his or her direction:

> The labour process, when it is the process by which the capitalist consumes labour-power, exhibits two characteristic phenomena. First, the worker works under the control of the capitalist to whom his labour belongs; the capitalist takes good care that the work is done in a proper manner, and the means of production are applied directly to the purpose, so that the raw material is not wasted, and the instruments of labour are spared, i.e. only worn to the extent necessitated by their use in the work.
>
> Secondly, the product is the property of the capitalist and not that of the worker, its immediate producer. Suppose that a capitalist pays for a day's worth of labour-power; then the right to use that power for a day belongs to him, just as much as the right to use any other commodity . . . . The use of a commodity belongs to its purchaser, and the seller of labour-power, by giving his labour, does no more, in reality, than part with the use-value he has sold.
>
> (Marx 1976, 291–2)

Under capitalism labour power becomes a commodity which can be bought and sold in the market. Like other commodities its value is determined for Marx by the 'socially necessary' labour time needed for its production, though spelling out what this means becomes rather more complex than is the case with other commodities such as tools, machines and raw materials:

> Labour-power exists only as a capacity of the living individual. Its production consequently presupposes his existence . . . the production of labour-power consists in his reproduction of himself or his maintenance. For his maintenance he requires a certain quantity of the means of subsistence. Therefore the labour-time necessary for the production of labour-power is the same as that necessary for the production of those means of subsistence; in other words, the value of labour-power is the

value of the means of subsistence necessary for the maintenance of the owner.

(Marx 1976, 274)

But during the course of his work the worker expends effort and
'his means of subsistence must be sufficient to maintain him in his
normal state as a working individual'. This may vary as between
societies and over time: 'the determination of the value of labour-
power contains a historical and moral element', but 'in a given
country at a given period, the average amount of the means of
subsistence necessary for the worker is a known *datum*' (275).
Further, the value spent in producing labour power must include
the expenses of education and training ('exceedingly small in the
case of ordinary labour-power') (276). And finally, as the worker is
mortal 'the labour-power withdrawn from the market by wear and
tear, and by death, must be continually replaced by, at the very
least, an equal amount of fresh labour-power. Hence the sum of
the means of subsistence necessary for the production of labour-
power must include the means necessary for the worker's replace-
ments, i.e. his children' (275).

In Marx's analysis, therefore, the value of the labour power
'consumed' by the capitalist in the course of employing the
worker, and consequently the price which on average the employer will have to pay to secure such work capacities, is determined by the socially necessary costs of producing, maintaining
and reproducing the worker who embodies that capacity. The
crucial characteristic of labour power, however, which for Marx
distinguished it from the other means of production, was that it
had the capacity to create new value, more value than was necessary merely to maintain and reproduce itself.

the value of labour-power, and the value which that labour-
power valorizes . . . in the labour process, are two entirely
different magnitudes; and the difference was what the capitalist
had in mind when he was purchasing the labour-power. . . .
What was really decisive for him was the specific use-value which
this commodity possesses of being a source not only of value,
but of more value than it has itself.

(Marx 1976, 300–1)

To put it in its most basic terms, the worker could recreate the value used up in the exercise of his (or her) labour power for a day (or week, etc.) by working for only part of that day (or week). If he or she worked for longer (if in Marx's terms they provided 'surplus labour'), the capitalist would gain the benefit of the extra value so created ('the surplus value'). Surplus value provided the capitalist's profits, and made capital accumulation possible, as well as providing for the payment of rent and interest where these were due. To use the terminology adopted by Marx, the capitalist 'labour process' is also and simultaneously a 'valorisation process'.

The employer would not have to pay extra for this 'surplus' because he or she had already paid the full cost of employing the worker.

> By paying the daily or weekly value of the labouring power of the workman, the capitalist has, therefore, acquired the right to use or make that labouring power work during the *whole day or week.* The working day or the working week has, of course, certain limits, but those we shall afterwards look more closely at . . . . The *value* of the labouring power is determined by the quantity of labour necessary to maintain or reproduce it, but the *use* of that labouring power is only limited by the active energies and physical strength of the labourer. The daily or weekly *value* of the labouring power is quite distinct from the daily or weekly exercise of that power . . . . The quantity of labour by which the *value* of the workman's labouring power is limited forms by no means a limit to the quantity of labour which his labouring power is apt to perform.
>
> (Marx 1958, 427)

It is an important part of Marx's argument that in the capitalist system it seems to the worker that he or she has been paid for the whole of their daily or weekly labour. 'Although one part only of the workman's daily labour is *paid,* while the other part is *unpaid,* and while that unpaid or surplus labour constitutes exactly the fund out of which *surplus value or profit* is formed, it seems as if the aggregate labour was paid labour' (Marx 1958, 429). This distinguishes capitalism from other modes of production. In the case of slavery, for example, it appears as if no part of the labour of the slave is paid for, though in reality part of the slave's work goes to meet the costs of his or her own maintenance. In contrast in the case of serfdom, it can be obvious that the peasant's work is divided between time spent on his own land providing for himself and his family, and unpaid labour on the lord's land. In the case of wage labour under capitalism the existence of such 'unpaid labour' is concealed by the wage form.

Having established the notions of surplus labour and surplus value in this way (and his discussion was, of course, very much longer and more complex than it is possible to indicate here) Marx described the ways in which capitalist employers could and did attempt to secure and increase the surplus value derived from their purchase of labour power, their employment of workers. The most basic consideration is the length of the working day, for the amount of surplus value produced will increase directly the longer the worker works over and above the minimum period necessary to restore the value of his or her labour power. The length of the working day was seen by Marx as indeterminate: it could not for long remain at a shorter period than was necessary to maintain the value of labour power, but, though there might be physiological limits, the maximum possible could not be established un-contentiously. Hence struggles over the length of the working day were a characteristic feature of the development of capitalist industry in the eighteenth and nineteenth centuries and have by no means disappeared today. Secondly, however, if workers could be made to work more *intensively* they could cover the costs of their labour power in a shorter period of time, leaving a longer propor-tion of the working day, also with this more intensive working, for the production of surplus value. These two types of surplus value were labelled 'absolute' and 'relative' by Marx.

> I call that surplus-value which is produced by the lengthening of the working day, *absolute surplus-value*. In contrast to this, I call that surplus-value which arises from the curtailment of the necessary labour-time, and from the corresponding alteration in the respective lengths of the two components of the working day, *relative surplus-value*.
>
> (Marx 1976, 432)

This distinction between absolute and relative surplus value is associated by Marx with a distinction between what he terms the 'formal' and the 'real subsumption of labour'. With the formal subsumption (or subordination) of labour to capital workers depend on the capitalist employer for both their means of production and their means of subsistence; but the production process itself may be little changed from that characteristic of pre-capitalist modes of production. In contrast the production of relative surplus value involves major and continuing changes in both the technical processes and the social organisation of work: the direct application of science and technology, an increasingly detailed division of labour, an increase in the scale of production and in the capital required, mechanisation, and the subordination of the worker to much greater and more detailed control by the capitalist employer (Marx 1976, 645, 1019–38).

The attempts by capitalist employers to maximise surplus value by maintaining or extending the length of the working day and/or intensifying labour, and the conflicts which result as workers resist, are central to Marx's understanding of the labour process under capitalism. They do not, however, exhaust the ways in which surplus value, and the accumulation of capital, may be increased. Marx identified the productivity of labour, which depended on the 'degree of development attained by the conditions of production', as a third influence on 'the relative magnitudes of surplus value and the price of labour power' (1976, 655). For example, if other conditions remain unchanged, Marx argued that increasing productivity will increase surplus value by reducing the value of labour power (by reducing the cost of the means of subsistence); workers will be able to create value equal to these costs in a shorter period of time (656–60). Similarly if the costs of labour power can be reduced, for example by employing unskilled workers instead of skilled, or women and children instead of men, surplus value can be increased; and mechanisation and/or the reorganisation of work can be very important in this context.

Marx (1976, esp. 781–802) also argued that increasing labour productivity and the changing 'organic composition of capital' (an increased use of fixed capital in relation to variable capital, labour power) would give rise to a 'relative surplus population' or 'industrial reserve army'. This mass of unemployed and irregularly employed workers makes an important contribution to capitalists' ability to exploit labour by ensuring that the supply of labour exceeds the demand for it, thereby keeping wages low.

The development of capitalist industry, in which these processes occurred, involved a number of distinct stages. The income of the small masters in handicraft trades depended as much or more on their own productive work as on any surplus value extracted from the labour of their apprentices and assistants. For Marx, 'capitalist production only really begins . . . when each individual capital simultaneously employs a comparatively large number of workers, and when, as a result, the labour-process is carried on on an extensive scale, and yields relatively large quantities of products' (1976, 439). 'Manufacture', as Marx termed it, initially involved merely the employment of large numbers of workers; the differences were quantitative. However, such an increase in scale made possible both cooperation between workers and, as a further but related step, an increased division of labour. Under the direct authority of the employer workers could be employed on a small part of the total task; their labour could be regulated by the flow of work through the factory; and, as a hierarchy of labour power developed, simpler tasks could be allocated to less skilled (and therefore cheaper) workers. Such tendencies were greatly increased by the introduction of 'machinery and large-scale industry'. Under both 'manufacture' and even more so with mechanisation this division of labour in detail – something Marx saw as specific to the capitalist mode of production – enriched the productive power of the 'collective worker' but at the cost of impoverishing the worker's individual productive powers (1976, 455–91).

Marx argued that the capitalist system compelled capitalist employers constantly to strive to augment their capital, to reduce the costs of production and increase the rate at which they extracted surplus value. The alternative was to be forced out of business by competitors who could undercut them. Thus the developments discussed above – lengthening the working day, intensifying labour, increasing the division of labour, mechanisation – are inherent in capitalism; but they are also measures likely to bring employers into conflict with their employees as workers resisted the cheapening of their labour power and the worsening of their conditions of employment.

Marx's writings, in *Capital* and elsewhere, are, of course, concerned with the development and characteristics of the social and economic system of a capitalist society as a whole, and not just with the structure and operation of industrial organisations in such a system. Nevertheless it is clear that his analysis provides a very rich source for anyone with the more limited interests. There have, of course, been important developments within capitalist societies since Marx wrote, many of which affect the structure and operation of industrial enterprises, for example changing patterns of ownership and control, and the growth of trade unions. These changes have been the source of continuing debates, particularly in relation to discussions of class structure, consciousness and action, debates which cannot be considered further here (see, for example, Dahrendorf 1959). Despite such arguments about the need to revise if not abandon Marx it remains surprising that Marx's writings on the labour process remained neglected for so long.

In his valuable introduction to the labour process debate Thompson attributes this neglect of Marx's discussion of the labour process to two main factors. In the first place there was the division in Marxist thought between 'economics' and 'politics', and what happened in the workplace was seen as necessarily restricted to 'economistic' demands and a limited trade union consciousness; the really important areas for thought and action were the political party and the wider class struggle. Secondly, in self-claimed 'socialist' societies from 1917 onwards the leaders, and most notably Lenin, accepted the methods and organisation of industrial work developed in the West as the technically most advanced (and as socially neutral); these methods could be adopted without question as long as there was state ownership and control of the means of production, distribution and exchange. Rather similarly the Labour party in Britain and other socialists here and elsewhere concentrated on obtaining political power through parliament, and on programmes of nationalisation, with little consideration of the organisation or control of work (Thompson 1983, 58–63).

A further factor can be added. As will be apparent from the account of it given above Marx's discussion of the labour process is based on the labour theory of value. This is dismissed as irrelevant, or worse, by most modern economists, and has been the subject of considerable controversy even amongst Marxists and others sympathetic to his approach (see for example Steedman *et al.* 1981). Most sociologists have hesitated to get involved in such stormy waters; Nichols, for example, more or less explicitly by-passes any such discussion (e.g. 1980, 35, 41); and – though of course this does not apply to Nichols – as a result the rest of Marx's discussion of the labour process has been neglected. It can be argued, however, that much of what Marx had to say about the relations between capital and labour, and employer and employee, remains of relevance whatever position one takes on his theory of value.

BRAVERMAN

Much of the impact created by the publication of *Labor and Monopoly Capital* can be attributed to the way in which Braverman combined in one book a number of rather different types of material. He restated in a straightforward and accessible way Marx's ideas about the nature of the labour process under capitalism, ideas which as we have seen had been largely neglected until this point; he extended that analysis to his own times, the era of 'monopoly capitalism', drawing attention especially to the ideas embodied in Scientific Management (or Taylorism) which he saw as the pervasive basis for the organisation and control of work in the twentieth century; and he provided a detailed account and discussion of the changing American occupational and class structure and of the ways in which paid work of all types was being 'degraded'. The book therefore combined a basically pessimistic and critical account of the changing nature of work, rich in example and corroborative detail, with an analysis which provided a fundamentally simple and highly plausible explanation of these trends. The account resonated with contemporary concerns about work and its discontents in the USA, and in other highly industrialised societies, and the explanatory framework appeared more powerful than any other currently available perspective.

For Braverman, as for Marx, production processes in capitalist societies are 'incessantly transformed under the impetus of the principal driving force of that society, the accumulation of capital' (Braverman 1974, 8–9). He rejected a simplistic reading of Marx as seeing the mode of production as technologically determined and emphasised the ways in which it is continually being worked out and developed. His account has a strong historical emphasis: 'the manner in which labor processes are organized and carried out is the "product" of the social relations we know as capitalist. But the shape of our society . . . is not an instantaneous creation of "laws" . . . . Every society is a moment in the historical process' (1974, 21).

Human work, argued Braverman, is distinguished from the work done by animals by the fact that it is 'conscious and purposive', not instinctual (46). It involves both conception and execution; but the link between these two can be broken: 'The unity of conception and execution may be dissolved' (51). Human labour is also indeterminate. Capitalism is distinguished as an economic system by the purchase and sale of labour power, but, following Marx, 'what the worker sells, and what the capitalist buys, is *not an agreed amount of labor, but the power to labor over an agreed period of time*' (54).

> It thus becomes essential for the capitalist that control over the labor process pass from the hands of the worker into his own. This transition presents itself in history as the *progressive alienation of the process of production* from the worker; to the capitalist, it presents itself as the problem of *management.*
>
> (58)

In the earlier stages of capitalism employers tried to avoid this problem of management by purchasing 'a definite quantity of work', using a variety of subcontracting and putting out systems. But this deprived the capitalist of much of the potential of human labour power. If the capitalist was to 'show a surplus and accumulate capital' he had to centralise employment (concentrate workers in one place) and exercise management which 'was far more complete, self-conscious, painstaking, and calculating than anything that had gone before' (65). As we have seen, in these circumstances a greatly increased division of labour was possible, the division of labour in detail, breaking the production process up into its constituent parts, which could then be allocated to largely unskilled and therefore cheaper workers (77–83).

To this point in his argument Braverman follows Marx closely, though his emphasis is somewhat different:

> The distinctive capacity of human labor power is therefore not its ability to produce a surplus, but rather its intelligent and purposive character, which gives it infinite adaptability and which produces the social and cultural conditions for enlarging its own productivity, so that its surplus product may be continuously enlarged.
>
> (56)

This emphasis is important for the next stage of the argument, the stress on the significance of Scientific Management.

Scientific Management is the name given to developments, initially in the USA, at the end of the nineteenth and the beginning of the twentieth centuries which involved the application of supposedly 'scientific' methods to production. It is associated particularly with the work of Frederick W. Taylor, who was its most notable exponent and leading publicist, but also involved a number of other important collaborators and followers. Within industrial sociology, following the work of people like Bendix (1956), Baritz (1960) and Rose (1975, 1988), and the authors of several text books, the main emphasis had been on Scientific Management as a set of ideas, which purported to provide an explanation of worker motivation and behaviour but were ideological in that they provided a justification for certain courses of action by management. These ideas had been a major target for the Human Relations movement from the 1920s onwards.

Braverman's emphasis was quite different. Scientific Management was seen not just or primarily as an ideology, but as the continuing basis for management practice in capitalist societies (and somewhat to his regret in state socialist societies like the USSR too). The innovations introduced by Taylor and other proponents of Scientific Management enabled employers to exercise much greater control over the labour process, to intensify work and to cheapen the cost of labour power. They were to be seen as the specific form taken by the capitalist control over the labour process under monopoly capitalism; and market pressures would ensure their general application. Thus although Scientific Management as a set of ideas might have been discredited (partly as a result of the attacks by social scientists in the Human Relations tradition as well as others), Scientific Management as practice had become part of the taken-for-granted assumptions of engineers, managers and others responsible for the design, organisation and control of work, a point which was also made by researchers at the Tavistock Institute of Human Relations (see Chapter 3, and Trist *et al.* 1963).

There is no need to repeat here the detailed, and very vivid, account of Taylor's work provided by Braverman (similar accounts can also be found elsewhere, for example Rose 1988, Pt 1). The crucial characteristics of Scientific Management for Braverman were threefold:

1 'The *dissociation of the labour process from the skills of the workers*' (1974, 113). All tasks, simple or complex, should be 'studied with the object of collecting in the hands of management at least as much information as is known by the worker who performs it regularly, and very likely more'. They should be subjected to systematic experiment to determine the quickest

and best way, and thus 'the labor process is to be rendered independent of craft, tradition and the workers' knowledge' (112–3).

2   *'The separation of conception from execution'* (114). The unity of the labour process is broken by this separation of mental from manual labour (mental labour, of course, can also be subjected to the same process of separating the conceptual elements from the routine execution of tasks); and the greater knowledge of and improvements in production become the exclusive property of management; workers have merely to undertake simplified jobs governed by simplified instructions (113–18).

3   'The *use of this monopoly over knowledge to control each step of the labour process and its mode of execution'* (119). All elements of the labour process should be pre-planned and pre-calculated; this process gives rise to the need for a special management staff, and a considerably developed supervisory structure, to ensure that workers receive the right instructions and carry them out in the manner which has been laid down (118–20).

The results of the application of these principles, according to Braverman, were to destroy craftsmanship and to bring about a progressive degrading of the work carried out by the majority of manual workers. In addition, however, 'the separation of hand and brain' necessarily called into existence 'a variety of new occupations, the hallmark of which is that they are found not in the flow of things but in the flow of paper' (126). The growing number of 'unproductive' workers inside the enterprise was accompanied by the growth in the number of workers outside the enterprise who were engaged in the 'realisation' rather than the production of surplus value – employees in marketing, advertising, banking, finance, retailing and so on. But Braverman argued that these 'new' skills and occupations would undergo the same process of degradation in due course, as the methods of scientific management were applied to the office (and indeed to other service occupations) as well as to the workshop.

Of necessity the worker was forced to become 'habituated' to these new conditions. The development of industrial psychology and the Human Relations movement were seen by Braverman as being largely a response to the problems managements faced in securing the adjustment of workers to the conditions of industrial work in the twentieth century, but he regarded their contribution as insignificant. The main means by which habituation was achieved was through the destruction of alternative sources of employment and a mixture of inducement and coercion to compel workers to accept the new conditions. Ford's introduction of the assembly line and then of the five dollar day were seen by Braverman as a classic example of what was involved (1974, 146–51). The former developed the fragmentation and machine pacing of work to the fullest possible extent; the relatively high level of pay offered secured a plentiful supply of labour with little alternative but to submit to work on such terms (see Beynon 1984, 31–9).

Braverman argued that the growth of Scientific Management was an aspect of the development of monopoly capitalism. The greater scale of capitalist enterprises and the increased resources this made available were preconditions for its development. For the capitalist system as a whole to function, however, other conditions were necessary, which also had implications for work and the occupational structure. Management hierarchies grew, absolutely and relatively, as an increasing number of functions became the concern of specialised administrative departments, and in particular the whole range of activities associated with marketing became enormously important. Outside the enterprise the activities of the state expanded inevitably, to regulate the economy and secure 'effective demand' (partly through 'permanent war mobilization'), and to provide services and welfare measures. As a consequence government employment also grew. And, as we have already noted, the distribution of the products of industry and the realisation of surplus value gave rise to massive increases in employment in the financial sector and in services generally (1974, Pt 3).

Further, but of particular interest, Braverman argued that there had developed what he called 'a universal market': more and more goods and services in contemporary society were becoming commodities, to be bought and sold. The conditions in which people could provide directly for their own needs tended no longer to exist; they were forced to seek paid employment to provide for themselves and their families, and increasingly this meant that both partners in a marriage would be employed. This 'commodification of social life' helped both to ensure a ready supply of labour for capitalist enterprises and to provide a market for their products in the form of wage earners who both needed to purchase such goods and services and had the means to do so (1974, 271–83 especially).

In the extensive discussions which have followed the publication of Braverman's book two related themes have been uppermost:

1 the question of the nature of capital's control over labour, the driving forces behind it, and, in particular, whether Braverman was right to identify Scientific Management as the only or the predominant strategy available to managements in capitalist societies; and

2 the questions of whether, how far, and why there has been and is an inherent tendency within capitalism to de-skill and degrade work.

These two clusters of problems provide convenient 'pegs' on which to hang a discussion of the debates about the labour process which have occurred since the mid-1970s, and a convenient framework within which a number of subsidiary issues can be discussed. Whilst Braverman's formulations remain important, and are likely to be referred to for some time to come, a very much more complex and less deterministic picture of the relations between capital and labour, and of industrial and other employing organisations, emerges from the many and diverse contributions to this debate.

Before turning to questions of control and consent, however, there is a rather different question which must be faced. Braverman's emphasis, like that of Marx, is on the specifically *capitalist* labour process. The tendencies he observed and analysed arose because of the pressures within the capitalist system as rival 'capitals' seek to remain viable in competition with each other. Braverman was aware, however, in a way Marx could not be (though he did not neglect the subject altogether), of the massive expansion of employment in the public sector (in government, etc.) and in the private sector (e.g. employment in finance) outside the 'productive' agricultural, extractive, manufacturing and (some) service industries. The analysis proposed by Marx and echoed by Braverman centres on the production and appropriation of surplus value. The question that arises in the context of the contemporary structure of employment is how relevant is such an analysis to those considerable areas of paid work where there is either no production and appropriation of a 'surplus' and/or indeed no production of 'use values' at all? Much service sector employment, for example, is concerned with the realisation of value (banks, financial institutions, advertising and marketing, etc.); those employed on such activities are not 'productive' and derive their incomes from the surplus produced by others, as do most of those employed in the public sector (see Gough 1972; and also Crompton and Gubbay 1977, Chs 5 and 6 especially).

A narrow view of Marx's and Braverman's ideas as relevant only to situations where the labour process is also a valorisation process (i.e. where surplus value is produced and appropriated) would restrict the applicability of the analysis to a steadily diminishing proportion of employment in societies like Britain. This appears to be advocated by certain scholars (see Brighton Labour Process Group 1977). Braverman's own discussion, however, stressed the major similarities between what are analytically separate types of employment in capitalist societies:

> Although productive and unproductive labor are technically distinct, although productive labor has tended to decrease in proportion as its productivity has grown, while nonproductive labor has increased *only as a result of the increase in surpluses thrown off by productive labor* – despite these distinctions, the two masses of labor are not otherwise in striking contrast and need not be counterposed to each other. They form a continuous mass of employment which, at present and unlike the situation in Marx's day, has everything in common.
>
> (Braverman 1974, 423)

Empirically it is also true that those employed in the public sector, as well as in financial and commercial enterprises, have been subject to much the same processes of control and degradation as those employed in, for example, private sector manufacturing industry. This was particularly true in the 1980s because of the stress on the reduction of public expenditure, and the privatisation of a number of formerly public sector activities; but it was the case even before 1979. For these reasons the line which will be taken here is that the account of the labour process provided by Braverman, as derived from Marx, cannot be restricted only to employment in manufacturing and a few other industries. Rather it should be regarded as potentially very generally applicable to employment in capitalist societies; indeed it can be applied to employment in state socialist societies too (Burawoy 1985). There are differences between 'productive' and 'unproductive' sectors of employment, and between private and public sector employment, but the nature of these differences is something which has to be established empirically, not asserted *a priori.*

CONTROL AND CONSENT

Much of the power and persuasiveness of Braverman's account of the development of the labour process came from its broad sweep, its apparent success in incorporating a large number of not obviously related developments within one overall framework. It has not been difficult for those sympathetic to his formulations concerning the nature of the capitalist labour process, and the historical tendencies which have flowed from it, to provide empirical evidence which appears to 'fit' into the framework offered. Thus, for example, an account of the reorganisation of the steel industry in the USA in the nineteenth century by Stone (1973) has been an oft-cited study of the ways in which management has de-skilled work in its quest for greater control and a real subordination of labour. Similarly many of the case studies on the labour process, in the volume of that title edited by Zimbalist (1979), provide comparable supportive examples. In the same way much of the criticism of Braverman's account has taken the form of detailed, often historical, studies of particular industries, occupations and/or locations where 'it didn't happen like that'. They have confronted the generalisations of *Labor and Monopoly Capital* with the uncomfortable reality of what actually happened in the engineering and cotton industries in Britain in the nineteenth century, for example (Elger 1982, 34–8; Penn 1982, 90–108; Burawoy 1985, 85–121), or the very mixed reception given to Scientific Management ideas and practice in Britain in the inter-war period (Littler 1982, 99–145).

Such empirical examples of cases which 'don't fit' are important, of course, in that they force attention to be given to the basic framework of ideas in an attempt to see why there should have been such 'exceptions' and whether they can be somehow explained within the terms of the original 'model'. The debates which are discussed below, however, cannot be effectively resolved by a piling up of examples on one side or the other; understanding can only really be advanced if the exploration of empirical cases is combined with a more theoretically oriented critique which attempts to expose inadequacies and contradictions in the original formulations. Whilst there will be a good deal of reference to empirical materials the discussion which follows will attempt to focus on these more general issues.

For example, Braverman, like Marx, saw the pressures for increasing control over the labour process as arising directly from 'the imperatives of capital accumulation as the fundamental dynamic . . . in capitalist societies' (Elger 1982, 23). Elger, however, has criticised Braverman for a failure adequately to locate this compulsion to control and has argued that there is a need for 'a more complex and historically located analysis of the relations between valorisation and accumulation and the development of the capitalist labour process' (34). In this connection, to give one example, he cites Hobsbawm (1964) as arguing that the uneven international adoption of Scientific Management, with the USA as a pioneer in comparison with Europe, was due to the fact employers in the USA 'confronted both higher wages and the competitive disadvantage of a lack of secure imperial markets' (42); in contrast, at least till the First World War employers in Britain paid relatively lower wages and benefited from the 'cushion' of imperialism, and consequently were not forced to seek ways of intensifying labour. Indeed if it is argued that the 'need' for control of the labour process derives from the imperatives of capital accumulation within a capitalist system, then, unless it can also be argued that this imperative bears equally on all firms, industries and/or societies at all times – and it cannot – there will be considerable differences for substantial periods of time in the degree to which control of the labour process is the central issue for employers; and there may well be 'space' for considerable variation in the means of control which are adopted.

In a parallel argument Littler (1982, 28–9) has pointed out that the fundamental compulsion of capital accumulation can be met in various ways at different times; control of the labour process is only one, albeit important, way of appropriating surplus value.

The assumption that increasing capital accumulation entails intensifying control of the labour process in an unmediated way is based on the idea of the continued centrality of labour and the labour process, but this may vary through different stages of capitalist development. It is important to realize that appropriation of surplus value may occur not only in the labour process, but through other mechanisms, namely in the sphere of circulation through pricing policy and via state taxation. It could be argued that under monopoly capitalism the centrality of control over labour diminishes and the extraction of surplus value now occurs via monopoly pricing and taxation (e.g. see Wright, 1975). Braverman fails to consider this point because, though the central aim of the book is to link the nature of the labour process and monopoly capital, the nature of this link remains obscure. Given a single overall dynamic of deskilling and intensifying capitalist control, the transition to monopoly capitalism does not in his account alter the logic of the labour process (Edwards 1978, 109).

(Littler 1982, 28–9)

It will not be possible to pursue this question further here (but see Friedman [1977a] for an important attempt to establish such connections). Two further general issues should, however, be identified at this stage. One of the most quoted features of Braverman's account has been his explicit disavowal of any consideration of the 'subjective' content of class: 'This is a book about the working class as a class *in itself*, not as a class *for itself*' (1974, 27). Such a limitation may be considered understandable, and even partly defensible, as a reaction against the sociological writing which defines concepts like 'class' and 'alienation' in solely 'subjective' terms (i.e. class becomes entirely a matter of 'class consciousness'; alienation becomes merely a question of the degree of job dissatisfaction). The limitation leads however to a fundamental weakness in Braverman's account: his neglect of worker resistance and opposition as a factor determining the nature of the labour process in capitalist societies. As we shall see this has important consequences for his whole discussion of control.

Secondly, and surprisingly in a Marxist analysis (though Braverman is not unique in this respect), there is very little awareness of contradiction in Braverman's account. The processes of increasing managerial control over the labour process, and the de-skilling of work which this implies, appear to have no undesirable consequences for capital, except and until the whole system is transformed by a socialist revolution. Like other social processes, however, attempts to control the labour process must have unintended consequences which conflict with employers' original intentions and may necessitate yet further measures if control is to be maintained. Thus, the creation of integrated production processes based on the detailed fragmentation and control of work, as in the assembly line, simultaneously creates a situation where small groups of workers may have considerable power to disrupt the whole production process. Or, to give another example, processes of de-skilling and specialisation, in a context where there are also pressures to reduce the size of the labour force, can run counter to the need many managements now recognise for a 'flexible' labour force with 'polyvalent' skills. And, as Elger (1982, 45–7) points out, much mechanisation (seen as the basis for a de-skilled and more highly productive labour force) created *semi-skilled* rather than unskilled workers, and they had some real power in the workplace and in the labour market. (See also Littler 1982, 3; Storey 1985.)

In an important recent paper Hyman (1987) has emphasised very forcefully the ways in which managements are faced with inherently contradictory demands which they have to respond to as best they can whilst also coping with the problems arising in the political and economic context in which they operate.

> For individual capitals – as for capital in general – there is no 'one best way' of managing these contradictions, only different routes to partial failure. It is on this basis that managerial strategy can best be conceptualised: as *the programmatic choice among alternatives none of which can prove satisfactory*.
>
> (Hyman 1987, 30)

Notwithstanding the difficulties of specifying the nature and means of managerial control, the need for control of the labour process is an aspect of the arguments developed by Braverman, and by Marx, which would be widely accepted by sociologists, including those who would be critical of other features of those arguments. It can be seen as derived from a fundamental feature of the employment relationship in that the employer can only buy the worker's capacity to work and has to ensure, over time and in the workplace, that that capacity is realised. As we have seen, however, it can be argued that the pressures to exercise this control may vary considerably between different industries and societies and/or over time. A further source of variation arises from the differences likely to exist in what Littler terms 'the recalcitrance of labour'. Not only can a universal recalcitrance not be assumed, but that assumption 'obscures the essential variability of worker resistance: some changes are resisted more than others, some groups resist more than others, some groups achieve a "negotiated order", whilst some groups become a privileged elite' (Littler 1982, 28). It is to an exploration of these variations within the overall control imperative that we now turn.

'Direct control' and 'responsible autonomy'

One of the earliest writers to pursue such issues both theoretically and empirically was Friedman (1977a, 1977b). He was one of the first to argue that the means of control identified by Braverman were not in fact the only strategies open to management, nor the most effective in all circumstances. Friedman's starting point was the need to explain 'the persistence of areas of deprivation alongside areas of prosperity within cities and regions in spite of the general prosperity in advanced capitalist societies from the late 1940s' (1977a, 3). This led him to look at the different situations of different firms within any one capitalist society. In any such society, he argued, competitive pressures are felt unequally, and this difference is increased with the development of monopoly capitalism. Within monopoly capitalism large firms tend to compete through sales efforts and cost reductions rather than through price competition. The managers in such firms are in a position where they can pursue alternative strategies for exercising control over their labour force (23–30). The choices they make are considerably influenced by the strength and nature of worker resistance to this control, resistance which will vary considerably but is more effective in so far as the growth in size of firms and factories increases the ability of workers to oppose managerial authority and as the influence of the reserve army of labour becomes less important, due, for example, to the 'drying-up of the latent reserve army' and/or to the establishment of full employment (45–50).

In contrast to the unilinear account of the development of capitalism provided by Braverman, in which worker resistance played no real part, Friedman suggested a significant role for such resistance and argued that it could affect the course of capitalist development other than by just destroying the capitalist mode of production other than by just destroying the capitalist mode of production as whole.

> What Marx did not study systematically was the possibility that technical and social changes might occur *under* the capitalist mode of production in response to the contradictory or self-

destructive forces created by capitalist accumulation. He did not carefully examine the means by which *contradictions are accommodated*, by which the mode of production is sustained.

(Friedman 1977a, 49)

Friedman suggested that there are two types of strategies which managers use to exercise authority over labour power – 'Responsible Autonomy and Direct Control'. Both have existed throughout the history of capitalism, but the coming of monopoly capitalism increased the importance of the responsible autonomy strategy, because of the increased strength of worker resistance, the greater resources available to management to experiment with new techniques, and their desire for greater stability within the labour force in the firm (78–9; see also Friedman 1977b). The strategies are distinguished as follows:

> The Responsible Autonomy type of strategy attempts to harness the adaptability of labour power by giving workers leeway and encouraging them to adapt to changing situations in a manner beneficial to the firm. To do this top managers give workers status, authority and responsibility. Top managers try to win their loyalty, and co-opt their organisations to the firm's ideals (that is, the competitive struggle) ideologically. The Direct Control type of strategy tries to limit the scope for labour power to vary by coercive threats, close supervision and minimising individual worker responsibility. The first type of strategy attempts to capture benefits particular to variable capital, the second tries to limit its particularly harmful effects and treats workers as though they were machines.
>
> (1977a, 78)

Friedman went on to argue, with particular reference to management-initiated changes in work organisation in the motor industry in Sweden (see 1977b, 46–7), that the loosening of top managers' *direct* control over workers' activity in order to reduce worker resistance may increase management control over productive activity as a whole (1977a, 84). In arguing in this way he indicated what other writers have developed and made more explicit: that control can be exercised at different 'levels' and in different ways, not just by direct surveillance on the shop or office floor. Braverman's apparent acceptance of Taylor's claim of a 'one best way' (for capital) was mistaken.

'Responsible autonomy' and 'direct control' strategies can and do co-exist in the same firm as well as in the same society. Indeed there may well be advantages in using both strategies, each in relation to different groups of workers, in order to overcome the rather different inflexibilities to which they are subject. The strategy of control through responsible autonomy is appropriate for the 'central' employees, those whose skills and abilities are, or have been made by worker organisation to seem, essential to the firm's long term profits; this strategy is the best way of securing such workers' willing cooperation and flexible working practices, but if their loyalty is to be secured they cannot easily be laid off even when demand falls. 'Peripheral' workers are more expendable, are typically less strongly organised, and can be hired and fired more easily; direct control can be applied to such employees (1977a, 108–114). The use of a responsible autonomy strategy is typically associated with the creation of an internal labour market within the firm (though Friedman uses this term with a rather different emphasis from many writers; see Friedman 1977a, 68; and cf. Doeringer and Piore 1971; Garnsey et al. 1985). Terms and conditions of employment, the terms of the effort bargain, and the possibilities of promotion for the workers with access to the internal labour market depend more on bargaining within the firm than on the forces of supply and demand in what Friedman calls 'the external labour power market'. As we shall see this distinction between the core and the peripheral labour force is a central feature of more recent discussions of flexibility and the 'flexible firm'.

The core and periphery distinction also applies to relations between firms. Large firms are able to treat a larger proportion of their workers as 'central' and to use responsible autonomy strategies, if they can establish cooperative relations with smaller supplier and distributor firms who provide the necessary flexibility when variations occur in levels of demand for their products or services. The costs of this flexibility are born by the smaller firms who are unable to treat many if any of their employees as 'central'; they therefore rely largely on direct control strategies. The relative security of employment, higher wages, and privileged terms and conditions of employment of the core workers in the larger firms are secured at the expense of the peripheral status of the less skilled non-core workers in the same firms and the doubly peripheral status of most workers in the smaller firms (1977a, 114–18).

Thus the discussion of managerial control strategies links directly to the phenomenon of labour market segmentation.

Friedman's work, which also included a lengthy discussion of the relevance of these ideas for an understanding of developments in the hosiery and car industries in Britain, is valuable in that he broke with the rather monolithic conception of capitalist control of the labour process offered by Braverman, and did so within an understanding of monopoly capitalism which was considerably more detailed and sophisticated than Braverman's own. In particular three aspects can be noted. There is an alternative to the direct control of the labour process which Braverman saw as reaching its full development in the form of Scientific Management; in appropriate circumstances managements can secure and retain control in another way, by allowing workers considerable areas of discretion and securing their loyalty and commitment by offering preferential terms and conditions of employment. Secondly, worker resistance has to be seen to be an important influence on the ways in which managements control the labour process; workers with power based on their skills and/or organisation (and often the one is a precondition for the other) can secure the greater status, authority and responsibility at work, and the associated relatively privileged terms of employment, which go with the use of a responsible autonomy strategy, especially where the firm has the extra room for manoeuvre available to most large firms under monopoly capitalism. Thirdly, Friedman's discussion links control of the labour process with processes of labour market segmentation, and in doing so indicates how the activities of workers and their organisations play some part in bringing about such divisions between more and less privileged members of the working class; the labour market is also an arena within which capital can control labour.

There remain however a number of important limitations to the understanding of capitalist control of the labour process offered in Friedman's account. Some of these will become apparent as alternative approaches are considered, but a few points can be made at this stage. In outlining a simple distinction between direct control and responsible autonomy strategies Friedman is oversimplifying the possibilities available to managements. The distinction is probably more appropriately seen as one of degree, a continuum rather than a dichotomy, but even if this is accepted (as it has been by Friedman [1984, 181]), it only represents one dimension of control. There are other aspects of the relations between capital and labour, within the firm and in the labour market, where managements may have choices which affect the ways in which they attempt to exercise control over the labour process. Further, the notion of strategy is much more problematic than Friedman suggested; there is a real question as to how far the means used by employers to control the activities of their employees within the employment contract are the result of the adoption of a conscious 'strategy' and how far they are the at least partially unintended consequences of actions taken for a variety of unrelated reasons.

Simple, technical and bureaucratic control

The assertion that Friedman's two strategies for control of the labour process have not exhausted the available possibilities can be supported by consideration of the work of Edwards. Although his account started with a contrast between three examples of different ways of organising work which coexisted in the contemporary USA, his book is an essentially historical account of the ways in which employers have attempted to control the work of their employees (Edwards 1979). The three main means he identified, whilst they also represent a challenge to Braverman's emphasis on Scientific Management as the strategy by which capital controls the labour process, are not altogether compatible with the two strategies proposed by Friedman. However his account is similar to Friedman's in two important respects. It, too, attempted to relate the means of management control to the changing nature of capitalism and in particular the development of monopoly capitalism; and his arguments also had important links with the ways in which labour markets are segmented.

In what Edwards termed the 'entrepreneurial firm' 'the personal power and authority of the capitalist constituted the primary mechanism for control' (Edwards 1979, 25). The employer, with the possible assistance of a few managers, watched over the entire operations of the firm and supervised worker activities directly. This simple control was 'direct, arbitrary and personal'; it was typical of small businesses in the nineteenth century operating in highly competitive markets, and remains the means of control typically used in small competitive businesses at the present time (34–6). However as firms grew in size and became geographically dispersed direct personal control was increasingly difficult. The increased visibility and arbitrariness of the unequal power relations between the employers and their hierarchy of 'hired bosses' and workers provoked opposition and challenges to the power of employers. Simple control came to be seen as increasingly unsatisfactory as a means of controlling the labour process in large corporations.

With the growth of monopoly capitalism, Edwards argued, the economy came to be dominated by a few hundred large corporations with tens or hundreds of thousands of employees. Such firms experimented with a variety of means of control: 'welfare capitalism'; Scientific Management; and company unions. Drawing on these failed 'experiments', however, the managers of large corporations developed two alternative ways of controlling the labour process each of which involved embedding 'the organization, coordination, and assignment of work tasks . . . in a larger structure of work' (90–110).

The first of these means was 'technical control'. This 'involves designing machinery and planning the flow of work to minimize the problem of transforming labor power into labor as well as to maximize the purely physically based possibilities of achieving efficiencies' (Edwards 1979, 112). The assembly line provides perhaps the most important single step in achieving technical control. In particular it provided for the direction and pacing of work, though quality control remained a problem to which a 'technical control' solution has only been found with the development of computer based feedback systems. Computer based systems also give methods of technical control much greater flexibility. However, technical control does not alter the need to discipline and reward workers in conventional ways. There is also a tendency for technical control to create more homogeneous, and more easily unionised, workforces whose strikes and other forms of action gain considerable strength from the integrated nature of the technology. In the light of disputes in the 1930s and 1970s Edwards concluded 'technical control can never again *by itself* constitute an adequate control system for the core firms' main industrial labor force' (129).

'Bureaucratic control' represents an attempt to overcome these deficiencies. It is

> embedded in the social and organizational structure of the firm and is built into job categories, work rules, promotion

procedures, discipline, wage scales, definitions of responsibilities, and the like. Bureaucratic control establishes the impersonal force of 'company rules' or 'company policy' as the basis
for control.

(131)

Impersonal rules and procedures provide for the direction, monitoring and rewarding/disciplining of the workforce. The large
number of different job categories and pay and other differentials
divides the workforce and undermines the basis for collective
action. The differentials also make possible the use of promotion
in the internal labour market of the firm as an important means of
reward. Because one of its main incentives for employees is the
provision of job security, however, the use of 'bureaucratic' means
of control introduces a considerable measure of inflexibility into
the utilisation of labour by the firm; to make employees redundant
would be to threaten the bases of control, yet even large corporations cannot be sure that this will never be necessary. 'Bureaucratic control is thus without contradiction only if capitalism itself
is without crisis' (Edwards 1979, 159).

Bureaucratic control, Edwards argued, is also likely to stimulate
demands for greater participation; 'job security and long-lasting
identification with the company' are conditions 'under which
demands for workplace democracy flourish' (153). Further, as
large corporations play down their 'private' capitalist enterprise
character and project themselves as essential social institutions,
they also invite greater public regulation and control; workers and
unions may turn to state action to place restrictions on corporate
activities (159–62).

Edwards linked the development of these three types of control
with segmentation in the labour market, an argument which is
considerably elaborated and somewhat modified in a later book
(Gordon *et al.* 1982). 'Simple control' is associated primarily with
the 'secondary labour market', the preserve of casual labour 'un-
fettered by any job structure, union, or other institutional constraints' (Edwards 1979, 167). 'Technical control' is associated
primarily with the 'subordinate primary market', jobs which offer
'some job security, relatively stable employment, higher wages,
and extensive linkages between successive jobs that the typical
worker holds', which are unionised, but which are also typically
'repetitive, routinised, and subject to machine pacing' (170–2).

'Bureaucratic control' is associated primarily with the 'independent primary market' containing jobs which differ from the 'subordinate primary market' in that they are better paid, involve 'general' rather than 'firm-specific' skills, tend to demand educational credentials and are likely to have occupational or professional standards for performance (174). There are, however, exceptions to all these linkages; and types of control are not seen as the only reason for labour market segmentation; racial and sexual discrimination also play an important part (177–83).

Friedman's and Edwards's formulations are important in a number of respects. They both saw 'direct' or 'simple' control as characteristic of earlier stages of capitalist development, though not everyone would agree that they were right to do so (e.g. Burawoy 1985, 125); they identified alternative means of controlling labour which become possible with the development of monopoly capitalism; and they linked these means of control to processes of segmentation in the labour market. Though their suggested alternatives, 'responsible autonomy' on the one hand, and 'technical' and 'bureaucratic' control on the other, do not correspond in any precise way, each of them is very different from Braverman's emphasis on Taylorism as *the* means of controlling the labour process in the twentieth century. Thus the rather monolithic and unilinear account of how capitalist industry develops, which Braverman derived from the work of Marx and extended into the era of monopoly capitalism, is challenged by accounts which suggest that there are alternatives and that the adoption of one means of control rather than another is related to one or more of a number of contextual factors, such as the nature of the market(s) for a firm's or industry's products.

Others have argued that labour market segmentation itself provides a means of controlling the labour process (e.g. Rose 1988, 328–9). It is a strategy of divide and rule, which runs directly counter to attempts to control the labour force by de-skilling it and making it more homogeneous. It does however enable managements to utilise existing social divisions, based on gender, ethnic origin, language, religion or whatever, to their own advantage by favouring one such group at the expense of others. Indeed, it is an important deficiency in Braverman's argument that he failed to see the proper significance of such divisions, especially gender, for managerial control of the labour process (Beechey 1982; Cockburn 1983).

The recognition of a plurality of means of controlling work is welcome and makes it possible to account for some of the apparent anomalies created by an uncritical acceptance of Braverman's position. Neither Friedman nor Edwards, however, can be said to have exhausted the possibilities for control over the labour process, nor to have identified all the conditions which may make one set of control measures necessary, or at least preferable in the eyes of employers, rather than another. To pursue such issues further demands that we give closer attention than has been done so far to the notion of 'control of the labour process'.

Levels of control

Like many other writers, Edwards made an important distinction between 'coordination' and 'control'. The former is essential in any production system where more than one or two people are involved; the activities of the various participants have to be meshed together if inefficiency or even chaos are to be avoided. 'Control', 'the ability of capitalists and/or managers to obtain desired work behaviour from workers' was for Edwards (1979, 17) a feature of class-based social systems, where the willingness of the worker to work cannot be taken for granted and where more or less coercive means may be needed to ensure that the 'labour power' purchased is transformed into 'labour'. The distinction between 'coordination' and 'control' is an analytical one, and the same observable activities may be one or the other or both. This has enabled many writers to emphasise the need for coordination in complex production systems and to overlook the more or less coercive aspects of management and supervision in all contexts where people are employed to produce goods or provide services (see also Burawoy 1979, 24). Edwards went on to suggest that a system of control can be thought of as consisting of three elements: direction; evaluation and supervision; and discipline and reward (1979, 18). This is helpful but limits control to activities close to the actual performance of work tasks. Controlling the labour process can involve a good deal more than that.

Any employing organisation can be seen to exercise control on a number of different 'levels'; and, equally important, at any one time the means of control used on one level can vary independently of those used on others. This point was made very effectively by Littler by drawing on Weber's discussion of bureaucracy. A bureaucracy is, among other things, a set of administrative arrangements for coordinating *and* controlling the activities of a large number of people. Weber's enumerations of the characteristics of bureaucracy can, Littler suggested, be separated into two main categories: 'those that describe the official's relationship to the organization and those that are largely concerned with the structure of control' (Littler 1982, 37). Thus to the control which can be built into the division of labour and the technology of production must be added control exercised at two further 'levels of structuration of work organization: . . . the formal authority structure of the factory, plus the monitoring system . . . [and] the wider framework of the capital/labour relationship arising from the relation of job positions to the labour market' (42).

Littler went on to argue that these three levels of structuration of the labour process can have 'relatively independent dynamics'; 'whilst there is a tendency for changes in job design, control structures and employment relations to go together this is only a tendency and not a necessity' (43). For example, the means of control advocated by Taylor emphasised the first two levels identified by Littler, the division of labour and job design, and the structure of control over task performance; they did not include any attempt to influence the employment relationship. Labour power was to be treated as a commodity; there need be a minimum of interaction between employer and employees outside the workplace, and no attempt to control workers by creating relations of dependence between them and their employer, as, for example, can be achieved by offering prospects of a career within the firm, or at least greater job security through the operation of an internal labour market. In other contexts employment relations have played an important part in securing control over the labour process; for example, when Ford introduced the five dollar day in 1913 the control which was built into the technology and division of labour on Taylorite lines was supplemented by an insistence on a minimum length of continuous employment and satisfactory personal habits at home and at work, to be monitored by the 'Sociological Department' (Littler 1982, 57; Beynon 1984, 35–7). Even more obviously the control over their employees exercised by large Japanese corporations depends on a 'corporate paternalism' which creates relations of employment dependence for workers on their employer (Littler 1982, 45, 57). In contrast 'Taylorism represents the bureaucratization of the structure of control, but not the employment relationship'; 'the major characteristic of Taylorite work organization is the lack of any notion of a career system' (58–9); without an internal labour market, or other appropriate means, enterprises organised on strictly Taylorite lines exercise little or no control through the employment relationship.

The notion of levels of control has also been used by Storey, together with the idea of 'circuits of control', to suggest that in any organisation there can be 'a cluster of devices, structures and practices' which form 'control configurations' that are best under-stood as the temporary outcomes of dialectical processes of securing control (or attempting to do so) (Storey 1985, 196–9). In this case 'levels' is used to refer to the different levels in the hierarchy of an organisation at which control may be exercised, and the ways in which they may be vertically reinforcing; whereas '"circuits of control" is more generic . . . and refers *also* to cases where controls are activated horizontally or indeed without any particular grading' (199). Storey emphasised, however, that a variety of means of control could be, and generally would be, used simultaneously: for example, 'new technology, job restructuring, new disciplinary practices, new welfare "styles" and the simple elimination of certain occupations and functions' (203); and that a dialectical framework for understanding is needed in order to comprehend the dynamics of control, as managers constantly respond to new challenges from the workforce, colleagues, competitors and the environments in which they operate. Storey's argument provides an important and useful critique of earlier attempts to provide 'definitive singular types of control', attempts which display a strong 'functionalist and deterministic streak' (207). It is right to stress that control is a complex and continuous process, where a range of possibilities exist which are not neces-sarily mutually exclusive and which have uncertain outcomes.

Factory regimes

Drawing on material from Britain, the USA, Eastern Europe and Africa, Burawoy provided an even more wide ranging account of the differing ways in which control over the labour process may be exercised; suggested how these may combine to form distinctive 'factory regimes'; and tried to identify the conditions necessary for the development of one sort of regime rather than another. He arrived at the notion of 'factory regime' by means of an elaboration of what he saw as inherent in the notion of a mode of production, placing particular emphasis on the *political* aspects of the social relations and processes involved. Though his account does provide a typology of 'regimes', and tends to suggest that certain general patterns of development can be discerned in history, which someone like Storey might regard as too restrictive and deterministic, Burawoy was at pains to suggest that developments in the future are wide open.

Burawoy drew on a complex set of analytical distinctions to characterise factory regimes, the different patterns of control, and of accommodation to that control, within capitalist enterprises. He made an overall distinction between two basic types of factory regime, the 'market despotic' and the 'hegemonic'. In the case of market despotism, which he regarded as representing 'Marx's prototypical factory regime', the employer is subject to the dictates of an unregulated competitive market, survival depends on the expenditure of labour on the shopfloor, and 'workers have no ways to defend themselves against the arbitrary whims of the manager or overseer' (Burawoy 1979, 194). 'Anarchy in the market leads to despotism in production' (Burawoy 1985, 89). However, three further conditions are also necessary: the real subordination of labour to capital, the workers' dependence on selling their labour power for wages, and state action limited to preserving the *external* conditions of production, and not regulating relations between capitalists or between capital and labour (89–90). Burawoy's own examination of the cotton textile industry in England, the USA and Russia in the nineteenth century suggested that it was the exception rather than the norm for all four of these conditions to be present, with the result that factory regimes tended to be 'patriarchal', 'paternalist' or a 'company state' rather than purely 'market despotic' (91–111).

'Hegemonic' regimes develop, according to Burawoy, when state intervention reduces workers' dependence on the sale of their labour power. This can occur in two ways: as a result of social insurance legislation which guarantees a minimum level of living independently of any participation in production; and state regulation of employer–employee relations in ways which limit managerial methods of domination (e.g. compulsory trade union recognition, grievance machinery, and so on) (125–6). As a result managements can no longer rely on the 'economic whip of the market' nor impose 'an arbitrary despotism' in the workplace, but have to persuade workers to cooperate. Such hegemonic regimes also differ from country to country according to the extent of state provision and regulation; and within any one country depending on the degree of competition, skill, technology and workers' resistance (126). Whilst the necessary 'consent' to the regime is derived partly from processes in the family, the school and elsewhere in the wider society, Burawoy emphasised particularly how the production process itself could generate consent, due to the fact that workers come to accept the rules which regulate their participation in production. Such rules, for example creating internal labour markets and/or institutionalising industrial conflict, although they limit managerial power, are acceptable to management if not welcomed by them; they reduce the uncertainties which otherwise occur with an external labour market and unregulated industrial conflict.

The final stage of Burawoy's argument was to suggest that with the extension of the operations of large-scale capitalist corporations to a world-wide scale hegemonic regimes can be transformed into a new 'hegemonic despotism'. Given a fragmented labour process, and greatly improved means of transport and communication, capital can be mobile to utilise pools of cheaper labour in less developed countries. Faced with the possibility that production will be moved elsewhere if they protest, workers are defenceless against threats of rationalisation, technical change and work intensification; they can be forced into concessions to avoid loss of their jobs (Burawoy 1985, 148–52). This conclusion provides what is a rather pessimistic view of the possibilities for action by labour, surprisingly pessimistic perhaps in the light of other aspects of Burawoy's work which will be discussed below.

Resistance

As we have seen Braverman largely discounted the question of the varying willingness and ability of workers to resist managerial control. Other writers, however, have given considerable attention to such considerations, and it is clear that in this respect Braverman's account is seriously deficient. As Storey has indicated, the possibility of worker resistance to managerial control introduces an important dynamic element into the discussion of control of the labour process. However, it is not simply a matter of trying to identify how employers respond to and try directly to counter the opposition their control measures may provoke. Control can also, and possibly more effectively, be exercised by limiting or removing as far as possible employees' means of resistance (e.g. curbs on trade union activities). Further, the 'recalcitrance' of labour, the degree of unwillingness to accept employment on the terms and subject to the controls provided by employers, is far from being constant in any case; and if this recalcitrance can be minimised, then control will be easier. This leads to the need to look more closely at the ambivalent nature of the employment relationship and the possibilities of securing 'consent', topics which will be discussed in the following section.

These deficiencies in Braverman's account were recognised early. Friedman, for example, argued that workers' potential or actual resistance to de-skilling and managerial control was a factor which might lead management to adopt a responsible autonomy strategy rather than try to exercise direct control. Worker resistance plays an important part in Edwards's and in Gordon *et al.*'s accounts of the successive attempts by capitalist employers in the USA to control the labour process. In an important discussion which linked labour market segmentation (its main focus) with Braverman's arguments concerning de-skilling Rubery pointed to the neglect of the role of worker organisation in the process of development of a structured labour market. Indeed in support of her general thesis that 'workers and worker organisation must be assigned an active role in the development of labour market structure', she argued that as workers organised in opposition to de-skilling 'to control entry into an occupation, firm or industry' they might well 'create segmentation in the external labour market' (Rubery 1980, 244, 260); such segmentation could, of course, be used by management to reassert control by 'buying off' the more privileged workers with preferential conditions of employment whilst exercising close control over the less skilled and unprotected who were excluded from the 'primary' labour market.

In addition to the theoretical cogency of their arguments all the above writers drew upon empirical evidence in support of the need to give worker resistance a significant place in any adequate account of managerial control of the labour process in capitalist society. Indeed the opposition which Taylor himself faced has been well documented, especially in relation to the attempts to introduce Scientific Management methods into US government arsenals (Aitken 1960; Littler 1982, 179–85). As well as commenting on the American case Littler (1982, 117–45) provided evidence of the considerable though not particularly successful opposition to the rationalisation of work, using the Bedaux system, in Britain during the inter-war period.

There does not yet appear to be, and may well never be, any comprehensive account of the circumstances under which workers, organised or unorganised, will resist management-initiated changes in the organisation and supervision of work, still less of their likely success. With the possible partial exception of productivity bargaining, trade unions in Britain have tended to neglect questions of work organisation and to concentrate on securing the best possible pay and other terms of employment for their members. They have sought compensation for management-initiated changes in work organisation rather than trying to secure improvements in the ways in which their members' work is or-ganised (Moore 1978). It is important, however, to try to indicate some of the ways in which managements may try to deal with worker resistance (or potential resistance), and in this way extend further the notion of control.

Hyman's (1987) discussion of managerial strategies provides a useful basis. Divisions within the workforce, whether between strata organised hierarchically or in terms of 'horizontal' divisions, can give management an advantage in securing control, though Hyman appeared less certain than some writers have been that such a situation resulted from a deliberate 'divide and rule' strategy. Such developments create costs (the need to motivate the less privileged workers, and to coordinate and manage their work; the cost of the relatively more privileged conditions which have to be provided for the core workforce); but they may be allowed or encouraged in order to maintain a stable, often skilled, workforce whilst also being able to deal with fluctuations in demand (38–9). In so far as worker resistance may be manifested through trade unions, managements can try to retain control by attempting to prevent workers organising and refusing to recognise and negoti-ate with their unions if and when they do; they can attempt to limit trade union bargaining to narrowly defined terms and conditions of employment whilst retaining all other areas as matters ex-clusively for themselves ('managerial prerogatives'); they can encourage the procedural regulation of collective bargaining in ways which make it more predictable; and they can try to 'incorp-orate' union representatives (shop stewards and/or officials) into just such a bureaucratic structure of rules and procedures and so to reduce or eliminate their 'radicalism' (43–7). Through policies to provide welfare benefits and to give employees greater job security and prospects, managements can attempt to 'obscure the commodity status of labour'; but in this area too such policies may well have contradictory consequences in that measures to minimise the extent to which workers are treated as just a factor of production may introduce unwelcome rigidities into the firm when workers have to be dismissed or re-allocated (42–3).

Control, and prevention, of resistance can extend beyond the employing organisation itself. The 'recalcitrance' of labour is in any case variable and dependent on workers' consciousness. If employees and potential employees can be persuaded to accept the legitimacy of managerial authority and the necessity, even the duty, of expending effort in working for a wage or salary under conditions determined by others, then managerial control will be very much easier. Many employers have been active in the communities from which their labour forces are recruited in order to encourage such attitudes. Firms which are important sources of employment locally can create dependence on the part of employees and potential employees which will reduce the likelihood of resistance in the workplace (see, for example, Maguire 1988; Warde 1989).

More generally, such considerations direct attention to the role of schools, and education and socialisation, in creating a potential workforce with the 'right' attitudes. There is no doubt that from the beginning mass education has operated in ways which tend to produce a suitably socialised labour force: perhaps partly unintentionally, as in the very structure of school itself with its hierarchical organisation, compulsory attendance and so on; and partly very consciously, as at times in the 1980s with the emphasis on the inculcation of a work ethic and the need for education seen as relevant to 'the real world' of business and industry. Whilst most individual employers and managers may have no active part in creating or maintaining such an educational system, organised industry and business, at local and national levels, can be and has been very influential. Organisations representing employers' interests are also influential in a more diffuse way in sustaining a climate favourable to 'business', one which, for example, values property rights, denigrates trade unionism, and emphasises the desirability of material growth and prosperity over other possible goals (equality, for example, or the environment) and the importance of priorities like 'efficiency' and profit if such goals are to be achieved. In so far as the mass media reflect such values (and they do do so, though not unambiguously nor to the complete exclusion of other positions) then they too play a part in forming a less 'recalcitrant' workforce.

The influences of socialisation are largely diffuse and rarely clear-cut. Indeed, as Willis's (1977) study of 'the lads' showed, the unintended consequences of action may be such that the outcome of socialisation is quite different from what one might have expected; in his research, which concerned school leavers entering unskilled manual work, rebellion against school and adult authority led to an initial commitment to paid work and an eagerness to enter jobs which were low skilled and physically demanding, rather than to the growth of a workforce which had to be coerced into employment. Socialisation into employment, and into an acceptance of the legitimacy of managerial authority, is difficult to observe empirically and to establish uncontentiously. Nevertheless its importance as a necessary prerequisite of a successfully functioning capitalist economy must be accepted. In one of the best analyses of what is involved Baldamus (1961, esp. 81–101) has stressed that without such processes one cannot explain how relatively stable day-to-day relations are possible between managers and supervisors, on the one hand, and workers, on the other; without the internalisation of work obligations and the institutionalisation of standardised expectations of wages and effort there would be continual acute conflicts over pay, work-loads, manning levels, output targets, and so on.

The need for control arises not just from technical requirements for the coordination of the activities of a number of people engaged in a common task, but from the inherent nature of employment in capitalist enterprises and capitalist societies, whereby the employer buys the worker's *capacity* to work and this has to be realised within the ongoing processes and social relations of production. Securing control of the labour process, however, is not just a matter of structures and processes in the workplace, however many 'levels' of control may be distinguished. The need for control can vary depending on the degree to which employees accept managerial authority and have internalised obligations to work for a wage or salary; the recalcitrance of labour is empirically variable. Control can therefore also be secured by means which assist the creation, maintenance, recruitment and reproduction of a labour force which is less 'recalcitrant'. Securing a 'cooperative' workforce, however, does not just depend on creating a consciousness among employees and potential employees which is favourable to management (and might be held to obscure workers' 'true' interests); or on establishing ideological hegemony for capitalist values in the wider society. It can also make use of ambiguities which are inherent in the relations between employer and employee, and try to maximise the elements of cooperation and consensus which are available within that relationship, and minimise or obscure the elements of conflict.

Consent

The ambivalent nature of the employer–employee relationship has been widely recognised in sociology for a long time. It has been acknowledged even within accounts of social relations at work which have been primarily focused on the conflicting interests of the two parties, and on the many ways in which they can be manifested. Put simply, on the one hand employers' profits (or the ability of non-profit making organisations to deliver a particular level of service whilst remaining within budget) depend on keeping wage costs as low as possible whilst ensuring that employees work as 'hard' as possible; the interests of the parties are in conflict. On the other hand, employees' livelihoods, as well as employers' profits, depend on the continuing success of the enterprise or organisation; both parties have this interest in common. This latter consideration was made very clear to Beynon during his study of Ford workers at Halewood. His tentative title for his book, *Never Buy a Ford*, met with a clear adverse reaction from shop stewards, and he commented: 'If people stopped buying Fords they'd be out of a job. Their battle with Ford is tempered by this concern. A concern that can only be remedied by a fundamental change in the entire basis of production' (Beynon 1973, 318).

Such consent to the existing organisation and control of work might rightly be considered somewhat coerced. As Braverman made clear it is conditioned by the absence of alternative ways of securing the means of existence. There is, however, another way in which the employment relationship necessarily involves cooperation and consent which is not subject to the same comment, and which represents a more fundamental criticism of the way in which the labour process was conceptualised by Braverman, and by Marx. In what is perhaps the most developed account of this argument Cressey and MacInnes (1980) focused on the theory of the 'real subordination of labour' (RSL). They suggested that the interpretation of this process offered by Braverman, and – explicitly or implicitly – by most other writers, exaggerates and misinterprets the nature and degree of control it is possible for capital to impose. Capital is seen as controlling labour 'materially' as well as formally; through forms of work organisation such as the assembly line 'it . . . actually materially controls what labour does' (8). This is to ignore, however, that the tendency towards the real subordination of labour is 'a process which is *internally* contradiction ridden' (11). If capital is to exploit labour's ability to create new value it cannot exercise the sort of comprehensive and absolute control over workers' activities which the idea of the real subordination of labour implies; rather it has to try to harness workers' subjectivity and 'powers of social productivity' to its own ends.

> For even though capital owns (and therefore has the right to 'control'), both means of production and the worker, in practice capital must surrender the means of production to the 'control' of the workers for their actual *use* in the production process. All adequate analysis of the contradictory relationship of labour to capital in the workplace depends on grasping this point.

And they continued:

> It is precisely because capital must surrender the use of its means of production to labour that capital must to some degree seek a cooperative relationship with it, unite labour with the means of production and maximise its social productivity and powers of cooperation. Here is the central point of our critique of R.S.L. The two-fold nature of the relationship of capital to labour in the workplace implies *directly contradictory* strategies for both labour and capital which in turn represent the working out of the contradiction between the forces and relations of production at the level of the workplace itself.
>
> (Cressey and MacInnes 1980, 14)

Cressey and MacInnes rejected Taylor's claim, which was not challenged by Braverman, that it was possible for employers to take over 'all the workers' subjectivity and skill' and to design and control the production process so that there was no need and no room for workers to exercise any initiative (17). In contrast they emphasised 'the dual nature of labour within capitalism' and the 'dual character of "control" itself'. Capital may be able 'to enforce valorisation and the production of commodities', but it continues to rely on labour's cooperation 'in order to get work performed at all' (19).

The argument that labour cannot be reduced to such a limited and mechanical place within the production process that there is no need and no space for any independent action on its part is a crucially important one. It is not a new argument. Though he wrote from within a different tradition of social theory the same point was made by Bendix (1956, 251):

> In modern industry the cooperation needed involves the spirit in which subordinates exercise their judgement. Beyond what commands can effect and supervision can control, beyond what incentives can induce and penalties prevent, there exists an exercise of discretion important even in relatively menial jobs, which managers of economic enterprises seek to enlist for the achievement of managerial ends.

If the arguments of Cressey and MacInnes, and of Bendix and others who have written in the same vein, are accepted, as they should be, then control of the labour process becomes a more complex and contradictory matter than it would otherwise be. Capitalist employers will necessarily be involved in trying to secure workers' consent whilst at the same time retaining control. Such a contradictory stance will be made easier if they can disguise the nature of their control activities. They may be helped in this by the fact that control as a means of extracting surplus value can be confused with control as coordination, something which is necessary in any large scale productive enterprise. Much of the writing about bureaucracy and organisations has failed to make this distinction at all clearly, and, not surprisingly, the same confusion is contained in much everyday 'common sense' discussion of organisations and employment.

Burawoy indicated the same contradictory nature of the capitalist production process when he wrote of the need to obscure and secure surplus value: 'the dilemma of capitalist control is to secure surplus value while at the same time keeping it hidden' (1985, 32; also 1978, 260). He suggested that this problem is met, in part, by the institutional separation of 'ownership and control', the dislocation of the relations in production from the relations of production, which makes capitalists generally invisible; by the ways in which the labour force is divided in terms of skill and other differences so that it fails to develop a 'collective consciousness'; and by the effects of 'bourgeois ideology' in obstructing the proletariat's 'capacity to recognise itself as a class opposed to capital' (1985, 32–3).

Though these considerations are important Burawoy also stressed the significance of other processes by which consent is secured, processes inherent in the labour process itself. He drew attention to the large body of evidence regarding the ways in which workers in practice adapt to the demands of industrial work, ways which frequently involve them in playing 'games' in the workplace. This is perhaps clearest in the case of 'making out' under payment by results, a phenomenon which has been very widely observed, though sometimes differently labelled (see, for example, Roy 1952, 1953; Lupton 1963; Burawoy 1979). In such situations workers gain 'relative satisfaction' from manipulating the rules to achieve their own goals regarding pay, levels of effort, how they spend their time at work, and so on. Burawoy suggested, however, that 'participation in games has the effect of concealing relations of production at the same time as coordinating the interests of workers and management'. 'The very act of playing a game produces and reproduces consent to the rules and to the desirability of certain outcomes . . . . Playing the game generates the legitimacy of the conditions that define its rules and objectives' (1985, 38). Though accounts of 'making out' may appear to show workers acting against management's interests, Burawoy argued that shop-floor management normally tolerated such 'games' because they made their job easier, and that in practice, though within limits, 'playing games' was in the wider interests of capital because it generated consent to the exercise of capitalist control. 'Coercion, of course, always lies at the back of any employment relationship, but the erection of a game provides the conditions in which the organization of active cooperation and consent prevails' (Burawoy 1979, 83).

Burawoy entitled his earlier book *Manufacturing Consent* which neatly encapsulates his argument that in producing commodities workers also reproduce the conditions and social relations which make possible the production of commodities, and that these conditions include the 'manufacture' of their own 'consent' to their (concealed) exploitation. In the light of such an argument management's control depends, in part, on toleration of activities which may appear initially and superficially to run directly contrary to their own interests. What Burawoy's argument illustrates is the complexity of the notion of 'control' and of the ways in which control may be secured. This is as it should be. The relatively simple account of capitalist control of the labour process put forward by Braverman cannot survive the criticisms to which it has been subjected and (at best) has to be modified and amended out of all recognition.

Braverman and those who followed his lead have been right to stress the centrality of control over the labour process for an understanding of capitalist work organisations, and indeed of all organisations where people are employed. In making this emphasis, however, there is a danger of failing to recognise that the pressure for control may vary very considerably over time and as between different firms and industries, partly because in some circumstances capital can be accumulated in other spheres than production. Braverman's analysis of the development and nature of the control of work in the twentieth century is much less satisfactory. It identified one, important, tendency but failed to recognise that this could and did coexist with many others, securing control by different combinations of means and on different levels; and that all 'strategies' of control are incomplete and contradictory. A major reason for this deficiency in the analysis can be attributed to Braverman's decision to ignore the subjective aspects of class and so to neglect the extent to which worker resistance influences the exercise of control, and at times undermines it. Remedying this deficiency directs attention to topics (ideology, consciousness) which were largely neglected in the earlier contributions to the labour process debate.

SKILL

The ways in which the debates about the control of the labour process have developed have far-reaching implications for the discussion of skill and of Braverman's thesis that there has been a 'degradation of work in the twentieth century'. If the Taylorite strategy of separating conception and execution, and fragmenting and 'de-skilling' both manual and white collar work, is no longer to be seen as *the* means by which managements in the era of monopoly capitalism control their employees, then the de-skilling and/or degradation of work is less likely to be a universal or even a very general experience. All or nothing views in this controversy can almost certainly both be dismissed. There remain, however, a number of important questions about the notions of 'skill' and 'de-skilling' which need to be addressed.

Defining skill

The definition of 'skill' is far from straightforward. Skill refers to mental and/or manual abilities and dexterities, largely acquired through education, training and/or experience. Commentators appear to agree, however, that such a definition leaves a number of important questions unanswered. First, as Cockburn (1983, 113) pointed out with reference to compositors, there is the distinction between 'skill that resides in the man himself, accumulated over time, each new experience adding something to a total ability' and 'the skill demanded by the job'; 'de-skilling' could be seen as applying to either, or both, of these conceptions of skill. The scarcity of skilled workers (not just men), however, which has in fact been seen as a deep-rooted problem in British society due to our poor provisions for training, would imply that jobs or tasks would have to be 'de-skilled' too, whereas the latter would not necessarily imply the former, at least in the short run. Second, Cockburn went on to distinguish 'de-skilling' from a more general 'degradation' of work (the term used by Braverman), adverse changes in 'earnings, hours, conditions and the extent of the division of labour' (117), and suggested that at least in the newspaper industry de-skilling of work in the 1950s, 1960s and 1970s went along with improvements in conditions of employment rather than an objective 'degradation of work'.

Thirdly, more important, and more difficult, is the distinction between skill as an objective, observable and measurable attribute or set of attributes of either a worker or a task, or both, and skill as something which is socially constructed and socially sustained. A notion like skill is always likely to be contestable and contested, but two factors increase this probability. Most skills other than simple manual dexterities consist of a number of diverse and incommensurable elements. It is very difficult if not impossible to devise ways of assessing or measuring them which will be generally acceptable and uncontroversial. Consider the everyday skill of driving a car and the difficulty of securing agreement as to whether any individual has acquired sufficient skill to be allowed to drive unsupervised, or – even more so – as to the relative abilities of experienced drivers. Major differences in skill may be established uncontroversially; it takes more skill to drive a Formula One racing car (or be a surgeon) than to drive a Mini to the shops (or be an operating theatre orderly); but many others remain open to argument. If one goes on to consider the relative level of skill of quite different types of work or worker – comparing the skill needed to drive a racing car with that needed to be a surgeon, for example – the problems can become even greater. The initial entry qualifications and the length of training may provide some guidance, but educational standards, training times and credentials are all used to boost the skill status of occupations, and to limit the numbers able to compete for jobs in the labour market. They may have little relationship to the 'real' skills required to do the job.

The difficulty of measuring, or assessing, and comparing most skills leaves space for arguments about skill. The importance of claims to be 'skilled', or to be doing 'skilled' work, for any individual's or group's social status, labour market opportunities and work situation make it highly likely that this 'space' will be used to contest skill definitions and differences. To establish a claim to be skilled is to secure material and symbolic resources and advantages in relation to employers and other categories of employees. Thus 'there is the political definition of skill: that which a group of workers or a trade union can successfully defend against the challenge of employers and of other groups of workers' (Cockburn 1983, 113). A successful claim to be skilled may be self-reinforcing in the sense that it brings the resources with which to defend that claim. Women workers, who have less power in the labour market and in the workplace, and are frequently less strongly organised, have greater difficulty than men in claiming skilled status for the jobs they customarily do (see Phillips and Taylor 1986).

Nevertheless the question arises of how far and for how long such a 'subjective' definition can be sustained when the mental and/or manual abilities of the workers, or the abilities needed for the jobs concerned, have declined. Littler (1982, 9–11) has suggested that there are two versions of the 'social construction theory of skill'. The strong one 'asserts that it is possible to label certain work activities as skilled *whatever the technical content*'. Such a view makes the de-skilling hypothesis 'largely irrelevant to the overall organization of production'. The weak version accepts that nearly all skilled jobs have some objective skill content but 'that it is strategic position within the production process combined with collective organization which gains the occupation a skilled label'. It is the weak version which seems more plausible, but that does not make the definition of skill very much easier. It also leaves open the possibility, indeed the likelihood given the relationship between gender and skill referred to above, that whereas all jobs labelled 'skilled' will have some skill content, not all jobs containing skill will be accepted as 'skilled'.

Two further issues remain. Firstly, in an important discussion Manwaring and Wood (1985) have introduced the notion of tacit skills – the working knowledge needed by all employees, however 'unskilled' in official terms, in order to be able to participate in the labour process. Tacit skills include the successful 'routines' acquired and internalised through experience on the job, the different degrees of awareness required in more and less familiar situations, and the cooperative skills needed because of the collective nature of the labour process. (A similar appreciation of what is required to be an effective worker is to be found in the discussion in Geer *et al.* [1968] of socialisation into a job, 'learning the ropes'.) As we have seen in the earlier discussion of control and consent, management need to secure their employees' active co-operation if work is to be done effectively and harnessing tacit skills is an important part of this process, one which must give pause to any claims that work has been simply 'de-skilled'.

Secondly, most discussions of skill, including Braverman's, see skill as including the degree of autonomy remaining to the worker. For example, Manwaring and Wood (1985, 192) wrote: 'Specialization overlaps with another differentiating feature of skill, the level of discretion in different jobs, and therefore the degree of autonomy open to the worker. Our conception of tacit skills suggests that there must always be some autonomy.'

The argument that all jobs include some autonomy is acceptable, and in practice skill and discretion often co-vary. Skilled manual workers (still more so surgeons) are expected both to utilise their knowledge and manual skills in successfully completing particular tasks (or operations), and to exercise their discretion: to take responsibility and make decisions as to how to proceed, when faced with unfamiliar, uncertain or unanticipated circumstances. The skill/knowledge is needed in order to be able to exercise that responsibility, but analytically it is more satisfactory to regard skill and discretion as distinct attributes (see Brown 1988). They do not always coincide, and the degradation of work may involve the loss of skill, or the loss of autonomy/discretion, or both. In his study of skill and the English working class, for example, More (1980, 24) focused his account on 'the manual skill and knowledge requirements of jobs', rightly seeing the discretion content ('in Marxian terms, the degree to which conception was integrated with execution') as a separate question. Similarly Littler (1982, 6–7), like More drawing on the work of Fox (1974) and Jaques (1967), distinguished between the number of tasks a worker has to do (the extent to which 'specialization' has taken place), and the discretionary content of jobs, and argued that they do not and need not coincide.

Historical changes in levels of skill

The difficulties in arriving at a satisfactory definition of skill are paralleled by the difficulties of providing an adequate account of the changing skill levels in work in the nineteenth and twentieth centuries. No such account will be attempted here, but some of the problems can be identified. In the first place there is the question of the starting point for the account, in relation to which subsequent changes gain their significance. Braverman's starting point was an understanding of the organisation of production in the pre-industrial period as predominantly carried out by craftsmen, workers who had both the necessary knowledge and manual skills and the autonomy on the job to produce the goods.

> From earliest times to the Industrial Revolution the craft or skilled trade was the basic unit, the elementary cell of the labor process. In each craft, the worker was presumed to be the master of a body of traditional knowledge, and methods and procedures were left to his or her discretion. In each such worker reposed the accumulated knowledge of materials and processes by which production was accomplished in the craft.
>
> (Braverman 1974, 109)

Critics have rightly pointed out that such a view not only provides a highly romanticised view of the craftsman, comparable to that of Mills (1951, 220–4), but is misleading as the sole starting point for an account of the transformation of work following the Industrial Revolution. Certainly some industries in the nineteenth century were dominated by craftsmen (skilled workers who had acquired their skills by means of apprenticeship), either pursuing traditional and pre-industrial skills in the changed context of the factory system or developing new skills on a craft basis. Some of these industries, notably many areas of engineering, experienced the sort of degradation of work outlined by Braverman: increasing mechanisation and the fragmentation of increasingly standardised tasks along Taylorite lines leading to much production work being done by non-skilled workers. The details of this process, however, are considerably more varied than is allowed for in Braverman's account (see, for example, More 1980, 1982; Penn 1982). In other 'craft' industries, such as printing and shipbuilding, the craftsman retained his place in the production process until much later in the twentieth century, though the nature of his skills may have changed (Cockburn 1983; Brown and Brannen 1970; Roberts 1988).

Many industries, however, including ones like coal mining, textiles, iron and steel, and the railways, which were at the centre of the process of industrialisation in Britain and elsewhere, were never organised along craft lines; the skilled workers employed in them acquired their skills other than by apprenticeship, and work was organised and controlled in a wide variety of ways, including much use of internal and external sub-contracting. The degree of collective control over work also varied in such industries, though typically the absence of apprenticeship weakened labour's ability to control entry and thereby increase its power in the labour market. In these industries, too, processes of 'de-skilling' have taken place in the twentieth century but in a variety of circumstances and with far from uniform effects (Littler 1982; Penn 1982). In yet other industries or branches of industry, especially but not only where women were employed in large numbers, work was never recognised as skilled; de-skilling in the sense of a separation of conception and execution and a fragmentation of tasks *previously carried out by craftsmen* could not therefore apply, though comparable processes did take place in many cases.

As might be expected in the light of our discussion of control, contemporary evidence provides an equally complex picture with no clear conclusion that there is a universal tendency towards de-skilling because of the use of a Taylorite strategy to attempt to

control the labour process. Indeed as we shall see in the conclusion to this chapter, there is some evidence of quite different
developments in recent years. Crompton and Jones (1982, 1984),
for example, have argued that much clerical work in banks, insurance and local government has been or is technically
'de-skilled', though the skill 'fiction' is maintained (by demanding
O levels for entry, for example) and there are at least notionally
opportunities for promotion via the internal labour market. The
situation is further complicated by the fact that these opportunities are markedly greater for male than for female employees,
though this situation may be changing. Studies of the introduction
of new, computer based, technology in other areas show a varied
set of outcomes indicating that managerial decisions as to how the
technology is to be used and work controlled can have significantly
different consequences for workers' autonomy and levels of skill
on the shop floor (Jones 1988; Elger 1990; Dankbaar 1988).

Braverman's periodisation of the transformation of industrial
work – a movement from pre-capitalist handicraft production
through manufacture and machinofacture to the full subordination of labour with automation and monopoly capitalism –
has also been criticised. It is seen as providing an analysis which is
too simple and monolithic; the course of developments in the past,
and particularly the extent to which de-skilling could be and was
used as a control strategy, has been much more varied than his
account allows for, and different forms of work organisation and
modes of control have coexisted at all times in the past, as indeed
they do today (Littler 1982, especially 20–35; Littler and Salaman
1982; Thompson 1983, 52–8).

More important, perhaps, is Lee's (1982) argument that a focus
on the changes taking place within particular occupations and
industries is seriously deficient because at a societal level the
question of levels of skill and the extent of de-skilling or enskilling
is determined much more by secular developments in the
industrial and occupational structure, the growth and decline of
industries and occupations. Industry shifts (absolute and relative
changes in the size of different industries) and cyclical shifts
(fluctuations in the level of economic activity) may have more far-
reaching effects on levels of skill in society at large (in so far as they
can be satisfactorily defined at all) than organisational and occupational changes within the enterprise itself. Lee concluded 'One
cannot in any case assume, without a great deal more comparative

research, that net skills in the working class as a whole are either rising or falling' (1982, 162). As was the case with his attractively simple generalisations about the control of the labour process, Braverman's generalisations about the degradation of work have to be modified out of all recognition to accommodate the complexities revealed by historical and contemporary investigations.

CONCLUDING DISCUSSION

In an important sense it was no part of Braverman's, or Marx's, intention to provide an account, still less a model, of industrial organisations. In this sense the perspective they offer is more closely comparable with the social action approach than with the systems thinking discussed in Chapters 2 and 3. As has been the case with the action approach too, although Braverman's work initiated a vigorous debate and a lot of research and writing, few of those who participated presented an overall account of the organisation or organisations they were studying; the focus was on particular aspects – managerial strategies, the organisation and control of work, de-skilling, and so on. Armstrong's (1989) discussion of managerial work provides an illuminating example of one important respect in which a conventional labour process account of organisations can be regarded as incomplete. Nevertheless there is no doubt that the labour process debate contributed greatly to our understanding of industrial organisations even if it left important aspects of those organisations largely unexplored. It provided insights from which future researchers, even those who do not share exactly the same presuppositions, can gain a great deal.

An important part of the attractiveness of Braverman's argument lay in the way it located an analysis of the organisation and control of work in industrial enterprises within an overall conception of the structure and dynamics of capitalist society. In contrast to closed systems thinking and the action approach to organisations in particular, the links between industrial organisations and their environments were built into the mode of analysis being proposed, not added on as an after-thought. The continuing pressures to expand capital by the creation and appropriation of new value were seen as leading to an imperative to control the labour process; and Taylorism was identified by Braverman as the control strategy in the era of monopoly capitalism. The most fundamental criticisms of Braverman's position can therefore be seen as those which argue that accumulation does not occur only within the labour process and that it is necessary to consider the whole 'circuit of capital'; and that there are alternative means and 'levels' of control such that Taylorism is only one of a number of possible 'strategies'.

If these arguments are seen as sound, as I think they should be, then one is faced with a very much less narrowly determined situation, one where there is room, conceptually, for agency and choice. Employers are not totally constrained by the imperatives of an advanced capitalist economy but, at least in principle, can choose between a variety of alternative strategies of control. Any control strategy consists of a variety of means and, within limits, these can be combined and recombined in different ways. The reactions and resistance of the actual or potential labour force exert an influence on the ways in which such choices are exercised. In trying to understand and explain the choices made by management and the degree of resistance offered by labour ideological factors are bound to be of importance. An approach, like Braverman's, which sees action as more or less entirely determined by the exigencies of the situation, and which explicitly excludes consideration of the 'subjective' content of class, will be seriously deficient. Because values and ideologies are important as influences on action, ideology is important in another context too: control can be exercised, at least in part, through ideological influences as well as through the techniques of Scientific Management, technical devices and/or other management actions. Such ideological influences may, for example, include paternalist employment policies which extend well beyond the workplace, or the use of gender, ethnic, religious and other divisions in the workforce to gain the commitment of the more highly favoured group(s).

Thus it seems that Littler's judgement (1982, 33–4) that 'there can be no theory of the capitalist labour process' is a sound one. It is not possible to argue that there is a clear overall pattern in twentieth century capitalist societies of a more or less universal degradation of work due to the increasingly general, and unavoidable, adoption of Scientific Management methods to control work. All that is possible is to provide accounts of the ways in which work has been organised and controlled in historically and culturally specific circumstances, and the reasons why a particular outcome is to be found in a specific case. Braverman's account is very insightful and may be appropriate in a considerable number of cases but it has to be seen as only one of a very much larger range of possibilities.

For those seeking a single overarching explanatory schema, and perhaps also the possibility of prediction, this will seem a disappointing conclusion to a lengthy discussion. It does, however, have certain welcome consequences. One of them is that much of the earlier research and writing, which enthusiasts for Braverman's approach have sometimes dismissed as theoretically ill-informed, misdirected and no longer relevant, can be more appropriately seen as still offering important insights and arguments regarding the organisation and control of work. More important, it becomes more easily possible to develop arguments which apply to employing organisations of all kinds and are not only applicable to capitalist enterprises in monopoly capitalist societies, as it can be suggested that Braverman's arguments are.

There are certain important elements to be retained from the whole labour process debate. Employment – the buying and selling of labour power – necessarily involves employers, or their agents, in exercising control if the employees' potential is to be realised in the work they do. Realising that potential also necessitates securing at least some measure of cooperation from employees. The employment relationship is an inherently ambivalent not to say contradictory one. An adequate understanding of any organisation which involves the employment of paid labour has to explore the ways in which managements attempt to secure this control, and the cooperation of their employees, and the reactions, possibly resistance, of employees of various sorts to their strategies. The labour process debate also demonstrates that the analysis has to extend outside the organisation to consider the ways in which labour power is produced and reproduced on a daily and a generational basis, which involves considering enterprises in their context – local, national and international – and issues like the gender division of labour. Organisations can not be analysed in isolation from the wider society.

Flexibility

As has been outlined in Chapter 1, the 1970s and 1980s have seen major changes in the composition of the labour force, the structure and distribution of employment, and the organisation and management of paid work. These changes will certainly challenge sociologists and others to reconsider their approaches to understanding industrial organisations and to utilise new concepts and models. One example of such developments is the notion of 'flexibility'. This term has gained considerable prominence in the 1980s and has been used in a variety of ways each of which captures something of the character of contemporary changes in employment. At the time of writing it seems unlikely that discussions of flexibility will grow to rival the labour process debate in size or importance, but a brief account of the arguments about flexibility can both bring the story more nearly up to date and reinforce some of the points which have just been made about the labour process debate.

A convenient starting point is the notion of 'the flexible firm' (Atkinson and Meager 1986). This is best considered as an ideal type accentuating certain features of employment relations in the 1980s and 1990s. The flexible firm is one which has attempted to secure three sorts of flexibility: numerical flexibility, the ability to change the size of the workforce quickly and easily in response to changes in demand; functional flexibility, the ease with which workers can be redeployed to different tasks to meet changes in market demand, technology or company policy; and pay flexibility, the extent to which the structure of pay encourages and supports the other two sorts of flexibility, and the level of pay reflects individual performance and the market rate for the skill in question (Atkinson 1985). Numerical and functional flexibilities are achieved primarily by dividing the workforce between a core with a real degree of security in exchange for willingness, and skills, to move between different tasks; and peripheral categories of workers without long term security of employment: part-time and fixed term contract workers, and sub-contractors, self-employed specialists, home workers and agency temporary workers outside the firm.

The notion of the flexible firm has aroused considerable controversy. Some of the criticisms are concerned with the concept itself, for example as to how far a number of disparate developments have been conflated to construct a supposed managerial strategy in a political context where some politicians and employers were keen to claim that a fundamental restructuring of employment was taking place (see, for example, Pollert 1988).

Others have been concerned with the extent to which it can be claimed that this sort of pattern of employment is at all widespread in Britain; the evidence for it is far from clear (see Brown 1990, 313–23; Hakim 1990). Indeed at the centre of the idea of a flexible firm there appears to be a distinction between core and periphery which parallels the familiar difference between responsible autonomy and direct control seen by Friedman (1977a, 1977b) as the two basic strategies available to capitalist employers.

A related, but theoretically more sophisticated notion has been the idea of flexible specialisation. The starting points for this idea lie in both the changing nature of consumer demand and the new possibilities offered by modern, especially electronic, technologies. In western capitalist societies, it is argued, consumers are no longer satisfied with readily available, relatively inexpensive, standardised goods and services but wish to have greater choice from a more highly differentiated range of products which also reflect changing fashion. It is possible to meet this demand through the use of computer based technologies and by employing a functionally flexible workforce, with polyvalent skills, in smaller enterprises able to produce small batches of higher quality goods (see Piore and Sabel 1984). Thus, as 'Fordist' mass production is transferred to low wage third world countries, 'post-Fordism' develops in the advanced capitalist societies of the West. Lane has pointed out, however, that certain preconditions, such as a surviving craft tradition and systems of industrial relations based on cooperation, may be necessary; and that such developments are likely to proceed in a more pronounced and consistent way in (West) Germany than in Britain, though even in Germany Taylorism has not been completely abandoned (Lane 1988, especially 142–3).

Flexible specialisation is far from being merely the creation of academic commentators. There are developments in firms, industries and industrial districts in most advanced capitalist societies which correspond to what is being claimed. What is more questionable is how widespread and significant the changes are; do they, in Piore and Sabel's phrase, represent 'a second industrial divide'? Indeed, could they do so given the continuing high levels of demand for cheap mass produced products and the absence so far of technologies which enable them to be provided without a great deal of work organised along traditional repetitive and labour intensive lines? There are few signs, in Britain especially, of managements being able or willing to make the necessary large-scale investment in equipment and, even more important, training to make possible widespread use of flexible specialisation strategies. Such strategies are appealing because they appear to benefit both producers (more skilled and rewarding work) and consumers (greater choice, better quality products), but wishful thinking is a dangerous basis for sociological generalisation.

What the discussion of flexibility does provide is one more illustration of alternatives to Taylorism as a basis for the organisation and control of work in the late twentieth century. It refers however to only one set of such alternatives and it is far from clear at the moment how influential they are going to be. The questions which emerged from the discussion of the labour process debate remain: what approach or perspective is likely to provide the most adequate framework for the analysis of industrial organisations, and what elements can be retained from the labour process debate, and indeed from any of the other perspectives which have been discussed? The concluding chapter will indicate, all too briefly, one possible answer to these questions.

Chapter 6

Conclusion

Our review of four approaches to the analysis of industrial organisations covers only a small proportion of the massive and continuously expanding literature on this subject. The frameworks which have been considered, however, provide some indication of the very different ways in which sociologists have tried to characterise organisations and explain the patterns of social relations and social action within them. Other writers have presented an even more highly differentiated picture. Morgan (1986), for example, organised his discussion around eight 'images of organization': as machines, as organisms, as brains, as cultures, as political regimes, as psychic prisons, as flux and transformation, and as instruments of domination. Each 'image' throws some light on the nature of organisations, but even this list does not exhaust the possibilities!

To some extent the approaches we have considered constitute a continuing debate about organisations. Arguments have been developed and approaches suggested with the explicit intention of repairing the perceived deficiencies of earlier theories. It may be possible to claim some degree of cumulation of ideas, that more recent writing shows an awareness of, and avoids, some of the weaknesses of earlier formulations. Each of the approaches can claim to make some contribution to a set of desiderata for a sociology of industrial organisations. On that basis one can sketch a minimum list of headings for such a set:

1 the systemic nature of organisations, both because of the intentions and actions of (powerful) members, and because the unintended as well as the intended consequences of social action structure organisational life; but organisations may best

be seen as a plurality of systems rather than as necessarily one system;

2 the ways in which organisational arrangements are contingent on the economic, legal, political, social and technological contexts;

3 the key problem for any organisation with employees of controlling those employees to ensure task performance to meet the (variable) demands of market and/or budget;

4 the variations possible in means, levels and locations of control, but the inevitability of contradictory consequences whatever controls are used;

5 the influences on action within organisations of members' values, priorities and expectations, and the ways in which these are influenced by factors and experiences outside, as well as inside, employment; and

6 the inevitability of conflicts of interest between individuals and groups within organisations and the nature of the mechanisms for resolving (or suppressing) such differences.

In other respects, however, the different writers must be seen as talking past each other, as deriving their arguments from discrepant and probably incompatible premises and assumptions. In these circumstances it is impossible to claim that we now have an agreed and coherent approach to the sociological analysis of organisations which somehow transcends the differences between these various perspectives. Any attempt to develop such a composite approach will inevitably have to choose between conflicting emphases, which have not so far been resolved, and therefore will itself be subject to criticism as a partial approach.

One way of categorising these discrepant demands is to see them as reflecting one or other side of a division which has been identified as running through contemporary social theory, and which in one form or another has been an issue for a very much longer time: the apparent incompatibility of a sociology based on social structure and a sociology based on social action. Dawe (1970, 214), for example, referred to 'two sociologies . . . grounded in the diametrically opposed concerns with two central problems, those of order and control . . . one views action as derivative of system, whilst the other views system as the derivative of action'. More recently Abrams (1982) and Giddens, in a series of books (1976, 1979, 1984), have tried to suggest ways in which this supposed incompatibility could be resolved. Abrams advocated a sociology which addressed the 'problematic of structuring' by transcending the conventional divisions between sociology and history. Giddens has developed the idea of 'structuration' as the central process in human society, and has referred to 'the recursive nature of social life': the ways in which 'the structured properties of social activity – via the duality of structure – are constantly recreated out of the very resources which constitute them' (1984, xxiii).

This dualism of structure and action underlies many of the problems raised by the approaches to organisational analysis discussed in previous chapters. A major criticism of systems thinking is its tendency to reify the system and its neglect of human agency. The emphasis on strategic choice as a necessary element in any contingency theory of organisations represents an assertion of the importance of social action in a context where structural factors were receiving overwhelming emphasis. The central issue in many of the criticisms of and modifications to labour process analysis has been the importance of individual and/or collective action, especially on the part of workers and their trade unions, in resisting the controls exercised by employers, and the recognition that employers have some possibilities of choice of strategy. In contrast the weakness of the 'action approach' to organisations has been its neglect of structure, its failure adequately to incorporate in analysis the technological and social structural conditions for action.

This book is not intended to offer a resolution of these complex issues, which need separate treatment. What can be attempted is to take some steps towards a sociology of industrial organisations, which draws on elements in the approaches considered in the earlier chapters, and which may be helpful in constructing a more satisfactory framework. Two notions especially, drawn respectively from developments within the action approach and the debates about the labour process, can perhaps contribute most to the formulation of a more adequate approach for understanding industrial organisations. They are the notion of organisation as 'negotiated order', and a focus on the employment relationship. The former accentuates the ways in which organisational structures need to be seen as continually (re)created by the actions and interactions of their members. It reflects the continuing processes of conflict, negotiation, bargaining and (at least temporarily) resolution of differences which characterise organisations and create the patterns of roles and relationships within them. The employment relationship focuses attention on the key issue around which this 'negotiation' will revolve: the regulation of the relations between employer and employee, which is necessary if work is to be done.

ORGANISATION AS NEGOTIATED ORDER

The initial formulation by Strauss and his colleagues (first published 1963) of the notion of an organisation as a 'negotiated order' was made when reporting findings from a study of a psychiatric hospital in the USA, but the concept can be applied much more generally. It belongs on the 'action' side of the 'structure/action' divide, but nevertheless provides perhaps the best starting point for attempts to develop an approach to organisational analysis which transcends that dichotomy. The authors wrote:

> order is something at which members of any society, any organization must work. For the shared agreements, the binding contracts – which constitute the grounds for an expectable, non-surprising, taken-for-granted, even ruled orderliness – are not binding and shared for all time . . . the bases of concerted action (social order) must be reconstituted continually, or, as remarked above, 'worked at'.
>
> Such considerations have led us to emphasize the importance of negotiation – the processes of give-and-take, of diplomacy, of bargaining – which characterizes organizational life.
>
> (1971, 103–4)

In the remainder of their account the authors elaborated on this initial statement of their perspective. They suggested that an organization such as a hospital is a 'locale' where employees drawn from different occupations (and other persons such as, in their case, patients) come together to work out their respective purposes. They will have different commitments, ideologies and ambitions reflecting differences in their occupational training and socialisation, their positions in the organisational hierarchy, and the stage reached in their careers; and different views as to the 'proper division of labour'. Such differences cannot be resolved by reference to any shared 'single, vaguely ambiguous goal' which is of mainly symbolic importance, nor by reference to the organisation's rules ('far from extensive, or clearly stated or clearly binding'); application of the rules needs judgement and they represent a resource to be used, stretched, broken, and so on. The resulting negotiation is 'patterned' in various ways: by implicit or explicit time limits to agreements, as stressed in the above quotation; in terms of the issues (in the case of hospitals, for example, programmes of treatment for patients, and the role of non-professionals); and by demands from outside agencies such as the state and professional associations. They concluded:

> The model presented has pictured the hospital as a locale where personnel, mostly but not exclusively professionals, are enmeshed in a complex negotiative process in order both to accomplish their individual purposes and to work – in an established division of labour – toward clearly as well as vaguely phrased institutional objectives. We have sought to show how differential professional training, ideology, career, and hierarchical position all affect the negotiation. . .
>
> (1971, 121)

Such a model is seen by its proponents as relevant to the study of 'corporations, universities and government agencies' which, like hospitals, also have complex divisions of labour.

In a largely sympathetic review and critique of 'negotiated order theory' Day and Day (1977) suggested that it has several important limitations. These include its neglect of the outside environment of an organisation, the structural features of the wider society. They argued that 'By necessity the theory will have to become much more politically, structurally, and historically grounded than it has been in the past' (140). Such criticism is justified. The approach represents an important corrective to overly structural accounts of organisations, and rightly emphasises the importance of the actions of and interactions between members in creating the order which is organisation. However, it fails to give sufficient attention to the conditions within which such action and inter-action take place. Yet all action is constrained to some extent, and action (and negotiation) within organisations such as industrial enterprises are only likely to be possible within more or less narrow limits which are not, or not easily, amenable to modification by the actors involved.

The emphasis in Strauss and his colleagues' formulation on the ways in which the 'order' within organisations is negotiated must therefore be complemented by an attempt to specify some of the conditions which provide the setting for such processes. Most important of all are the technical and, especially, economic exigencies which industrial organisations have to meet if they are to remain viable as enterprises which produce goods and/or services within the constraints of the market(s) and/or the limits of the budget. The starting point for exploring the technical and economic constraints on action within industrial organisations is probably the product (or service); what is being, or is to be produced, and for whom, sets limits to organisational structure and operation. Though technological requirements in relation to a particular product rarely determine social relations and the organisation of production in any complete sense they are likely to impose some limits on what is possible. These limits may well be made tighter by the constraints of the markets within which the organisation operates: the markets for capital, raw materials and/or other supplies, and labour, and for the sale of the product or service. Large and powerful organisations may be able to dominate, even control, some or all of the markets in which they operate, but for most organisations these factor and, especially, product markets represent more or less intractable conditions of action.

The situation for what Jaques termed 'grant income' organisations is slightly different in that they may not be subject to product market constraints, if they do not sell their goods or services, though they are unlikely to escape factor market constraints (e.g. the costs of materials, labour, etc.). What replaces the product market in such cases are the budgetary limits put on their resources by the controlling agency, often, of course, government. These may vary over time in quite marked ways, just as the conditions of action for 'earned income' enterprises can differ over time and between different firms, industries, countries, and so on.

Political processes are of considerable importance for governmental and quasi-governmental organisations, but political processes and institutions, and especially the state, influence all industrial organisations: very directly through legislation and regulation, less directly by means of incentives, sanctions and influence; so too do the activities of associations of employees (trade unions, professional associations) and the institutions of industrial relations, which provide the framework for bargaining between employers and employees, or their respective representatives. Much of this 'negotiation' typically takes place 'outside' industrial organisations, though there are variations over time and as between industries and societies as to the extent to which this is the case. As Flanders (1970, 86) has rightly pointed out such industrial relations activity is a rule making process, institutionalised means of job regulation. What Flanders failed to pursue is the ways in which the agreements reached between trade union officials and employers' representatives, or between managers and shop stewards, during processes of collective bargaining, are themselves negotiated and renegotiated in the day-to-day interaction of managers, supervisors and employees in the workplace.

Historical and cultural influences can be crucial, even if difficult to establish. Organisations, and the industries and economies of which they are a part, have histories during which relations and procedures have become institutionalised, allocations of resources have been established and some courses of action have come to be seen as legitimate or at least normatively preferred. Marx (1973, 146) asserted the importance of history, and recognised the duality of structure and action, in a much quoted sentence:

> Men make their own history, but not of their own free will; not under circumstances they themselves have chosen but under given and inherited circumstances with which they are directly confronted.

Comparative studies of organisations have demonstrated the importance of the differences in culture within and between societies for any account of organisational characteristics. The case of Japanese industrial organisations and management, where cultural differences are regarded as one important factor in accounting for differences from the West, is the most obvious example of a more general phenomenon.

Thus the negotiating of 'order' in organisations takes place within conditions of action which are largely 'given' so far as most if not all members of the organisations are concerned. Recognition that this is so should go some way to remedy a further weakness of the approach as suggested by Strauss and his colleagues. This is their failure to acknowledge adequately that although all members of an organisation (even patients in a mental hospital) are able to negotiate the conditions of their participation to some extent, they cannot do so to the same extent; some are much more powerful than others, and can draw on more and possibly more varied resources – material and/or ideational – to secure their own preferred outcome to any 'negotiation'. Whilst the hierarchies which are characteristic of most organisations both embody and perpetuate such differences in power, they are often also reinforced from sources external to the organisation such as other organisations, professional associations and trade unions, and the state.

EMPLOYMENT RELATIONS

Industrial organisations have in common that they are composed of people engaged under contracts of employment. They exist because and in so far as those who establish and/or control them are able to employ others to undertake work. The employment relationship is a central and inescapable feature of such organisations. Like all legal agreements employment contracts typically do not state explicitly the full range of expectations, rights and obligations which are implied. As compared with contracts which regulate the buying and selling of other commodities, however, employment contracts which regulate the buying and selling of labour power have certain other important distinctive features. In the first place, the exchange of wages or salaries for work is not one which can take place instantaneously; it implies a continuing relationship between employer and employee in order for the work to be done for which the payment is to be made. Secondly, the contract itself is normally remarkably indeterminate or 'open-ended'; it typically does not and possibly cannot state in more than very general terms the nature of the employee's obligations, the work he or she is expected to do in return for payment.

The buying and selling of most commodities, whether expensive and complex like a house or a car, or simple and everyday like purchasing a newspaper, involves a transaction which takes place at a precise point in time. In contrast, employment involves employees entering into a continuing relationship with the purchasers of their labour power because it is only over time that they can 'deliver' the work for which they are being paid. Moreover it is very difficult, if not impossible, for the employer to specify in advance precisely what is expected of the employee; this can only be worked out in the continuing day-to-day relations which the employment contract establishes. It is difficult because of the costs of trying to specify in advance all that employees might be expected to do during their hours of employment (which typically are specified) (see Marsden 1986, 22). It may be inherently impossible because of the problems of including in a contract a meaningful and enforceable statement of the quantity and quality of work which is being demanded: how hard the employee is to work, and what standards of performance are required. Lupton and Bowey indicate some of the problems involved:

> The contract of employment between an employer and an employee hardly ever specifies exactly what the employee undertakes to do during each hour or day of his employment. It is neither possible nor desirable to define every action and sequence of actions precisely, because the employer usually seeks a degree of freedom to direct the work-force to perform tasks which are appropriate to the changing demands of customers, the availability of materials, breakdowns of machinery or equipment and so on. And the employee seeks a degree of freedom to respond as he thinks fit. The limits within which these freedoms may be exercised are sometimes written into a contract and sometimes 'understood', but in either case custom and practice will further elaborate what it is reasonable for the employer to demand of the employee and vice versa.
>
> (1974, 74)

These continuing relationships between employer and employee are also relations of authority, of super- and sub-ordination. To accept employment is to enter into a situation involving loss of freedom and autonomy, of being prepared, within whatever limits, to do as one is told. Without such power employers would be unable to ensure that the work for which they are paying would actually be done as and when they wish it to be done. Much of the administrative apparatus of large-scale employing organisations can be seen as comprising the means of 'closing' the employment contract and ensuring the performance to desired standards of the tasks for which workers are being employed. The exercise of authority would be needed in any circumstances in order to ensure that tasks were completed to time and in a coordinated way. It is all the more necessary, from the employer's point of view, because the interests of employer and employee are in conflict.

This conflict derives from the fact that whereas for the employee the wage or salary is income, for the employer it is a cost. For any employer providing goods or services in a competitive market there will be pressures to contain or reduce labour costs, and if this is not done there is a danger that the enterprise will be forced out of business. For employers in the public sector there are more or less equivalent restrictions on labour costs arising from finite budgets within which demands for goods or services, which are always likely to be expanding, have to be met. The conflict is not only about the size of the wage packet or salary cheque, however, but also concerns what work the employee is required to do, their levels of physical and mental effort, the responsibilities they are to carry, and so on. In this way the employer's exercise of authority, and the employee's defence of a degree of autonomy on the job, are equally a source of conflict. The terms of the employment contract include both pay and other rewards, and the contribution which the employee is expected to make to the employing enterprise. Both may be contentious.

Examination of the employment relationship emphasises the central and unavoidable place which the processes of controlling the activities of employees must have in any analysis of industrial organisations. The problem of transforming 'labour power' into 'labour', to use Marx's terms, or of realising the potential to work which is all that can be secured through contracts of employment, is not of course the only problem faced by employers. They also have to obtain capital, negotiate with suppliers, secure markets, control cash flow, calculate profit and loss, and so on. As most accounts of organisation structures recognise these are basic activities which are likely to be differentiated and allocated to specialists at an early stage in the growth of an organisation. That in itself, however, means employing others and ensuring that the tasks for which they are to be paid are completed in a satisfactory manner. Indeed, there are likely to be special problems in controlling the work of managers and professionals (see Armstrong 1989).

The employment relationship is an inherently ambivalent one. Employer and employee have conflicting interests in both parts of the employment contract: the contribution to be expected from the employee, and the pay and other rewards to be exchanged for that contribution. They have shared interests in the continued viability of the organisation itself on which both parties depend. The conflicting interests cannot be resolved at the moment of agreeing the contract of employment within the sphere of the labour market: it has to be worked out within the organisation as part of the ongoing interaction between the two parties. Only in the process of actually carrying out the work for which the employee has been hired can the employee's contribution finally be specified in any determinate way. The contested nature of the employees' contributions – how hard they are working, how skilled and responsible their work is – make it highly likely that the employment relationship will have to be continually renegotiated as circumstances change. Over time such relationships may, of course, become more highly institutionalised; and there are likely to be pressures to regulate employment relations and impose normative sanctions on the parties so as to prevent disruptive consequences developing from the ongoing processes of conflict and negotiation. Such social controls are unlikely to be complete or to last indefinitely.

Analysis along these lines, it is suggested, could provide the bases for an approach to understanding industrial organisations which was capable of at least recognising the claims of both sides of the structure/action dichotomy. It recognises that order is created by the actions and interactions of organisational members and that the resultant organisation itself constitutes the conditions and resources for such action and interaction. It also both seeks to explore the contexts for those processes, and suggests that attention should be focused on the employment relationship as the central issue around which negotiative processes take place. Any attempt to apply these ideas would inevitably involve looking at processes in organisation(s) over time and would therefore go some way to meeting Abrams's demand that sociology be historical.

EMPLOYMENT AND WORK

It remains to return to questions raised in the opening chapter about the definition and delimitation of the scope of industrial sociology. One of the major sources of difficulty in providing a coherent account of the field(s) to be covered within the 'sociology of industry' is in the word 'industry' itself. It is an imprecise term, with a variety of meanings and connotations, and only with difficulty can it be seen as designating an institutional area or a set of social relations or a type of organisation which has some clear features in common, and which is demarcated from other such areas or types. One dictionary definition, for example, nicely encapsulates the problem: it refers to 'a particular branch of productive labour, a trade or manufacture'. Such a definition must exclude much of the public sector (civil service, local government, education, health, etc.) and, it could be argued, much of the service sector more generally (are banking, insurance, advertising, and so on 'productive'?). Yet in terms of the problems normally considered within industrial sociology – the nature of industrial organisations, relations between employers and employees, management, work groups, and so on – there are enough common features between (say) the engineering industry, banking and the health service to make it desirable to extend 'industrial' sociology to cover them all.

A focus on the employment relationship would obviate these difficulties and provide theoretically defensible grounds for considering engineering, banking, the health 'industry' and so on within a common framework. What all these areas of activity have in common is that they are providing goods and/or services and that people are employed to carry out the necessary work. Sociological analysis which focused on employment could have a certain coherence. There are, of course, important differences between manufacturing and service industries, and private and public sectors, which such analysis will identify, but such differences would provide the possibility of comparisons which could aid the analysis of phenomena which also have analytically relevant features in common.

The search for analytically illuminating comparisons, and for coherence and comprehensiveness in a field of study, make a further step desirable. The employment relationship is only one context within which work can be carried out. Although it is the most important context in our sort of society (industrial), in terms of human history as a whole work by peasants, slaves, serfs, artisans, and 'self-employed' merchants, traders and businessmen and women, has been quantitatively much more significant. A focus on the employment relationship would provide an appropriate point of reference for the topics discussed in this book (the perspectives considered have all been concerned with organisations which are centred on employment). Comparison with other settings for and types of work – domestic work, voluntary work, the 'work' of criminals, and so on – can, however, greatly increase our understanding of the nature of employment and of organisations of employees.

As is also the case for 'employment', there are difficulties in giving 'work' a completely watertight definition. Some activities (or, in the case of employment, relationships) may be hard to classify; there will always be 'grey' areas. Work can refer to any of an enormous range of activities many of which may, in certain contexts, be regarded as recreation, play or leisure. Work refers to any physical and mental activities which transform materials into a more useful form, provide or distribute goods or services to others, and extend human knowledge and understanding. Many such activities – craft 'work', for example – may be carried out for their own sake as part of people's leisure or recreation. These and other activities are work when they are done for reasons that are instrumental, directed towards meeting one's own or other's needs; they are work when they involve providing goods and/or services for which others are willing to pay, or for which the provider would otherwise have to pay. A definition of work therefore involves reference to both the activity and the purpose for which that activity is being carried out.

Defined in this sort of way it becomes clear both that many work tasks can be performed in any of a variety of settings – within social relations of employment, domestically, on a voluntary basis, and so on; and that historically and contemporaneously specific work activities do move between such settings (see especially Pahl 1984). Industrial sociology focuses on only one such setting and, though in other respects it could provide a more satisfactory point of reference, a sociology of employment would do the same. Attention is directed to the paid work people do and the ways in which it is allocated, organised and controlled. There are very good grounds, however, for suggesting that the more basic question is how members of a society provide for their material needs: through employment to earn a wage or salary, through work within the family and household, through 'do it yourself', by means of shared endeavour with family, friends and/or neighbours, and so on. Employment is then placed in a broader context, one which can both provide useful comparisons between paid and other forms of work, and allow some assessment of the significance of employment in society as a whole.

This brief concluding discussion has taken us some way from the large-scale industrial organisations with which this book began. In whatever directions sociology develops more generally, it is likely that such organisations will continue to attract the scholarly attentions of sociologists and others, and rightly so. A sociology of work, which includes within it study of the social relations of employment and of the organisations within which people are employed, will, I believe, provide a fruitful framework for carrying forward the task of understanding industrial organisations.

Bibliography

Abrams, P. (1982) *Historical Sociology*, Shepton Mallet, Somerset, Open Books.

Acton Society Trust (1951) *Training and Promotion in Nationalised Industry*, London, Allen & Unwin.

Aitken, H.G.J. (1960) *Taylorism at Watertown Arsenal*, Cambridge, Mass., Harvard University Press.

Albrow, M. (1968) The study of organizations – objectivity or bias?, in J. Gould (ed.) *Penguin Social Sciences Survey 1968*, Harmondsworth, Middx, Penguin, 146–67.

Albrow, M. (1970) *Bureaucracy*, London, Macmillan.

Aldrich, H.E. (1972) Technology and organisational structure: a re-examination of the findings of the Aston Group, *Administrative Science Quarterly*, 17, 1, 26–43.

Allen, V.L. (1971) *The Sociology of Industrial Relations*, London, Longman.

Allen, V.L. (1975) *Social Analysis. A Marxist critique and alternative*, London, Longman.

Amsden, A.H. (ed.) (1980) *The Economics of Women and Work*, Harmondsworth, Middx, Penguin.

Armstrong, P. (1989) Management, labour process and agency, *Work, Employment and Society*, 3, 3, 307–22.

Atkinson, J. (1985) Flexibility and the workforce: a good night out?, *Work and Society*, 9, 2–4.

Atkinson, J. and Meager, N. (1986) *Changing Working Patterns. How companies achieve flexibility to meet new needs*, London, National Economic Development Office.

Bakke, E.W. (1950) *Bonds of Organization*, New York, Harper.

Bakke, E.W. (1959) Concept of social organization, in M. Haire (ed.) *Modern Organization Theory*, New York, Wiley.

Baldamus, W. (1961) *Efficiency and Effort*, London, Tavistock.

Baldamus, W. (1976) *The Structure of Sociological Inference*, London, Martin Robertson.

Banks, J.A. (1963) *Industrial Participation. Theory and practice: a case study*, Liverpool, Liverpool University Press.

Banks, J.A. (1974) *Trades Unionism*, London, Collier-Macmillan.

Baritz, L. (1960) *The Servants of Power*, New York, Wiley.

Barron, R.D. and Norris, G.M. (1976) Sexual divisions and the dual labour market, in D.L. Barker and S. Allen (eds) *Dependence and Exploitation in Work and Marriage*, London, Longman, 47–69.

Bechhofer, F. (1973) The relationship between technology and shop-floor behaviour, in D.O. Edge and J.N. Wolfe (eds) *Meaning and Control*, London, Tavistock.

Beechey, V. (1982) The sexual division of labour and the labour process: a critical assessment of Braverman, in S. Wood (ed.) *The Degradation of work? Skill, deskilling and the labour process*, London, Hutchinson, 54–73.

Beechey, V. (1986) Women's employment in contemporary Britain, in V. Beechey and E. Whitelegg (eds) *Women in Britain Today*, Milton Keynes, Open University Press.

Beechey, V. (1987) *Unequal Work*, London, Verso.

Bendix, R. (1956) *Work and Authority in Industry*, New York, Wiley (1963 edition, New York, Harper and Row).

Bennett, R. (1974) Orientation to work and some implications for management, *Journal of Management Studies*, 11, 2, 149–62.

Bennett, R. (1978) Orientation to work and organizational analysis: a conceptual analysis, integration and suggested application, *Journal of Management Studies*, 15, 2, 187–210.

Berger, P. and Luckmann, T. (1967) *The Social Construction of Reality*, London, Allen & Unwin.

Berle, A.A. and Means, G.C. (1932) *The Modern Corporation and Private Property*, New York, Macmillan.

Von Bertalanffy, L. (1950) The theory of open systems in physics and biology, *Science*, 111, 13 January, 23–9.

Beynon, H. (1973) (2nd edition 1984) *Working for Ford*, Harmondsworth, Middx, Penguin.

Beynon, H. and Blackburn, R.M. (1972) *Perceptions of Work. Variations within a factory*, Cambridge, Cambridge University Press.

Beynon, H. and Nichols, T. (1971) Modern British sociology and the affluent worker, unpublished paper.

Bion, W.R. (1961) *Experiences in Groups and other Papers*, London, Tavistock.

Blackburn, R.M. and Mann, M. (1979) *The Working Class in the Labour Market*, London, Macmillan.

Blain, I. (1964) *Structure in Management. A study of different forms and their effectiveness*, London, National Institute of Industrial Psychology (Report No. 17).

Blau, P.M. (1955) (revised edition 1963) *The Dynamics of Bureaucracy*, Chicago, University of Chicago Press.

Blau, P.M. (1956) *Bureaucracy in Modern Society*, New York, Random House.

Blau, P.M. and Scott, W.R. (1963) *Formal Organizations*, London, Routledge & Kegan Paul.

Blauner, R. (1964) *Alienation and Freedom*, Chicago, Chicago University Press.

Bottomore, T. (1963) *Karl Marx. Early writings*, London, C.A. Watts & Co.

Bottomore, T. (1979) Marxism and sociology, in T. Bottomore and R.

Nisbet (eds) *A History of Sociological Analysis*, London, Heinemann, 118–48.

Bottomore, T. and Nisbet, R. (eds) (1979) *A History of Sociological Analysis*, London, Heinemann.

Boulding, K.E. (1956) General systems theory – the skeleton of science, *Management Science*, 2, 197–208.

Brannen, P. (1983) *Authority and Participation in Industry*, London, Batsford.

Braverman, H. (1974) *Labor and Monopoly Capital*, New York, Monthly Review Press.

Brighton Labour Process Group (1977) The capitalist labour process, *Capital and Class*, 1, Spring, 3–26.

Brown, C., Guillet de Monthoux, P. and McCullough, A. (eds) (1976) *The Access Casebook*, Stockholm, Teknisk Högskolelitteratur.

Brown, J.A.C. (1954) *The Social Psychology of Industry*, Harmondsworth, Middx, Penguin.

Brown, R.K. (1965) Participation, conflict and change in industry. A review of research in industrial sociology at the Department of Social Science, University of Liverpool, *Sociological Review*, 13, 3, 273–95.

Brown, R.K. (1967) Research and consultancy in industrial enterprises. A review of the contribution of the Tavistock Institute of Human Relations to the development of industrial sociology, *Sociology*, 1, 1, 33–60.

Brown, R.K. (1974) The attitudes to work, expectations and social perspectives of shipbuilding apprentices, in T. Leggatt (ed.) *Sociological Theory and Survey Research*, London, Sage.

Brown, R.K. (1976) Women as employees: some comments on research in industrial sociology, in D.L. Barker and S. Allen (eds) *Dependence and Exploitation in Work and Marriage*, London, Longman, 21–46 (reprinted with a postscript in D. Leonard and S. Allen [eds] *Sexual Divisions Revisisted*, London, Macmillan, 1991, 122–52).

Brown, R.K. (1984) Work: past, present and future, in K. Thompson (ed.) *Work, Employment and Unemployment*, Milton Keynes, Open University Press, 261–75.

Brown, R.K. (1988) The employment relationship in sociological theory, in D. Gallie (ed.) *Employment in Britain*, Oxford, Blackwell, 33–66.

Brown, R.K. (1990) A flexible future in Europe? Changing patterns of employment in the United Kingdom, *British Journal of Sociology*, 41, 3, 301–27.

Brown, R.K. and Brannen, P. (1970) Social relations and social perspectives amongst shipbuilding workers – a preliminary statement, *Sociology*, 4, 1 and 2, 71–84 and 197–211.

Brown, R.K., Brannen, P., Cousins, J.M. and Samphier, M.L. (1972) The contours of solidarity: social stratification and industrial relations in shipbuilding, *British Journal of Industrial Relations*, 10, 1, 12–41.

Brown, R.K., Curran, M.M. and Cousins, J.M. (1983) *Changing Attitudes to Employment?*, Research Paper No. 40, London, Department of Employment.

Brown, W. (1962) *Piecework Abandoned*, London, Heinemann.

Brown, W. (1965) *Exploration in Management,* Harmondsworth, Middx, Penguin (first published London, Heinemann, 1960).

Brown, W. (1973) *The Earnings Conflict,* London, Heinemann.

Brown, W. (1974) *Organization,* Harmondsworth, Middx, Penguin (first published London, Heinemann, 1971).

Brown, W. and Jaques, E. (1964) *Product Analysis Pricing,* London, Heinemann.

Brown, W. and Jaques, E. (1965) *Glacier Project Papers,* London, Heinemann.

Buckley, W. (1967) *Sociology and Modern Systems Theory,* Englewood Cliffs, New Jersey, Prentice Hall.

Bulmer, M. (ed.) (1975) *Working Class Images of Society,* London, Routledge & Kegan Paul.

Burawoy, M. (1978) Towards a Marxist theory of the labour process: Braverman and beyond, *Politics and Society,* 8, 3 and 4, 247–312.

Burawoy, M. (1979) *Manufacturing Consent. Changes in the labor process under monopoly capitalism,* Chicago, Chicago University Press.

Burawoy, M. (1985) *The Politics of Production. Factory regimes under capitalism and socialism,* London, Verso.

Burns, T. (1962) The sociology of industry, in A.T. Welford, M. Argyle, D.V. Glass and J.N. Morris (eds) *Society. Problems and methods of study,* London, Routledge & Kegan Paul, 185–215,

Burns, T. (1963) Industry in a new age, *New Society,* 31 January 1963, 17–20 (reprinted in D.S. Pugh [ed.] *Organization Theory,* Harmondsworth, Middx, Penguin, 43–55).

Burns, T. (1967) The comparative study of organizations, in V.H. Vroom (ed.) *Methods of Organizational Research,* Pittsburgh, Pittsburgh University Press, 113–70.

Burns, T. (1969) On the plurality of social systems, in T. Burns (ed.) *Industrial Man,* Harmondsworth, Middx, Penguin, 232–49 (first published in J.R. Lawrence [ed.] *Operational Research and the Social Sciences,* London, Tavistock, 1966).

Burns. T. and Stalker, G.M. (1961) *The Management of Innovation,* London, Tavistock.

Burrell, G. and Morgan, G. (1979) *Sociological Paradigms and Organisational Analysis,* London, Heinemann.

Carter, M.P. (1968) Report on a survey of sociological research in Britain, *Sociological Review,* 16, 1, 5–40.

Child, J. (1969) *British Management Thought. A critical analysis,* London, Allen & Unwin.

Child, J. (1970) More myths of management organization?, *Journal of Management Studies,* 7, 3, 376–90.

Child, J. (1971) Review of J. Woodward, 'Industrial Organization: behaviour and control', *Sociology,* 5, 1, 127–30.

Child, J. (1972) Organizational structure, environment and performance: the role of strategic choice, *Sociology,* 6, 1, 1–22.

Child, J. (1977) Organizational design and performance: contingency theory and beyond, *Organization and Administrative Science,* 8, 2, 169–83.

Child, J. (1984) *Organizations: A guide to problems and practice*, London, Harper and Row (2nd edn).

Child, J. (1988) On organizations in their sectors, *Organization Studies*, 9, 1, 13–19.

Child, J. and Ellis, T. (1973) Predictors of variation in managerial roles, *Human Relations*, 26, 2, 227–50.

Child, J. and Mansfield, R. (1972) Technology, size and organization structure, *Sociology*, 6, 3, 369–93.

Cicourel, A. (1964) *Method and Measurement in Sociology*, New York, Free Press.

Clark, P.A. (1972) *Organizational Design. Theory and practice*, London, Tavistock.

Clegg, H.A. (1950) *Labour Relations in London Transport*, Oxford, Blackwell.

Clegg, S.R. (1990) *Modern Organizations. Organization studies in the postmodern world*, London, Sage.

Clegg, S. and Dunkerley, D. (1980) *Organization, Class and Control*, London, Routledge & Kegan Paul.

Cockburn, C. (1983) *Brothers. Male dominance and technological change*, London, Pluto Press.

Cohen, P.S. (1968) *Modern Social Theory*, London, Heinemann.

Collins, O., Dalton, M. and Roy, D. (1946) Restriction of output and social cleavage in industry, *Applied Anthropology*, 5, Summer, 1–14.

Collins, O., Dalton, M. and Roy, D. (1948) The industrial ratebuster, a characterisation, *Applied Anthropology*, 7, Winter.

Coombs, R. (1978) 'Labor and Monopoly Capital', *New Left Review*, 107, 79–96.

Cotgrove, S. and Box, S. (1966) Scientific identity, occupational selection and role strain, *British Journal of Sociology*, 17, 1, 20–8.

Cotgrove, S. and Box, S. (1970) *Science, Industry and Society*, London, Allen & Unwin.

Craib, I. (1984) *Modern Social Theory. From Parsons to Habermas*, Brighton, Wheatsheaf.

Cressey, P. and MacInnes, J. (1980) Voting for Ford: industrial democracy and the control of labour, *Capital and Class*, 11, 5–33.

Crompton, R. and Gubbay, J. (1977) *Economy and Class Structure*, London, Macmillan.

Crompton, R. and Jones, G. (1982) Clerical 'Proletarianisation': myth or reality?, in G. Day (ed.) *Diversity and Decomposition in the Labour Market*, Aldershot, Gower, 125–45.

Crompton, R. and Jones, G. (1984) *White Collar Proletariat. De-skilling and gender in clerical work*, London, Macmillan.

Crouch, C. (1977) *Class Conflict and the Industrial Relations Crisis*, London, Heinemann.

Crouch, C.J. and Pizzorno, A. (eds) (1977) *The Resurgence of Class Conflict since 1968*, London, Macmillan, 2 vols.

Cunnison, S. (1966) *Wages and Work Allocation*, London, Tavistock.

Cunnison, S. (1982) The Manchester factory studies; the social context, bureaucratic organisation, sexual divisions and their influence on patterns of accommodation between workers and management, in R. Frankenburg (ed.) (1982) *Custom and Conflict in British Society*, Manchester, Manchester University Press, 94–139.

Cutler, T. (1978) The romance of 'labour', *Economy and Society*, 7, 1, 74–95.

Dahrendorf, R. (1958) Out of Utopia: towards a re-orientation of sociological analysis, *American Journal of Sociology*, 64, 2.

Dahrendorf, R. (1959) *Class and Class Conflict in an Industrial Society*, London, Routledge & Kegan Paul (originally published Germany, 1957).

Daniel, W.W. (1969) Industrial behaviour and orientation to work – a critique, *Journal of Management Studies*, 6, 3, 366–75.

Daniel, W.W. (1970) *Beyond the Wage-Work Bargain*, London, Political and Economic Planning.

Daniel, W.W. (1971) Productivity bargaining and orientation to work – a rejoinder to Goldthorpe, *Journal of Management Studies*, 8, 3, 329–35.

Daniel, W.W. (1973) Understanding employee behaviour in its context: illustrations from productivity bargaining, in J. Child (ed.) *Man and Organization*, London, Allen & Unwin, 39–62.

Dankbaar, B. (1988) New production concepts, management strategies and the quality of work, *Work, Employment and Society*, 2, 1, 25–50.

Davies, C., Dawson S. and Francis, A. (1973) Technology and other variables: some current approaches to organization theory, in M. Warner (ed.) *The Sociology of the Workplace*, London, Allen & Unwin.

Davis, H. (1979) *Beyond Class Images*, London, Croom Helm.

Davis, L.E. and Taylor, J.C. (eds) (1972) *Design of Jobs*, Harmondsworth, Middx, Penguin.

Dawe, A. (1970) The two sociologies, *British Journal of Sociology*, 21, 2, 207–18.

Dawe, A. (1979) Theories of social action, in T. Bottomore and R. Nisbet (eds) *A History of Sociological Analysis*, London, Heinemann, 362–417.

Day, R. and Day, J.V. (1977) A review of the current state of negotiated order theory: an appreciation and a critique, *The Sociological Quarterly*, 18, Winter, 126–42.

Dennis, N., Henriques, F. and Slaughter, C. (1956) *Coal is our Life*, London, Eyre & Spottiswoode.

DSIR/MRC (Department of Scientific and Industrial Research and Medical Research Council) (1958) *Final Report of the Joint Committee on Human Relations in Industry 1954–57* and *Report of the Joint Committee on Individual Efficiency in Industry 1953–57*, London, HMSO.

Doeringer, P.B. and Piore, M.J. (1971) *Internal Labor Markets and Manpower Analysis*, Lexington, Mass., D.C. Heath.

Donaldson, L. (1985) *In Defence of Organization Theory. A reply to the critics*, Cambridge, Cambridge University Press.

Donaldson, L. (1988) In successful defence of organization theory: a routing of the critics, *Organization Studies*, 9, 1, 28–32.

Donaldson, L., Child, J. and Aldrich, H. (1975) The Aston findings on centralization: further discussion, *Administrative Science Quarterly*, 20, 3, 453–60.

Dunlop, J. (1958) *Industrial Relations Systems*, New York, Holt.

Edwards, R. (1978) Social relations of production at the point of production, *Insurgent Sociologist*, 8, 2–3, 109–25.

Edwards, R. (1979) *Contested Terrain. The transformation of the workplace in the twentieth century*, London, Heinemann.

Eldridge, J.E.T. (1971) *Sociology and Industrial Life*, London, Nelson.

Eldridge, J.E.T. (1980) *Recent British Sociology*, London, Macmillan.

Eldridge, J.E.T. (1983) Review of S. Wood (ed.) *The Degradation of Work?* and C. Littler, *The Development of the Labour Process in Capitalist Society*, *British Journal of Industrial Relations*, 21, 3, 418–20.

Elger, A.J. (1975) Industrial organizations – a processual perspective, in J.B. McKinlay (ed.) *Processing People. Cases in organizational behaviour*, London, Holt, Rinehart & Winston, 91–149.

Elger, A.J. (1982) Braverman, capital accumulation and deskilling, in S. Wood (ed.) *The Degradation of Work?*, London, Hutchinson, 23–53.

Elger, T. (1990) Technical innovation and work reorganisation in British manufacturing in the 1980s: continuity, intensification or transformation?, *Work, Employment and Society*, Special Issue, May, 67–101.

Elliott, D. (1974) The organization as a system, in *Structure and System: basic concepts and theories*, People and Organizations Units 3–6, DT352, Milton Keynes, The Open University, 76–98.

Emery, F.E. (1959) *Characteristics of Socio-technical Systems*, London, Tavistock Institute of Human Relations, Document No. 527 (reprinted in part in L.E. Davis and J.C. Taylor [eds] *The Design of Jobs*, Harmondsworth, Middx, Penguin, 1972, 177–98).

Emery, F.E. (ed.) (1969) *Systems Thinking*, Harmondsworth, Middx, Penguin.

Emery, F. and Thorsrud, E. (1976) *Democracy at Work*, Leiden, Martinus Nijhoff.

Emery, F.E. and Trist, E.L. (1960) Socio-technical systems, in C.W. Churchman and M. Verhulst (eds) *Management Sciences – Models and Techniques*, Vol. 2, London, Pergamon, 83–97 (and in F.E. Emery [ed.] *Systems Thinking*, Harmondsworth, Middx, Penguin, 1969, 281–96).

Emery, F.E. and Trist, E.L. (1965) The causal texture of organizational environments, *Human Relations*, 18, 1, 21–32 (and in F.E. Emery (ed.) *Systems Thinking*, Harmondsworth, Middx, Penguin, 1969, 241–57).

Emery, F.E. and Trist, E.L. (1972) *Towards a Social Ecology*, London, Plenum Press.

Emmett, I. and Morgan, D.H.J. (1982) Max Gluckman and the Manchester shopfloor ethnographies, in R. Frankenberg (ed.) *Custom and Conflict in British Society*, Manchester, Manchester University Press, 140–65.

Engels, F. (1958) Introduction to K. Marx 'Wage labour and capital', in K. Marx and F. Engels, *Selected Works*, Vol. 1, Moscow, Foreign Languages Publishing House, 70–8.

Etzioni, A. (1960) Two approaches to organizational analysis: a critique and a suggestion, *Administrative Science Quarterly*, 5, 2, 257–78.

Etzioni, A. (1961) *A Comparative Analysis of Complex Organizations*, New York, The Free Press.

Faunce, W.A. (ed.) (1967) *Readings in Industrial Sociology*, New York, Appleton-Century-Crofts.

Flanders, A. (1965) *Industrial Relations: what is wrong with the system?*, London, Institute of Personnel Management (reprinted in A. Flanders [1970] *Management and Unions*, London, Faber & Faber, 83–128).

Flanders, A. (1970) *Management and Unions. The theory and reform of industrial relations*, London, Faber & Faber.

Flanders, A. and Clegg, H.A. (eds) (1954) *The System of Industrial Relations in Great Britain*, Oxford, Blackwell.

Fox, A. (1966) *Industrial Sociology and Industrial Relations*, Royal Commission on Trade Unions and Employers' Associations, Research Paper No. 3, London, HMSO.

Fox, A. (1971) *A Sociology of Work in Industry*, London, Collier-Macmillan.

Fox, A. (1973) Industrial relations: a social critique of pluralist ideology, in J. Child (ed.) *Man and Organization*, London, Allen & Unwin, 185–233.

Fox, A. (1974) *Beyond Contract: work, power and trust relations*, London, Faber & Faber.

Fox, A. (1980) The meaning of work, in G. Esland and G. Salaman (eds) *The Politics of Work and Occupations*, Milton Keynes, Open University Press, 139–91.

Fox, A. (1990) *A Very Late Development. An autobiography*, Coventry, Industrial Relations Research Unit, University of Warwick.

Frankenberg, R. (ed.) (1982) *Custom and Conflict in British Society*, Manchester, Manchester University Press.

Friedman, A. (1977a) *Industry and Labour. Class struggle at work and monopoly capitalism*, London, Macmillan.

Friedman, A. (1977b) Responsible autonomy versus direct control over the labour process, *Capital and Class*, 1, Spring, 43–57.

Friedman, A. (1984) Management strategies, market conditions and the labour process, in F.H. Stephen (ed.) *Firms, Organization and Labour*, London, Macmillan, 176–200.

Friedmann, G. (1955) *Industrial Society. The emergence of the human problems of automation*, Glencoe, Ill., Free Press.

Friedmann, G. (1961) *The Anatomy of Work*, London, Heinemann.

Gabriel, Y. (1978) Collective bargaining: a critique of the Oxford school, *Political Quarterly*, 49, 3, 334–48.

Gallie, D. (1985) Directions for the future, in B. Roberts, R. Finnegan and D. Gallie (eds) *New Approaches to Economic Life. Economic restructuring: unemployment and the social division of labour*, Manchester, Manchester University Press, 512–530.

Garnsey, E. (1981) The rediscovery of the division of labour, *Theory and Society*, 10, 337–58.

Garnsey, E., Rubery, J. and Wilkinson, F. (1985) Labour market structure and work-force divisions, in R. Deem and G. Salaman (eds) *Work, Culture and Society*, Milton Keynes, Open University Press, 40–76.

Garrett, A. (1987) The Quest for Autonomy: Sociology's advocatory dimension, unpublished Ph.D. thesis, University of Durham.

Geer, B., Haas, J., ViVona, C., Miller, S.J., Woods, C. and Becker, H.S.

(1968) Learning the ropes, in I. Deutscher and J. Thompson (eds) *Among the People*, New York, Basic Books, 209–33.

Gerth, H.H. and Mills, C.W. (eds) *From Max Weber: essays in sociology*, London, Routledge & Kegan Paul.

Giddens, A. (1976) *New Rules of Sociological Method*, London, Hutchinson.

Giddens, A. (1979) *Central Problems in Social Theory*, London, Macmillan.

Giddens, A. (1984) *The Constitution of Society*, Cambridge, Polity.

Glaser, B. and Strauss, A. (1968) *The Discovery of Grounded Theory*, London, Weidenfeld & Nicolson.

Goldthorpe, J.H. (1959) Technical organization as a factor in supervisor–worker conflict, *British Journal of Sociology*, 10, 3, 213–30.

Goldthorpe, J.H. (1965) Orientation to work and industrial behaviour among assembly-line operatives: a contribution towards an action approach in industrial sociology, unpublished paper to Conference of University Teachers of Sociology.

Goldthorpe, J.H. (1966) Attitudes and behaviour of car assembly workers: a deviant case and a theoretical critique, *British Journal of Sociology*, 17, 3, 227–244.

Goldthorpe, J.H. (1970) The social action approach to industrial sociology: a reply to Daniel, *Journal of Management Studies*, 7, 2, 199–208.

Goldthorpe, J.H. (1972) Daniel on orientations to work – a final comment, *Journal of Management Studies*, 9, 2, 266–73.

Goldthorpe, J.H. (1977) Industrial relations in Great Britain: a critique of reformism, in T. Clarke and L. Clements (eds) *Trade Unionism under Capitalism*, London, Fontana, 184–224 (first published 1974, *Politics and Society*).

Goldthorpe, J.H. and Lockwood, D. (1963) Affluence and the British class structure, *Sociological Review*, 11, 2, 133–63.

Goldthorpe, J.H., Lockwood, D., Bechhofer, F. and Platt, J. (1968) *The Affluent Worker: Industrial attitudes and behaviour*, Cambridge, Cambridge University Press.

Goldthorpe, J.H., Lockwood, D., Bechhofer, F. and Platt, J. (1969) *The Affluent Worker in the Class Structure*, Cambridge, Cambridge University Press.

Gordon, D.M., Edwards, R. and Reich, M. (1982) *Segmented Work, Divided Workers*, Cambridge, Cambridge University Press.

Gough, I. (1972) Marx's theory of productive and unproductive labour, *New Left Review*, 76, 47–72.

Gouldner, A.W. (1955) *Patterns of Industrial Bureaucracy*, London, Routledge & Kegan Paul.

Gouldner, A.W. (1957–8) Cosmopolitans and locals: towards an analysis of latent social roles, *Administrative Science Quarterly*, 2, 281–306 and 444–80.

Gouldner, A.W. (1959a) Organizational analysis, in R.K. Merton (ed.) *Sociology Today*, New York, Basic Books, 400–27.

Gouldner, A.W. (1959b) Theoretical requirements of the applied social sciences, *American Sociological Review*, 22, 335–46.

Gray, J.L. (1976) *The Glacier Project: Concepts and critiques*, New York, Crane Russak & Co./London, Heinemann.

Greenwood, R. and Hinings, C.R. (1976) A research note – centralisation revisited, *Administrative Science Quarterly*, 21, 1, 151–5.

Gregory, D. (ed.) (1978) *Work Organization. Swedish experience and British context*, London, Social Science Research Council.

Grieco, M. (1981) The shaping of a work force: a critique of the Affluent Worker study, *International Journal of Sociology and Social Policy*, 1, 1, 62–88.

Guest, R.H. (1962) *Organizational Change*, Homewood, Ill., Dorsey Press.

Hackman, J.R. (1981) Sociotechnical systems theory: a commentary, in A.H. Van de Ven and W.F. Joyce (eds) *Perspectives on Organizational Design and Behaviour*, New York, Wiley.

Hakim, C. (1990) Core and periphery in employers' workforce strategies: evidence from the 1987 ELUS survey, *Work, Employment and Society*, 4, 2, 157–88.

Hamilton, P. (1983) *Talcott Parsons*, Chichester and London, Ellis Horwood & Tavistock.

Haralambos, M. (1980) *Sociology: Themes and perspectives*, London, University Tutorial Press.

Herzberg, F. (1968) *Work and the Nature of Man*, London, Staples Press.

Heyworth Committee (1965) *Report of the Committee on Social Studies* (Chairman: Lord Heyworth), London, HMSO, Cmnd. 2660.

Hickson, D.J. and MacDonald, K.M. (1964) A scheme for the empirical study of organizational behaviour, *International Journal of Production Research*, 3, 1, 29–34.

Hickson, D.J. and McMillan, C.J. (eds) (1981) *Organization and Nation*, The Aston Programme IV, Farnborough, Hants, Gower.

Hill, S. (1981) *Competition and Control at Work. The new industrial sociology*, London, Heinemann.

Hinings, C.R. (1988) Defending organization theory: a British view from North America, *Organization Studies*, 9, 1, 2–7.

Hinings, C.R., Pugh, D.S., Hickson, D.J. and Turner, C. (1967) An approach to the study of bureaucracy, *Sociology*, 1, 1, 61–72.

Hirszowicz, M. (1981) *Industrial Sociology. An introduction*, Oxford, Martin Robertson.

Hobsbawm, E.J. (1964) *Labouring Men*, London, Weidenfeld & Nicolson.

Hopkins, T.K. (1966) Review of *Industrial Organization: Theory and practice*, by Joan Woodward, *Administrative Science Quarterly*, 11, 2, 284–9.

Hyman, R. (1975) *Industrial Relations. A Marxist introduction*, London, Macmillan.

Hyman, R. (1977) *Strikes*, 2nd edition, Glasgow, Fontana/Collins.

Hyman, R. (1987) Strategy or structure: capital, labour and control, *Work, Employment and Society*, 1, 1, 25–55.

Hyman, R. and Brough, I. (1975) *Social Values and Industrial Relations. A study of fairness and inequality*, Oxford, Blackwell.

Ingham, G.K. (1967) Organizational size, orientation to work and industrial behaviour, *Sociology*, 1, 3, 239–58.

Ingham, G.K. (1970) *Size of Industrial Organization and Worker Behaviour*, Cambridge, Cambridge University Press.

Inkson, K., Payne, R. and Pugh, D.S. (1967) Extending the occupational environment: the measurement of organizations, *Occupational Psychology*, 41, 33–47.

Jaques, E. (1951) *The Changing Culture of a Factory*, London, Tavistock.

Jaques, E. (1956) *Measurement of Responsibility*, London, Heinemann.

Jaques, E. (1967) *Equitable Payment*, Harmondsworth, Middx, Penguin (first published 1961, London, Heinemann).

Jaques, E. (1976) *A General Theory of Bureaucracy*, London, Heinemann.

Jones, B. (1988) Work and flexible automation in Britain: a review of developments and possibilities, *Work, Employment and Society*, 2, 4, 451–86.

Jönsson, B. (1978) Production design and works organization in Volvo, in D. Gregory (ed) *Work Organization. Swedish experience and British context*, London, Social Science Research Council, 61–7.

Katz, D. and Kahn, R.L. (1966) *The Social Psychology of Organizations*, New York, Wiley.

Kelly, J. (1968) *Is Scientific Management Possible?*, London, Faber & Faber.

Kelly, J.E. (1978) A reappraisal of sociotechnical systems theory, *Human Relations*, 31, 12, 1069–99.

Kent, R.A. (1981) *A History of British Empirical Sociology*, Aldershot, Gower.

Klein, L. (1976) *New Forms of Work Organisation*, Cambridge, Cambridge University Press.

Knights, D., Willmott, H. and Collinson, D. (eds) (1985) *Job Redesign. Critical perspectives on the labour process*, Aldershot, Gower.

Landsberger, H.A. (1958) *Hawthorne Revisited*, Ithaca, NY, Cornell University Press.

Lane, C. (1988) Industrial change in Europe: the pursuit of flexible specialisation in Britain and West Germany, *Work, Employment and Society*, 2, 2, 141–68.

Lassman, P. (1974) Phenomenological perspectives in sociology, in J. Rex (ed.) *Approaches to Sociology*, London, Routledge & Kegan Paul, 125–44.

Lawrence, P.R. and Lorsch, J.W. (1967a) Differentiation and integration in complex organizations, *Administrative Science Quarterly*, 12, 1, 1–47.

Lawrence, P.R. and Lorsch, J.W. (1967b) *Organization and Environment*, Boston, Mass., Harvard Graduate School of Business.

Lee, D. (1982) Beyond de-skilling: skill, craft and class, in S.Wood (ed.) *The Degradation of Work?*, London, Hutchinson, 146–62.

Littler, C.R. (1982) *The Development of the Labour Process in Capitalist Societies*, London, Heinemann.

Littler, C.R. and Salaman, G. (1982) Bravermania and beyond: recent theories of the labour process, *Sociology*, 16, 2, 251–69.

Littler, C.R. and Salaman, G. (1984) *Class and Work*, London, Batsford.

Lockwood, D. (1958) *The Blackcoated Worker*, London, Allen & Unwin.

Lockwood, D. (1960) The 'new working class', *Archives Européennes de Sociologie*, 1, 2, 248–59.

Lockwood, D. (1966) Sources of variation in working class images of society, *Sociological Review*, 14, 3, 249–67.

Lockwood, D. and Goldthorpe, J.H. (1962) The manual worker: affluence, aspirations, and assimilations, unpublished paper, British Sociological Association annual conference, Brighton.

Lupton, T. (1963) *On the Shop Floor*, Oxford, Pergamon.

Lupton, T. and Bowey, A.M. (1974) *Wages and Salaries*, Harmondsworth, Middx, Penguin.

Lupton, T. and Cunnison, S. (1964) Workshop behaviour, in M. Gluckman and E. Devons (eds) *Closed Systems and Open Minds*, Edinburgh, Oliver & Boyd.

Mackay, L. (1982) Sociology for Industry? A study of the diffusion and use of industrial sociology in industry, unpublished Ph.D. thesis, University of Durham.

Mackenzie, G. (1974) The 'Affluent Worker' study: an evaluation and critique, in F. Parkin (ed.) *The Social Analysis of Class Structure*, London, Tavistock.

McKinlay, J.B. (ed.) (1975) *Processing People. Cases in organizational behaviour*, London, Holt, Rinehart & Winston.

Maguire, M. (1988) Work, locality and social control, *Work, Employment and Society*, 2, 1, 71–87.

Mann, M. (1973) *Workers on the Move*, Cambridge, Cambridge University Press.

Mansfield, R. (1973) Bureaucracy and centralization: an examination of organizational structure, *Administrative Sciences Quarterly*, 18, 4, 477–88.

Manwaring, T and Wood, S. (1985) The ghost in the labour process, in D. Knights, H. Willmott and D. Collinson (eds) *Job Redesign: critical perspectives on the labour process*, Aldershot, Gower.

Marsden, D. (1986) *The End of Economic Man? Custom and competition in labour markets*, Brighton, Wheatsheaf.

Marx, K. (1958) Wages, price and profit, in K. Marx and F. Engels *Selected Works*, Vol. 1, Moscow, Foreign Languages Publishing House, 398–447.

Marx, K. (1973) The Eighteenth Brumaire of Louis Bonaparte, in *Surveys from Exile*, Harmondsworth, Middx, Penguin, 143–249.

Marx, K. (1976) *Capital*, Vol. 1, Harmondsworth, Middx, Penguin.

Maslow, A.H. (1943) A theory of human motivation, *Psychological Review*, 50, 370–96 (reprinted, abridged, in V.H. Vroom and E.L. Deci [eds] *Management and Motivation*, Harmondsworth, Middx, Penguin, 1970, 27–41).

Mayntz, R. (1964) The study of organizations. A trend report and bibliography, *Current Sociology*, 13, 3, 95–156.

Mayo, E. (1933) *The Human Problems of an Industrial Civilization*, New York, Macmillan (reprinted 1946).

Mayo, E. (1949) *The Social Problems of an Industrial Civilization*, London, Routledge & Kegan Paul.

Mennell, S. (1980) *Sociological Theory: uses and unities*, second edition, Walton-on-Thames, Nelson.

Merton, R.K. (1957) Patterns of influence: local and cosmopolitan influentials, in R.K. Merton, *Social Theory and Social Structure*, Glencoe, Ill., Free Press.

Miller, E.J. (1959) Technology, territory and time, *Human Relations*, 12, 243–72.

Miller, E.J. (1975a) The open-system approach to organizational analysis, with specific reference to the work of A.K. Rice, in G.H. Hofstede and

M.S. Kassem (eds) *European Contributions to Organization Theory*, Assen, Netherlands, Van Gorcum.

Miller, E.J. (1975b) Socio-technical systems in weaving, 1953–1970: a follow-up study, *Human Relations*, 28, 4, 349–86.

Miller, E.J. and Rice, A.K. (1967) *Systems of Organization*, London, Tavistock.

Mills, C.W. (1951) *White Collar*, New York, Oxford University Press.

Mindlin, S.E. and Aldrich, H. (1975) Interorganizational dependence: a review of the concept and a reexamination of the findings of the Aston group, *Administrative Science Quarterly*, 20, 3, 382–92.

Moore, R. (1978) Work organisation: a trade union perspective, in SSRC, *Research Needs in Work Organization*, London, Social Science Research Council, 80–95.

Moore, W.E. (1979) Functionalism, in T. Bottomore and R. Nisbet (eds) *A History of Sociological Analysis*, London, Heinemann, 321–61.

Moore, W.E. and Feldman, A.S. (1960) *Labor Commitment and Social Change in Developing Areas*, New York, Social Science Research Council.

More, C. (1980) *Skill and the English Working Class, 1870–1914*, London, Croom Helm.

More, C. (1982) Skill and the survival of apprenticeship, in S. Wood (ed.) *The Degradation of Work?*, London, Hutchinson, 109–21.

Morgan, G. (1986) *Images of Organization*, Beverly Hills, Ca. and London, Sage.

Mouzelis, N.P. (first edition 1967) (1975) *Organisation and Bureaucracy*, second edition, London, Routledge & Kegan Paul.

Mumford, E. and Banks, O. (1967) *The Computer and the Clerk*, London, Routledge & Kegan Paul.

National Institute of Industrial Psychology (1951) *The Foreman. A study of supervision in British industry*, London, Staples.

National Institute of Industrial Psychology (1952) *Joint Consultation in British Industry*, London, Staples.

Nichols, T. (1969) *Ownership, Control and Ideology*, London, Allen & Unwin.

Nichols, T. (1976) Management, ideology and practice, in Open University, *Politics of Work and Occupation 2*, People and Work, Units 15–16 (DE351), Milton Keynes, Open University Press, 5–27.

Nichols, T. (ed.) (1980) *Capital and Labour. A Marxist primer*, Glasgow, Fontana.

Nichols, T. and Armstrong, P. (1976) *Workers Divided. A study in shopfloor politics*, Glasgow, Fontana/Collins.

Nichols, T. and Beynon, H. (1977) *Living with Capitalism. Class relations and the modern factory*, London, Routledge & Kegan Paul.

Pahl, R.E. (1984) *Divisions of Labour*, Oxford, Blackwell.

Parker, S.R., Brown, R.K., Child, J. and Smith, M.A. (1967) (fourth edition, revised, 1981) *The Sociology of Industry*, London, Allen & Unwin.

Parsons, T. and Smelser, N.J. (1956) *Economy and Society*, London, Routledge & Kegan Paul.

Pasmore, W., Francis, C. and Haldeman, J. (1982) Sociotechnial systems:

a North American reflection on empirical studies of the seventies, *Human Relations*, 35, 12, 1179–204.

Paterson, T.T. (1955) *Morale in War and Work: An experiment in the management of men*, London, Max Parish.

Payne, R. and Pugh, D. (1971) Organizations as psychological environments, in P.B. Warr (ed.) *Psychology at Work*, Harmondsworth, Middx, Penguin, 374–402.

Penn, R. (1982) Skilled manual workers in the labour process, 1856–1964, in S. Wood (ed.) *The Degradation of Work?*, London, Hutchinson.

Perrow, C. (1970) *Organizational Analysis. A sociological view*, London, Tavistock.

Pettigrew, A.M. (1973) *The Politics of Organizational Decision-making*, London, Tavistock.

Phillips, A. and Taylor, B. (1986) Sex and skill, in *Feminist Review* (ed.) *Waged Work, A Reader*, London, Virago (first published *Feminist Review*, 6, 1980).

Piore, M.J. and Sabel, C. (1984) *The Second Industrial Divide: Prospects for prosperity*, New York, Basic Books.

Platt, J. (1984) The Affluent Worker revisited, in C. Bell & H. Roberts (eds) *Social Researching – Politics, Problems, Practice*, London, Routledge & Kegan Paul, 179–98.

Pollert, A. (1988) The 'flexible firm': fixation or fact?, *Work, Employment and Society*, 2, 3, 281–316.

Prandy, K., Stewart, A. and Blackburn, R.M. (1982) *White-Collar Work*, London, Macmillan.

Pugh, D.S. (1966) Modern organization theory: a psychological and sociological study, *Psychological Bulletin*, 66, 4, 235–51.

Pugh, D.S. (ed.) (1971) *Organization Theory*, Harmondsworth, Middx, Penguin.

Pugh, D.S. (1981) The Aston program perspective, and Response to Starbuck, in A.H. Van de Ven and W.F. Taylor (eds) *Perspectives on Organization Design and Behaviour*, New York, Wiley, 135–66 and 199–203.

Pugh, D.S. and Hickson, D.J. (eds) (1976) *Organizational Structure in its Context*, The Aston Programme I, Farnborough, Hants, Saxon House.

Pugh, D.S., Hickson, D.J., Hinings, C.R., MacDonald, K.M., Turner, C. and Lupton, T. (1963) A conceptual scheme for organizational analysis, *Administrative Science Quarterly*, 8, 3, 291–315.

Pugh, D.S., Hickson, D.J. and Hinings, C.R. (1964) *Writers on Organizations. An introduction*, London, Hutchinson.

Pugh, D.S. and Hinings, C.R. (eds) (1976) *Organizational Structure, Extensions and Replications*, The Aston Programme II, Farnborough, Hants, Saxon House.

Pugh, D.S., Mansfield, R. and Warner, M. (1975) *Research in Organizational Behaviour: A British survey*, London, Heinemann.

Pugh, D.S. and Payne, R.L. (eds) (1977) *Organizational Behaviour in its Context*, The Aston Programme III, Farnborough, Hants, Saxon House.

Purcell, J. and Sisson, K. (1983) Strategies and practice in the management of industrial relations, in G.S. Bain (ed.) *Industrial Relations in Britain*, Oxford, Blackwell.

Ramsay, H. (1982) Participation for whom? A critical examination of worker participation in theory and practice, unpublished Ph.D. thesis, University of Durham.

Rex, J.A. (1961) *Key Problems of Sociological Theory*, London, Routledge & Kegan Paul.

Rice, A.K. (1958) *Productivity and Social Organization*, London, Tavistock.

Rice, A.K. (1963) *The Enterprise and its Environment*, London, Tavistock.

Rice, A.K. (1970) *The Modern University*, London, Tavistock.

Robbins Report (1963) *Higher Education. Report of the Committee . . . under the Chairmanship of Lord Robbins*, London, HMSO, Cmnd. 2154.

Roberts, I. (1988) A question of construction. Capital and labour in Wearside shipbuilding since 1930, unpublished Ph.D. thesis, University of Durham.

Roberts, K., Cook, F.G., Clark, S.C. and Semeonoff, E. (1977) *The Fragmentary Class Structure*, London, Heinemann.

Roethlisberger, F.J. and Dickson, W.J. (1939) *Management and the Worker*, New York, Wiley (reprinted 1964).

Rose, M. (1975) *Industrial Behaviour. Theoretical development since Taylor*, London, Allen Lane.

Rose, M. (1988) *Industrial Behaviour. Research and control*, Harmondsworth, Middx, Penguin.

Ross, M.S. (1958) Organized labour and management; Part II: The United Kingdom, in E.M. Hugh-Jones (ed.) *Human Relations and Modern Management*, Amsterdam, North-Holland, 100–32.

Roy, D. (1952) Quota restriction and goldbricking in a machine shop, *American Journal of Sociology*, 57, March, 427–42.

Roy, D. (1953) Work satisfaction and social reward in quota achievement, *American Sociological Review*, 18, October, 507–14.

Royal Commission on Trade Unions and Employers' Associations (1968) *Report* (Chairman: Lord Donovan), London, HMSO, Cmnd. 3623.

Rubery, J. (1978) Structured labour markets, worker organization and low pay, *Cambridge Journal of Economics*, 2, 1, 17–36 (reprinted in A.H. Amsden [ed.] *The Economics of Women and Work*, Harmondsworth, Middx, Penguin, 1980, 242–70).

Sadler, P.J. and Barry, B.A. (1970) *Organisational Development: Case studies in the printing industry*, London, Longman.

Salaman, G. (1974) *Community and Occupation. An exploration of work/leisure relationships*, Cambridge, Cambridge University Press.

Salaman, G. (1979) *Work Organisations. Resistance and control*, London, Longman.

Sayles, L.R. (1958) *Behaviour of Industrial Work Groups*, New York, Wiley.

Schein, E.H. (1965) *Organizational Psychology*, Englewood Cliffs, New Jersey, Prentice-Hall.

Schneider, E.V. (1957) *Industrial Sociology*, New York, McGraw-Hill.

Scott, J. (1979) (second edition 1985) *Corporations, Classes and Capitalism*, London, Hutchinson.

Scott, W.H. (1952) *Industrial Leadership and Joint Consultation*, Liverpool, Liverpool University Press.

Scott, W.H. (1958) The factory as a social system, in E.M. Hugh-Jones (ed.) *Human Relations and Modern Management*, Amsterdam, North Holland, 18–42.

Scott, W.H., Banks, J.A., Halsey, A.H. and Lupton, T. (1956) *Technical Change and Industrial Relations. A study of the relations between technical change and the social structure of a large steelworks*, Liverpool, Liverpool University Press.

Scott, W.H., Mumford, E., McGivering, I.C. and Kirkby, J.M. (1963) *Coal and Conflict. A study of industrial relations at collieries*, Liverpool, Liverpool University Press.

Seear, N. (1962) Industrial research in Britain, in A.T. Welford, M. Argyle, D.V. Glass and J.N. Morris (eds) *Society: Problems and methods of study*, London, Routledge & Kegan Paul, 171–83.

Selznick, P. (1957) *Leadership in Administration*, Evanston, Ill., Row, Peterson.

Sheldrake, P.F. (1971) Orientations towards work among computer programmers, *Sociology*, 5, 2, 209–24.

Silverman, D. (1968) Formal organizations or industrial sociology: towards a social action analysis of organizations, *Sociology*, 2, 2, 221–38.

Silverman, D. (1970) *The Theory of Organisations*, London, Heinemann.

Silverman, D. (1972) Some neglected questions about social reality, in P. Filmer, M. Phillipson, D. Silverman and D. Walsh, *New Directions in Sociological Theory*, London, Collier Macmillan, 165–81.

Silverman, D. (1975) Accounts of organizations – organizational 'structures' and the accounting process, in J.B. McKinlay (ed.) *Processing People. Cases in organizational behaviour*, London, Holt, Rinehart & Winston, 269–302.

Silverman, D. and Jones, J. (1973) Getting in: the managed accomplishment of 'correct' selection outcomes, in J. Child (ed.) *Man and Organization*, London, Allen & Unwin, 63–106.

Silverman, D. and Jones, J. (1976) *Organizational Work. The language of grading, the grading of language*, London, Collier-Macmillan.

Smith, J.H. (1959) New ways in industrial sociology, *British Journal of Sociology*, 10, 3, 244–52.

Smith, J.H. (1961) *The University Teaching of the Social Sciences: Industrial Sociology*, Paris, UNESCO (Introduction by J-D.Reynaud).

Smith, J.H. (1987) Elton Mayo and the hidden Hawthorne, *Work, Employment and Society*, 1, 1, 107–120.

Sofer, C. (1972) *Organizations in Theory and Practice*, London, Heinemann.

Social Science Research Council (1978) *Research Needs in Work Organization*, A working party report to the Management and Industrial Relations Committee, London, SSRC.

Stansfield, R.G. (1981) Operational research and sociology: a case-study of cross-fertilizations in the growth of useful science, *Science and Public Policy*, 8, 4, 262–80.

Starbuck, W.H. (1981) A trip to view the elephants and rattlesnakes in the garden of Aston, in A.H. Van de Ven and W.F. Joyce (eds) *Perspectives on Organization Design and Behaviour*, New York, Wiley, 167–98.

Steedman, I. (ed.) (1981) *The Value Controversy*, London, Verso.

Stone, K. (1973) The origin of job structures in the steel industry, *Radical America*, 7, 6, 19-24.

Storey, J. (1985) The means of management control, *Sociology*, 19, 2, 193–211.

Strauss, A., Schatzman, L., Ehrlich, D., Bucher, R. and Sabshim, M. (1971) The hospital and its negotiated order, in F.G. Castles, D.J. Murray and D.C. Porter (eds) *Decisions, Organizations and Society*, Harmondsworth, Middx, Penguin, 103–23 (first published 1963 in E. Friedson [ed.] *The Hospital in Modern Society*, London, Macmillan, 147–69).

Tannenbaum, A.S. (1966) *Social Psychology of the Work Organization*, London, Tavistock.

Thompson, P. (1983) *The Nature of Work. An introduction to debates on the labour process*, London, Macmillan.

Thurley, K.E. and Hamblin, A.C. (1963) *The Supervisor and his Job*, Problems of Progress in Industry No.13, Department of Scientific and Industrial Research, London, HMSO.

Thurley, K.E. and Wirdenius, H. (1973) *Supervision: A reappraisal*, London, Heinemann.

Thurley, K.E. and Wood, S. (eds) (1983) *Industrial Relations and Management Strategy*, Cambridge, Cambridge University Press.

Touraine, A. (1962) An historical theory in the evolution of industrial skills, in C.R. Walker (ed.) *Modern Technology and Civilization*, New York, McGraw-Hill.

Townsend, P. (1979) *Poverty in the United Kingdom*, Harmondsworth, Middx, Penguin.

Tréanton, J.-R. and Reynaud, J.-D. (1964) Industrial Sociology 1951–62, A trend report and bibliography, *Current Sociology*, 12, 2, 123–245.

Trist, E.L. (1960) *Socio-technical Systems*, Tavistock Institute of Human Relations, Document No. 572, mimeo.

Trist, E.L. (1981) The socio-technical perspective. The evolution of socio-technical systems as a conceptual framework and as an action research program, in A.H. Van de Ven and W.F. Joyce (eds) *Perspectives on Organization Design and Behaviour*, New York, Wiley.

Trist, E.L. and Bamforth, K.W. (1951) Some social and psychological consequences of the longwall method of coal getting, *Human Relations*, 4, 1, 3–38.

Trist, E.L., Higgin, G.W., Murray, H. and Pollock, A.B. (1963) *Organizational Choice*, London, Tavistock.

Turner, A.N. and Lawrence, P. (1966) *Industrial Jobs and the Worker*, Cambridge, Mass., Harvard University Press.

Turner, B.A. (1971) *Exploring the Industrial Subculture*, London, Macmillan.

Udy, S.H. Jr. (1959) *Organization of Work*, New Haven, Conn., Human Relations Area Files Press.

Udy, S.H. Jr. (1965) The comparative analysis of organizations, in J.G. March (ed.) *Handbook of Organizations*, Chicago, Rand McNally.

Undy, R., Ellis, V., McCarthy, W.E.J. and Halmos, A.M. (1981) *Change in Trade Unions*, London, Hutchinson.

University of Liverpool, Department of Social Science (1954) *The Dock Worker. An analysis of conditions of employment in the Port of Manchester,* Liverpool, Liverpool University Press.

Van de Ven, A.H. and Joyce, W.F. (eds) (1981) *Perspectives on Organization Design and Behaviour,* New York, Wiley.

Warde, A. (1989) Industrial discipline: factory regime and politics in Lancaster, *Work, Employment and Society,* 3, 1, 49–63.

Warmington, A., Lupton, T. and Gribbin, C. (1977) *Organizational Behaviour and Performance. An open systems approach to change,* London, Macmillan.

Warner, W.L. and Low, J.O. (1947) *The Social System of the Modern Factory,* New Haven, Conn., Yale University Press.

Warr, P. and Wall, T. (1975) *Work and Well-being,* Harmondsworth, Middx, Penguin.

Watson, T.J. (1980) (second edition, 1987) *Sociology, Work and Industry,* London, Routledge & Kegan Paul.

Weber, M. (1947) *The Theory of Social and Economic Organization,* Glencoe, Ill., The Free Press/London, Collier-Macmillan.

Weber, M. (1968) *Economy and Society,* New York, Bedminster Press.

Wedderburn, D. (1972) What determines shop-floor behaviour?, *New Society,* 20 July, 128–30.

Wedderburn, D. and Crompton, R. (1972) *Workers' Attitudes and Technology,* Cambridge, Cambridge University Press.

Welford, A.T., Argyle, M., Glass, D.V. and Morris, J.N. (eds) (1962) *Society: problems and methods of study,* London, Routledge & Kegan Paul.

Westergaard, J.H. (1970) The rediscovery of the cash nexus. Some recent interpretations of trends in British class structure, in R. Miliband and J. Saville (eds) *The Socialist Register 1970,* London, Merlin Press.

Whelan, C.T. (1984) Employment conditions and job satisfaction: the distribution, perception and evaluation of job rewards among male employees in Dublin, unpublished Ph.D. thesis, University of London.

Whittington, C. and Bellaby, P. (1979) The reasons for hierarchy in social services departments: a critique of Elliott Jaques and his associates, *Sociological Review,* 27, 3, 513–39.

Whyte, W.F. (1955) *Money and Motivation,* New York, Harper.

Willis, P. (1977) *Learning to Labour,* London, Saxon House.

Wilson, N.A.B. (1973) *On the Quality of Working Life,* Department of Employment Manpower Paper No. 7, London, HMSO.

Wood, S. (ed.) (1982) *The Degradation of Work? Skill, deskilling and the labour process,* London, Hutchinson.

Wood, S. (1987) The deskilling debate, new technology and work organization, *Acta Sociologica,* 30, 1, 3–24.

Woodward, J. (1958) *Management and Technology,* Problems of Progress in Industry No. 5, Department of Scientific and Industrial Research, London, HMSO (reprinted in T. Burns [ed.] *Industrial Man,* Harmondsworth, Middx, Penguin, 1969, 196–231).

Woodward, J. (1964) Industrial behaviour – is there a science?, *New Society,* 8 October.

Woodward, J. (1965) *Industrial Organization: Theory and practice*, London, Oxford University Press.

Woodward, J. (ed.) (1970) *Industrial Organization: Behaviour and control*, London, Oxford University Press.

Wright, E.O. (1975) Alternative perspectives in Marxist theory of accumulation and crisis, *Insurgent Sociologist*, 6, 1, 5–39.

Wynn, P.S. (1980) Motivation, orientations and the action perspective: an alternative framework, *Journal of Management Studies*, 17, 3, 251–60.

Wynn, P.S. (1983) Job motivation – a new framework, unpublished D.Phil. thesis, University of Oxford.

Zimbalist, A. (ed.) (1979) *Case Studies on the Labor Process*, New York, Monthly Review Press.

Name index

Abrams, P. 31, 84, 229–30, 238
Acton Society Trust 17
Aitken, H.G.J. 207
Albrow, M. 30, 32, 93, 97
Aldrich, H.E. 117, 118
Allen, V.L. 166
Amsden, A.H. 171
Armstrong, P. 167, 222, 237
Aston University see University of
   Aston
Atkinson, J. 225

Bakke, E.W. 105
Baldamus, W. 62, 153, 210
Bamforth, K.W. 63–4, 69
Banks, J.A. 24, 50, 51
Banks, O. 50
Baritz, L. 127, 185
Barron, R.D. 171
Barry, B.A. 103
Bechhofer, F. 154
Beechey, V. 18, 201
Bellaby, P. 62
Bendix, R. 94, 185, 213
Bennett, R. 142
Berger, P. 159
Berle, A.A. 23
Bertalanffy, L. von 42, 64
Beynon, H. 14, 101, 139, 149, 154,
   167, 173, 203, 211
Bion, W.R. 55
Blackburn, R.M. 144, 149, 150,
   151, 154, 171
Blain, I. 103–4

Blau, P.M. 30, 52, 54
Blauner, R. 104, 130, 172
Bottomore, T. 14, 172
Boulding, K.E. 42
Bowey, A.M. 236
Box, S. 142, 149, 153
Brannen, P. 24, 220
Braverman, H. 14–15, 37–8, 163,
   166–8, 174, 183–97, 222–4; on
   control of labour force 201–2,
   206–7, 211–12, 215; on
   degradation of work 38, 216,
   219, 220, 221, 222
Brighton Labour Process Group
   167, 189
Brough, I. 29, 62
Brown, C. 9
Brown, J.A.C. 10, 52
Brown, R.K. 16, 18, 46, 76, 101,
   142, 143, 153, 220, 226
Brown, W. 35, 40, 56–63, 83, 85
Buckley, W. 43, 44
Bulmer, M. 139, 155
Burawoy, M. 166, 189, 190, 202,
   204–6, 213–15
Burns, T. 7, 103; on change 54,
   80–1, 95–6; on chief executives
   31; on conflict 86; on
   institutions 21, 36, 54–5, 94–7,
   104, 123; on sociological
   method 19, 90
Burrell, G.: on contingency
   theory 92, 122, 124; on
   functionalism 41, 42, 81–2, 160;

Subject index